A Philosophy of Political Myth

In this book, Chiara Bottici argues for a philosophical understanding of political myth. Bottici demonstrates that myth is a process, one of continuous work on a basic narrative pattern that responds to a need for significance. Human beings need meaning in order to master the world they live in, but they also need significance in order to live in a world that is less indifferent to them. This is particularly true in the realm of politics. Political myths are narratives through which we orient ourselves, and influence the way we act and feel about our political world. Bottici shows that in order to come to terms with contemporary phenomena, such as the purported clash between civilizations, we need a Copernican revolution in political philosophy. If we want to save reason, we need a new understanding of myth.

Chiara Bottici is a Research Fellow in political philosophy at the University of Florence. The author of *Uomini e Stati*, she has contributed to the *Journal of Political Philosophy, Iride, Epoché: A Journal for the History of Philosophy*, and the *European Journal of Social Theory*.

D1609820

A Philosophy of Political Myth

CHIARA BOTTICI

University of Florence and European University Institute

CAMBRIDGE
UNIVERSITY PRESS

CAMBRIDGE UNIVERSITY PRESS
Cambridge, New York, Melbourne, Madrid, Cape Town, Singapore,
São Paulo, Delhi, Dubai, Tokyo, Mexico City

Cambridge University Press
The Edinburgh Building, Cambridge CB2 8RU, UK

Published in the United States of America by Cambridge University Press, New York

www.cambridge.org
Information on this title: www.cambridge.org/9780521182751

First published 2007
First paperback edition 2010

A catalogue record for this publication is available from the British Library

Library of Congress Cataloging in Publication Data
Bottici, Chiara.
A Philosophy of political myth / Chiara Bottici.
    p.   cm.
Includes bibliographical references and index.
ISBN 978-0-521-87655-1 (hardback)
1. Political science – Philosophy. 2. Myth.
3. Mythology – Political aspects. I. Title.
JA71.b584   2007
320.01–dc22   2006034141

ISBN 978-0-521-87655-1 Hardback
ISBN 978-0-521-18275-1 Paperback

To B. for the political myths he gave me

Contents

Introduction

Contemporary political philosophy tends to depict politics as an activity involving rational individuals. For instance, the image of politics that emerges from John Rawls' *Theory of Justice* or Habermas' *Between Facts and Norms*, perhaps the two major works of political philosophy of the last fifty years, is that of a sphere of human life in which one can count on the rationality of the actors involved. However rationality is conceived, either as rationality with regard to ends and values, or as communicative rationality, the image of politics resulting from these works is that of an activity which can and should be guided by rational procedures.

Nevertheless, when one looks at the everyday activity that goes under the heading of "politics", one is confronted with quite a different picture.[1] People involved in this activity are not so easily persuaded to adopt rational procedures of communication and decision. Therefore, a purely rational model of society risks being a model for a world that does not exist.

Indeed, quite often, people seem to act on the basis of arational elements, some other kinds of powerful symbols and images of the world, which are not taken into account by a purely rational image of politics.

---

[1] Clearly, the purpose of both Habermas and Rawls is not to give an account of everyday politics but to propose a model for it. All the same, they both implicitly suggest with their models that politics is an activity where one can count on the rationality of the actors involved.

The twentieth century, with the rise of totalitarianism and its two world wars, contains countless examples. While the grandiose parades of totalitarian regimes exhibited the power of arational elements, such as myths and symbols, in a patent way, there seems to be reason to suspect that these elements still manoeuvre among us. Despite the fact that their presence is not always conspicuous, they might still be there, exercising their power in a more subtle way.

Scholars of different disciplines have long recognised the political role played by arational elements. Sociologists, historians and anthropologists, each in their own way, have devoted an important part of their work to the analysis of these kinds of phenomena. Anthropologists have always had to deal with such issues. As external observers catapulted into remote regions of the world, they were, perhaps, in the best position to do so: the foreignness of the "primitives" made their myths and symbols conspicuous to the anthropologists' eyes. Furthermore, in the study of traditional societies, the presence of such phenomena seemed to be the obvious consequence of the fact that politics could hardly be separated from religion in those cultures.[2]

Historians, too, have long dealt with such phenomena, at least from the time of Bloch's *The Royal Touch* (1973) and Kantorowicz's seminal work on medieval political theology, *The King's Two Bodies* (1957). These two works, in particular, by starting from the observation that rulers share some properties with gods, opened the path for a new line of study on the mythical and symbolic dimensions of power. But all these studies were still confined to traditional societies, in which the influence of myths and symbols could still be attributed to the proximity between politics and religion that characterises these societies.

Sociology has also dealt with these topics for a long time: one just has to think of the founding fathers of this discipline, Durkheim and Weber.[3] On the other hand, precisely by moving from Weber's

---

[2] See, for instance, the classical Malinowski (1992) or, more recently, Geertz (1983). However, both Geertz and Malinowski deal with myths under the general category of symbolism and do not focus specifically on the concept of political myth.

[3] On this point, see, in particular, Eisenstadt's collection of Weber's works on charisma and institution building (Weber 1969). However, Weber's concept of charisma refers to the belief in the exceptional qualities of the leader, and does not focus on the specific notion of political myth.

prediction of the transformation of the spirit of modernity into an iron cage (*stahlhartes Gehäuse*), one could think that modern politics, as a consequence of its increasing rationalisation and bureaucratisation, had become immune to the influence of myths and symbols: in a rationalist iron cage, there seems to be little room for them. If modern politics is deemed to have become the business of bureaucratic "specialists without spirits" (Weber 1976: 182), one could easily be tempted to conclude that there is no more need for myths and symbols.[4]

Rather recently, a number of new studies focusing on the mobilising power of modern myths and symbols have emerged. The rise of identity politics and the revival of nationalism in recent decades have, perhaps, rendered manifest that, to paraphrase Geertz, the extraordinary has not gone out of modern politics, however much of the banal may have entered it (Geertz 1983: 143). As well, the emphasis both on constructivism and on the linguistic turn have given rise to a new interest in the symbolic dimensions of social phenomena. As a consequence, titles such as "The invention of x" or "The symbolic construction of y and z" are quite common today.[5] The result of this new emphasis is that there is now a striking number of publications whose titles contain the word "myth" and/or the word "symbols".

The exponential number of publications on this topic would suggest the existence of a refined and consolidated theoretical framework for their use. However, there is not one yet. The aim of this book is to help to fill this gap and the way in which it does so is by proposing a "philosophy of political myth". The purpose of this proposition of a philosophy of political myth is not only to propose a new theory of political myth, but also to provide this theory with a philosophical framework that addresses the questions of what political myths are and why we need them.

Indeed, while there exists a vast theoretical literature that deals with the symbolic dimension of power in general, the different forms of political symbolism are rarely dealt with separately. To deal with these phenomena under headings such as "the extraordinary" or "political

---

[4] In reality, at some points, Weber himself seems to be aware of the possibility of new prophets: see, for instance, the end of *The Protestant Ethic and the Spirit of Capitalism* (Weber 1976).

[5] See, for example, *The Invention of Tradition* by the historians Hobsbawm and Ranger (1983) and *The Symbolic Construction of Community* by the anthropologist Cohen (1985).

symbolism" (Geertz 1983) can be misleading, because it might suggest
that all that is not rational is symbolic or extraordinary. Works such as
The Symbolic Uses of Politics (Edelman 1976) or *The Construction of Society*
(Cohen 1985) quite often end up unifying very different phenomena
under their very general categories – and this, in its turn, has led to the
conflation of myth with the much more general category of symbolism.

The problem, however, is that myths and symbols do not coincide.
Despite the fact that myths operate with symbols, the two concepts of
myth and symbol must be kept separate: to conflate the two would be to
lose the specificity of myth. Myths operate through symbols, but not all
symbols are myths: the sequence of letters of a mathematical equation
is also a symbol, but nobody – or only a few – would argue that it is a
myth. As Cassirer argues, symbols, in this sense, are the transcendental
conditions of the human mind: myth, science, language itself, these
are all "symbolic functions", that is, functions of the human mind
through which only the multiplicity of experience can be grasped and
communicated (Cassirer 1977).

It is precisely the conflation between these concepts that has generated most of the confusion surrounding this topic. In turn, this has
also generated a great reluctance to use the concept of myth at all –
particularly in relation to the realm of politics. Why make recourse
to a concept as cumbersome as myth, and not resort instead to other
concepts such as "tales", "narratives" or "legends"?

Much of this book is devoted to showing that to make recourse to
such substitutes is neither possible nor necessary. It is not possible,
because all of the alternatives are inadequate to convey the semantic
complexities of the concept of myth. Indeed, the word myth has been
used – and abused – in so many different and various ways. Faced
with the varieties of the conceptions of myth, Cassirer, more than
fifty years ago, recalled the scene of the witch's kitchen in Goethe's
Faust: Faust, waiting for the drink by which he shall regain his youth,
stands in front of an enchanted glass and has the wonderful vision of
a woman of supernatural beauty. Faust is enraptured and spellbound,
but Mephisto, standing at his side, scoffs at his enthusiasm because he
knows that what Faust has seen is not a real woman but only a creature of his mind (Cassirer 1973: 5). Myth, Cassirer suggests, is a sort of
enchanted mirror in which scholars have found the objects with which
each is most familiar: the linguists found a world of signs and names;

the psychologists a product of the unconscious; the philosophers both the opposite of philosophy and a form of primitive philosophy; and so on. Hence, the varieties of the conceptions of myth, and the complexity of the semantic area covered by the term as well. When faced with this complexity, one cannot simply disregard it.

Indeed, it is precisely because of this complexity that none of these alternatives are suitable. A myth is not a simple tale, because there are plenty of tales that are not mythical. *The Canterbury Tales* by Geoffrey Chaucer are not myths – they might have referred to myths, they might have worked as myth in the past, but they do not seem to operate as myths any longer. Myth is not co-extensive with the concept of narrative, either: it suffices to think of all the failed myths, that is, all the narratives that did not succeed in acquiring the status of myth. Neither is a myth a legend, because there are myths that are not legends, and vice versa. We can talk of the "myth of the French Revolution", but nobody would talk of the "legend of the French Revolution". At least, those who use the expression "the legend of the French revolution" mean something different from what is understood by "the myth of the French revolution".

Finding a substitute for myth is not only impossible, it is also unnecessary. With regard to *political* myth, there is now, indeed, a vast literature that examines from different perspectives the role that myths play in politics. Still, there is a striking asymmetry in the state of the art on this topic. On the one hand, there is an ever growing amount of literature that deals with specific case studies – beginning with the pioneering studies of the 1960s by Norman Cohn and Eric Hobsbawm on the role of eschatological myths in peasant rebellion (Cohn 1970; and Hobsbawm 1963), and the long series of studies on nationalism.[6] On the other hand, there are very few theoretical studies that clarify the different uses of the concept of political myth and even fewer that address the question of why this concept should be used at all.

In particular, while there is an overwhelming number of historical and sociological works that deal with specific case studies, political philosophy seems to be reluctant to accept the concept of political myth as an object of specific inquiry. Moreover, most of the (few) contemporary

---

[6] On myth and nationalism, there is now a vast literature. See, for example, Smith 1986; 1991; 1999, and Stråth 2000.

works that have undertaken this task have done so by approaching political myth through general categories such as "political symbolism" or, recently, "veil politics" (Wingo 2003). It is to this latter concept that Wingo, by criticising Rawls's liberalism, had recourse in order to vindicate the importance and legitimacy of elements such as monuments, flags, national heroes, political myths and rituals (Wingo 2003). According to Wingo, not only do "veils" operate in liberal democratic societies, but it could not be otherwise: they are a crucial means of both political persuasion and propaganda. Moreover, in his view, "veils" are not incompatible with the principle of individual autonomy if they meet the criterion of consensus from all sectors of a nation.

The problem, though, with this view is that by unifying such different phenomena as flags, rituals, national heroes, and political myths under the heading of "veil politics", not only does one lose the specificity of political myth, but one also risks ending up in a generalised defence of all sorts of "veils". For instance, it is disputable whether the cult of national heroes, which Wingo mentions among the possible forms of "veil", is compatible with the principle of autonomy.

The reluctance of political philosophy to focus specifically on the concept of political myth is particularly striking in light of the richness of the philosophical studies on the concept of myth. If the philosophical literature on political myth is very limited, the literature on myth without further qualification is endless. Myth has been the object of much Western speculation: the other side of philosophy; the side against which philosophy has defined itself as an intellectual enterprise; but also the cumbersome other side that has continually recurred throughout the centuries, despite all attempts to rationalise it. Notwithstanding the pervasiveness of myth, both the enlightened thinkers who argue for the dismissal of mythical thinking and the nostalgic romantics who advocate its renovation have rarely expressly dealt with *political* myth.

Indeed, there is not a vast tradition of philosophies of political myth. This may be due to the fact that it is only under the conditions of modernity that the specifically *political* role played by myth emerges as a topic. While political myths are hardly distinguishable from religious myths in archaic societies, in modern societies, with the separation of politics from its religious anchorage, on the one hand, and its democratisation on the other, the role of specifically *political* myths becomes conspicuous. As Sorel argues, when it comes to explaining typically modern phenomena such as major social movements, the fact that the people participating in them represent their action in the form of grand narratives that depict their success, becomes so evident that there seems to be little need to insist on the role of political myth (Sorel 1975: 22).

In spite of this conspicuousness, there seems to be something in the concept of political myth that renders it recalcitrant to a philosophical treatment. Indeed, if one looks for the classical theories of political myths, one discovers that philosophers themselves have focused on specific political myths rather than on political myth in general. Most noticeably, the theories of political myth that can be derived from the two most important philosophical works on the topic, namely, Sorel's *Reflections on Violence* (1975) or Cassirer's *The Myth of the State* (1973), are encapsulated in reflections on singular political myths: the proletarian general strike, and the myth of the Aryan race respectively. It seems as if political myths have an intrinsically particularistic nature, and this has not favoured the proliferation of a philosophical reflection on this topic.

However, there is nothing that, a priori, prevents a philosophical treatment of political myth. In particular, the debate on myth that took place in Germany in the 1970s focused on this particularistic nature of myth. Among the philosophers who participated in this debate, Hans Blumenberg best captured this in his theory of myth as "work on myth" (Blumenberg 1985). For this reason, Blumenberg's philosophical reflections on myth provide the ideal platform for a theory of political myth that specifically addresses their particularistic nature. A myth, Blumenberg concluded, is not a product that is given once and for all, but is instead a process of the continual reworking of a basic narrative core or *mythologem.* Blumenberg conveyed this idea through the German expression *Arbeit am Mythos,* which literally means "work on myth". If myth consists of the work on myth, not only are there no single myths, which are given once and for all, but the same *mythologem* also changes over time because, on each occasion, it is reappropriated[7] by different needs and exigencies. In order to work as a

---

[7] On Blumenberg's concept of reappropriation (*Umbesetzung*), see Blumenberg 1971 and Leghissa 2002.

myth, a narrative must always answer a need for significance (*Bedeut-samkeit*). If it cannot do so, it simply ceases to be a myth (Blumenberg 1985).

Blumenberg, however, puts forward his theory more through a phenomenological analysis of single myths than through the development of a systematic theory. Furthermore, he mainly focuses on literary myths and does not specifically deal with political myths: the political scope of his theory remains, in general, in the background and is not explicitly problematised. The overall German debate on myth (*Mythosdebatte*), the philosophical debate that took place in Germany from the 1970s onwards, rich as it is in theoretical insights does not, however, systematically focus on political myth.

My aim in this book is to construct a philosophical framework for a theory of political myth understood as "work on myth". In this way, I situate it between philosophical theories of myth, on the one hand, and the social science literature on political myth, on the other. Among the latter, together with the huge body of literature devoted to single case studies, there are also works specifically devoted to political myth. None of them however, has treated political myth as a process rather than as an object. Most of them remain therefore incomplete from different points of view.

For instance, both Lincoln's *Discourse and the Construction of Society* and Flood's *Political Myth* aim to build a theory of political myth.[8] However, both Lincoln and Flood treat political myth as an object, and, in particular, as an object that advances a claim to truth – and this approach, as we will see, is essentially flawed. Lincoln defines myths as those kinds of narratives that possess credibility and authority, in which a narrative possessing authority is "one for which successful claims are made not only to the status of truth, but, what is more, to the status of *paradigmatic* truth" (Lincoln 1989: 24). Similarly, Flood, who understands political myth as the synthesis of political ideology and religious myths, defines it as "an ideologically marked narrative which purports to give a *true* account of a set of past, present, or predicted

---

[8] Other works are conceived as surveys of existing theories. For instance, Tudor discusses the various theories of myth with the explicit intent of an introductory work, i.e., simply to draw attention to a common, but often neglected, type of political argument (Tudor 1972).

political events, and which is accepted as valid in its essential by a social group" (Flood 1996: 44, emphasis mine).

However, to define myth, in general, and political myth, in particular, in terms of its claim to "truth" means to bring it to a terrain that is not its own. As Wittgenstein pointed out many years before the publication of these works, a myth is not a scientific hypothesis about the constitution of the world: it does not aim to put forward a theory and cannot, therefore, be approached from the standpoint of its claim to truth (Wittgenstein 1979). Following Wittgenstein's philosophy of language, it may be said that to interrogate myths from the standpoint of their true or false account means to assume too limited a view of what human language and meanings are about: human beings are ceremonious animals, who, with their language, perform innumerable actions that are not based on any hypothesis about the constitution of the world (Wittgenstein 1979).

One could, perhaps, simply reject the theories of political myth of both Flood and Lincoln, on the basis of Wittgenstein's philosophical criticism towards the approach to myth that they endorse. Readers wishing to follow this route may skip the first part of this book and begin their reading at Chapter 4. This chapter first reconstructs Wittgenstein's critique of Fraser's *Golden Bough*, and shows thereby the shortcomings of an approach to myth in terms of truth; second, by discussing Wittgenstein's philosophy of language, the chapter points to an alternative view of language and meaning, one that is better suited to a theory of political myth.

The problem, however, remains that both Flood's and Lincoln's theories contain important remarks with regard to the way in which political myths work within a society: a philosophy of political myth would be enormously impoverished if it refused to engage with them. Moreover, these views also seem to reflect quite a common attitude towards myth. This comes as no surprise if one considers that what characterises the social sciences is precisely the fact that they take their objects as given, and, therefore, tend to rely on concepts as they emerge from everyday language.

Indeed, if we open the *Oxford English Dictionary* at the entry on "myth", we read: "1a A purely fictitious narrative usually involving supernatural persons, actions, or events, and embodying some popular idea concerning natural and historical phenomena; 1b in generalized use, also an untrue or popular tale, a rumour. 2. A fictitious or imaginary person or object" (Simpson and Weiner 1989; vol. X, 177). In both meanings 1 and 2, myth is characterised in terms of "fictitiousness" and "untruth", where "fictitious" – according to the *Oxford English Dictionary* – does not simply mean "artificial", but also "counterfeit", "arbitrarily devised", "feigned to exist", "imaginary", and "not real" (Simpson and Weiner 1989: vol. V, 873). Thus, three features seem to characterise the common use of the term: fictitiousness, unreality, and untruth.

Faced with the common usage of the term, one cannot simply refer to Wittgenstein and Blumenberg. In particular, a philosophy of political myth situates itself between social sciences and philosophy, and therefore, if it cannot simply ignore the former, which tend to take their objects as given, it can have recourse to philosophy, which typically puts its objects in question. With regard to the definition of myth in terms of its claim to truth, the approach adopted here is philosophical and consists of reconstructing the genealogy of this view of myth (Part I), and showing why contemporary thinking has the means for going beyond its presuppositions (Part II).

The genealogical method, as Nietzsche defined it in his *On the Genealogy of Morality*, consists precisely in facing the problem of the meaning of a certain formation by looking at the circumstances in which it was created and at the values that were at stake in this process (Nietzsche 1994: 5). In this sense, a genealogy of myth is not a reconstruction of the history of myth, but rather a *critique* of a certain view of myth aimed at discovering what its presuppositions are.

To this end, Chapter 1 moves from the recognition that in the Greek Homeric culture *mythos* simply meant word and was used as a synonym of *logos*. In contrast to the narrative of the birth of philosophy as an exit from myth, this chapter argues that, until the fourth century BC, no opposition between *mythos* and *logos* is attested. Even if the two terms had begun to be separated by the time of the sophists (fifth century BC) – *mythos* specialising in the meaning of "tale" and *logos* in that of "discourse, calculation", they were not yet counterpoised from the point of view of their relationship to truth. Philosophers themselves, at least up to Plato, did not disdain to have recourse to myth. Even if the professionalisation of philosophy brought with it a critical stance on the part of certain philosophers towards the old mythological tradition, not even in Aristotle is there an identification of myth with untruth and unreality. Instead, for Aristotle, *mythoi* are the constitutive elements of poetry, whose essence is the *mimesis* of reality.

Clearly, it is a particular conception of truth and reality that is at stake here: the ancient Greeks conceived of truth as *aletheia*, literally "unhiddenness", and it is only against this conception of the truth that we can understand the plurality of Greek myths: while this plurality is a scandal to us and we keep asking ourselves, "Did they really believe in their myths?", their view of the truth simply allowed a plurality of myths and of variants within a *mythologem* to coexist. And it is only because this plurality has been lost that the view of myth as untruth and unreality was able to emerge.

Chapter 2 reconstructs one of the crucial moments for the development of the attitude to treating myths from the point of view of their claim to truth. When the *logos* became the revealed Word of a unique God, the plurality of truths of ancient myths began to be condemned as deceitful. Indeed, in the monotheistic religion of the Book (*Biblos*), there seems to be something that is fundamentally hostile to the plurality of myth. This chapter argues that this consists of an absolute claim to truth and uniqueness that leaves no space for the recognition of the polytheistic world of myth. In this way, the sacred *logos* finds itself caught in a dialectic, in which, by condemning the plurality of myths, it presents itself as Holy History, that is, as History in the singular, and thereby denies its own possible mythical nature. But, as we will see, once the principle of the free interpretation of the sacred *logos* comes to be fully developed, it cannot but lead to the recognition of the mythical nature of the sacred *logos* itself, and, therefore, to the recognition of a plurality of histories.

Another crucial moment in the development of the common view of myth is represented by the dialectic of the Enlightenment that is analysed in Chapter 3. Following the thesis sustained by Horkheimer and Adorno more than fifty years ago, this chapter explores the dialectic into which any absolutism of scientific *logos* risks falling (Adorno and Horkheimer 1997). In particular, it argues that the Enlightenment, by condemning myth for its subjectivity, hides the fact that myth is already "enlightenment" insofar as it concerns the telling and the finding out of the origins of things. In this way, the Enlightenment reinforces that separation between the knowing subject and the known object upon which scientific *logos* itself rests. It is from the point of view of the Enlightenment that myths are condemned not just as untruth, but also as imaginary and thus unreal. The mistake here is to consider myth as a source of heteronomy and therefore as an obstacle for the modern project of individual autonomy. Myths are not necessarily heteronymous, because imagination can also be "radical", that is, it can also be a means for the critique.

Romantic approaches to myth, with their call for a rehabilitation of myth understood as the vehicle for a divine revelation, simply invert the axiological value of the dichotomy of myth versus reason upon which Enlightenment itself rests, instead of radically questioning it. Both Enlightenment and Romanticism are understood here as ideal-types rather than as historical processes. The critique put forward by this genealogy is meant to be a critique of an always possible attitude towards myth, and not a critique of historical processes that are of course always more complex than what can emerge in a few pages.

On a more historical ground, Chapter 4 shows that the reflections on the nature of language and meaning that have followed the so-called linguistic turn have not only gone beyond the presuppositions of the dialectic of Enlightenment, but also beyond the very opposition between an enlightened and a romantic view of myth. In particular, the philosophy of Wittgenstein, who is a central author of the linguistic turn, has definitely shown that any distinction between an expressive and a designative view of language is essentially flawed because meanings are only possible through language-games in which no distinction between the two views can be drawn.

Chapter 5, moving from both the genealogy of myth and the discussion of Wittgenstein's philosophy, tries to delineate a possible approach to myth that escapes both the dialectic of the sacred *logos* and that of the Enlightenment. In contrast to the criticism raised by the *logos* against the plurality of myth, Chapter 5 argues, first, in favour of an *interrelational* approach to myth, that is, of an approach that, following Blumenberg, focuses on the "work on myth" (*Arbeit am Mythos*); and second, in contrast to the Enlightenment's discourse about the unreality of myth, it proposes to adopt a *phenomenological* approach that leaves the problem of reality in parentheses. The chapter continues by pointing to four fundamental features of the work on myth: 1) myth operates with figurative means; 2) it is not limited to a particular set of contents; 3) it takes place around a narrative; and 4) it provides what Blumenberg has called "significance" (*Bedeutsamkeit*).

Blumenberg's concept of significance is discussed in Chapter 6. Myths provide names through which the unknown first becomes masterable, but they also provide narratives, which, by inserting events into a plot, can produce and reproduce significance. This leads back to Gehlen's characterisation of human beings as "not yet determined animals": human beings, in contrast to other animals, are not adapted to a specific environment. As a consequence, not only they are open to the world (*weltoffen*), and thus exposed to all sorts of stimulations from which they must seek relief through the creation of meaning, but they also interrogate themselves over the conditions of their own existence and must therefore provide significance to these conditions in order to fight the indifference of the world. As Kerényi has also pointed out, the function of myth is not simply to provide names for things, but, more specifically, to ground (*begründen*) them.

Chapter 7 serves as a passage from the preparatory parts, which deal with myth in general, to the parts specifically devoted to analysing the role that myth, thus conceived, plays in politics. In particular, to assume that, since political modernity has liberated politics from its religious anchorage, it must also have liberated it from myth means to take the point of view of the Enlightenment, which assimilates myth and religion under the heading of superstition. Myths, however, are not religion, and thus they can be a possible means of *critique*. By exploring the work of one of the most powerful myths of modern political theory, the myth of the state of nature, and the way in which the work on this myth changes between different authors and contexts, the chapter concludes that myth is not, in principle, incompatible with the idea of autonomy, and that, as Rousseau's uses of this myth shows, it can be an important means for critique. By doing so, this chapter advances a claim that recurs more or less explicitly in many points in the text: political myths can and should be a means for autonomy.

This view of political myth clashes with the view emerging from Cassirer's treatment of myth. Cassirer's view is discussed in Chapter 8, which is devoted to reconstructing the classical theories of political myth. This chapter prepares the terrain for the subsequent discussion of the definition of political myth. In particular, after rejecting Cassirer's definition of political myth as collective desire personified, because it is too dependent on the totalitarian model on the one hand, and on the premises of the Enlightenment on the other, the chapter focuses on Sorel's theory of political myth, as it emerges in his discussion of the general strike. With his emphasis on the *pouvoir moteur* of myth, which makes sense – we would say significance – of the present by providing a vision of a future catastrophe, Sorel points to the fact that myth is not a description of things, but a determination to act. However, he does so from the point of view of a problematical theory of two selves.

Exploring modern political theory, one can find another philosopher whose reflections on these topics provide crucial insights for a philosophy of political myth. Spinoza's political thinking stands as an anomaly in modernity not only due to his detailed analysis of the symbolic conditions for the preservation of power, but also because he combines it with a radical theory of democracy. In his reconstruction of the role played by prophecy in the constitution of the ancient nation of Israel, Spinoza points out that prophecy is a creation of the imagination understood as an idea produced on the basis of present or past bodily impressions. Prophecy is valid because the prophet is morally certain of his knowledge and this moral certainty is derived from the fact that he belongs to a community whose rules and laws he embodies. While myth is a form of regression into a primitive form of consciousness for Cassirer, and a means of progress for Sorel, Spinoza seems to conclude that myths can be a means for both. Myths operate in all societies, but where they differ is in the degree to which these mythical beliefs are subject to open and free discussion.

Chapter 9 concludes that a political myth can be defined as the work on a common narrative by which the members of a social group (or society) provide significance to their political experience and deeds. Thus, what makes a political myth out of a simple narrative is not its content or its claim to truth, but first, the fact that this narrative coagulates and produces significance, second, that it is shared by a group, and third, that it can come to address the specifically political conditions in which this group operates. This chapter represents the point of arrival of this work, that is, the point where the theory prepared for by the preceding chapters is put forward. The subsequent discussion is therefore simply meant to position this view within the debates of the social sciences, by analysing the relationship between political myth and other related concepts. The remaining part of the chapter argues that political myths thus understood are analytically distinct from ideology on the one hand, and utopia on the other.

Chapter 10 examines the consequences that this definition of political myth implies for the relationship between political myth and historical narratives. Even if both are constitutive of what Castoriadis called the social imaginary, and even if they are quite often intermingled, the two categories must be kept separate: when we say that a certain historical narrative is a political myth, we mean that this narrative has come to work in a particular way, namely as a narrative that provides significance to certain political experiences and deeds.

Finally, Chapter 11 looks at the role that myth plays in the constitution of common identity. By criticising Schmitt's view of political myth as a symptom of the national energy, this chapter maintains that myth is not only the product, but also the producer of common identities. Against Schmitt's holistic treatment of identity, in this chapter I argue for a distinction between different forms of identity – identity with an adjective: personal, social, cultural, and political, and so on, – albeit without ignoring the possible interactions among them. It is precisely the work on political myth, which can play a crucial role in the construction of common identities, that stresses how problematic it can be to separate cultural identity from political identity. Indeed, there are narratives that do not contain anything political per se, but that, within certain contexts, can come to create significance and to contribute to the shaping of common political identities.

The same argument emerges again in Chapter 12, with the analysis of some possible sites for the work of political myths today. This is, properly speaking, the task of a sociology of political myth understood as work on myth, for the construction of which we can only advance some suggestions herein. In particular, this final chapter puts forward some hypotheses as to the forms that political myths could assume under the contemporary conditions of a global society of spectacle. As the analysis of political myths such as that of the clash between civilisations suggests, there are reasons to suspect that it is precisely in our epoch, which aspires to get rid of the grand political narratives, that the work of political myth has become much more insidious than it has ever been in the past.

A theory of political myth can hardly avoid the normative question of how and when the critique of political myths is possible. The present philosophy of political myth points out that political myths are the product of a universal human need for significance and that they can and should be a means for critique and thus for autonomy. The task of a future sociology of political myth, understood as work on myth, will be to spell out in what conditions political myths are respectively a means for liberation or for oppression.

I

A GENEALOGY OF MYTH

According to common usage, myth is defined in terms of its untruth and unreality.[1] The task of a genealogy of myth is to reconstruct the presuppositions of such a view. Following Nietzsche's definition of the genealogical method (Nietzsche 1994), a genealogy must address the question of "what is x?" by simultaneously asking "why do we conceive of it in this way?". As Nietzsche pointed out, a genealogy faces the problem of *meaning* by looking at the *circumstances* in which it was created and thus at the *values* that were at stake in its creation (Nietzsche 1994: 5).[2]

In this sense, genealogy is a form of *critique* (Nietzsche 1994: 8). In contrast to the typically modern type of philosophical critique, it does not, however, aim at providing a transcendental fundament. The latter, according to Nietzsche, can easily turn into the opposite of the critique, that is, into the hypostatisation of a particular view and of the values that it presupposes (Nietzsche 2002: 75–92). In contrast, as Nietzsche puts it in his letter to Overbeck on 4 January 1888, the genealogical method aims to set up a critique of a given formation through the "artificial isolation" of some of its different hotbeds (*verschiedenen Entstehungsheerde*) (Nietzsche 1984: 224, trans. mine).

[1] See, for instance, the term "myth" in the *Oxford English Dictionary* (Simpson and Weiner 1989: vol. X, 177).
[2] On the relationship between meaning and values in Nietzsche's genealogical method, see Deleuze 2006: 1–3.

Consequently, a genealogy of myth must not be understood as either a history of myth or as a simple reconstruction of its origins. Insofar as it aims at isolating some of the different hotbeds that generated the view of myth as untruth and unreality from which we started, a genealogy does not focus on the continuity of history, but rather on its discontinuities.

In their *Dialectic of Enlightenment*, Adorno and Horkheimer put forward the thesis of a mutually dialectic constitution of myth and *logos* (Adorno and Horkheimer 1997). As has been observed, the approach they developed in this book is an example of a Nietzschean genealogy (Habermas 1987: 106–30). However, whereas they applied the genealogical method to the Enlightenment (*Aufklärung*) in order to show how it constitutes itself by rejecting myth, a genealogy of myth starts from myth and looks at the ways in which it was produced.

In particular, the following genealogy of myth focuses on the ways in which myth is related to the *logos* understood in different ways – first as *logos* without further specification (Chapter 1), then as *sacred logos* (Chapter 2), and, finally, as *scientific logos* (Chapter 3). This has many important consequences that will become clear later on. For now, suffice it to say that, while Adorno and Horkheimer move from the Enlightenment (*Aufklärung*), that is modern rationality, and then project it back to the Greek *logos*, in order to show the continuity between the two, a genealogy of myth moves from the Greek *mythos* and then tries to reconstruct the discontinuities of its genealogy.

Starting from the Greek *mythos* may appear arbitrary from the point of view of its spatial and temporal limitation (Jamme 1999). A reply to this objection is implicit in the concept of genealogy I have sketched. A genealogy does not aim at any kind of exhaustiveness – in either space or time – or at setting up a comparison between the ways in which different cultures across the globe have conceived of myth. It merely seeks to question a certain view of myth, namely a view that identifies it with "unreality and untruth", and then, by looking for its discontinuities, tries to put forward a critique of its presuppositions.

In particular, Chapter 1 aims to show that no association of myth with untruth and unreality is present in ancient Greece. To this end, the chapter criticises the traditional image of the birth of philosophy as an exit from myth and points out that not even in Aristotle or Plato is there a myth versus logos dichotomy.

This is the consequence of a different approach to the question of truth and reality, one which allowed the plurality of truths of myth to simply coexist. The emergence of the view of myth as untrue and unreal is the clearest sign that this plurality has been lost. There are two fundamental moments in this process: the rise of the monotheistic religion of the Book (Chapter 2), and the emergence of an "enlightened" view of the world (Chapter 3). Both of them must be understood as ideal-types rather than as historical process. Indeed, the critique put forward by a genealogy is meant to be a critique of always possible attitudes, and not a critique of historical processes, which would in any case be too complex to be analysed within the space of this work.

1

Mythos and *Logos*

Mythos is a Greek word which originally meant "word, speech". According to certain etymologists, it derives from a popular expression constituted by the onomatopoeic sound *mu-* (the sound that we produce with a closed mouth), and the common suffix *-thos*.[1] In the Homeric poems, *mython eeipe* is, for instance, the standard expression used to mean "he or she said", without adding any further connotations (Tebben 1994: 902; 1998: 1155).[2] In these poems, the primary meaning of the term is that of "word, speech", even though, as secondary meanings, the term is used in the sense of "public speech", and also "dialogue, conversation" or "tale, narration" (Liddell, Scott, and Stuart 1968: 1151).

By the time of the composition of the Homeric poems – a time that most interpreters place around the eighth century BC, the semantic area of the Homeric *mythos* corresponded to the area that would later be covered by the term *logos*.[3] Indeed, whereas the term *logos* is

---

[1] For a discussion of this etymology, see the entries "*mu-*" and "*mythos*" in Chantraine's *Dictionnaire Etymologique de la langue grecque* (Chantraine 1984: 717–18).

[2] In the 153 occurrences of *mytho** in the *Odyssey*, we have *mytho* eeipe* 20 times and *mytheomai*, "to tell, to speak", 37 times (Tebben 1994: 902); in the *Iliad*, there are 146 occurrences of *mytho**: the expression *mytho* eeipe* occurs 33 times and the verb *mytheomai*, "to tell", appears 20 times (Tebben 1998: 1155).

[3] According to some interpreters, in Homer *mythos* would designate a specific kind of speech, i.e. an authoritative speech act – the prototype being the public oration of the poet (Martin 1989). Despite these divergences, scholars agree on the basic meaning,

almost absent in the Homeric poems – there are only two occurrences, one in the *Iliad* (XV, 393) and one in the *Odyssey* (I, 56) – the term progressively came into common usage up to a point when it took the semantic place once occupied by *mythos*. At the same time, *mythos* began to express the additional meaning of "tale". According to Chantraine, this passage is fully attested in the works of the tragedians and of Plato: it is at this point that the term *mythos* tends to specialise in the sense of "narrative", "subject of a tragedy" (Chantraine 1984: 718; trans. mine).

Thus, a genealogy of myth starts with *mythos* meaning simply "word, speech", as synonymous with *logos*, and ends with the common view of *mythos* and *logos* as opposites, as false and true discourse respectively. What happened in between? Which forces determined such a passage? The aim of this chapter is to show that no dichotomy of *mythos* versus *logos* is attested by the ancient Greek sources, such a dichotomy being, rather, a later interpretation of the modern rationality in search of its origins. Not only is it the case that the so-called birth of philosophy did not represent an exit from the world of myth, as many argued, but not even in Plato or Aristotle is there a definitive association of *mythos* with false discourse. This, as we will see, is the consequence of a different attitude towards the question of the "truth" and "reality" of myth, one that simply allowed a plurality of truths to coexist.

According to a common view, however, it is the birth of philosophy that, by giving rise to a fundamentally new approach towards the world, determined the eclipse of the old mythological tradition and relegated the semantic ambit of *mythos* to that of pure "fiction". In this view, the activity initiated in the Ionia of the seventh century BC by the first "naturalist philosophers"[4] represented the exit from the world of myth. For the first time, thinkers such as Thales, Anaximander and Anaximenes searched for a rational underlying principle of the world

---

"word, speech", and therefore on the semantic proximity of the two areas *mythos, mytheomai* and *logos, legein* – as is attested by the expressions that combine the two areas, such as the previously mentioned *mythos* *eeipe*, or the verb *mythologeuo*, which simply means "to tell words" (Liddell, Scott, and Stuart 1968: 1150).

[4] As we will see later on, this is Aristotle's definition. Indeed, it was Aristotle who attributed to these figures both the title of first philosophers and that of "naturalist" philosophers.

(*arché*) – identifying it first with water (Thales), then with *apeiron*[5] (Anaximander) and finally with air (Anaximenes). In so doing, they rejected all mythological explanations and opened the Western road from "*mythos* to *logos*" (Nestlé 1942).

The narrative of the Greek "birth of philosophy" was linked with the idea of a Western development from "*mythos* to *logos*". *From Myth to Logos* was the title of Nestlé's very influential book and it captures well ideas that were widespread at the beginning of the twentieth century (Nestlé 1942; Burnet 1920). These views, which were elaborated in an epoch of crisis, served not only to provide an identity for the so-called European or Western civilisation, but also to supply an ideological covering for its political expansionism. In other words, the argument concerning Europe as the birthplace of philosophy was used to justify the superiority of Western civilisation: even when the argument did not take the explicit form of a panegyric upon "the extraordinary intelligence of Greek men", the fathers of European civilisation (Burnet 1920: 10), it still lent itself to providing an ideological justification for European colonialism.[6]

The idea of a "Western road from *mythos* to *logos*" is still widespread. Kirk adds a question mark to the title of his essay "From Myth to Philosophy?" and thus vindicates his perplexities about the narrative of the "birth of philosophy" as a linear development from *mythos* to *logos* (Kirk 1970; 1974: 277ff.). All the same, he still maintains that the birth of philosophy does imply the dismissal of myth. As he radically concludes in his essay: "the organic use of myths has to disappear before philosophy becomes even a remote possibility" (Kirk 1974: 279).

This, however, contrasts with the continuity that has been observed between the mythical tradition and the theories of the Ionians. For instance, Vernant recognised that there are some similarities between

---

[5] The term *to apeiron* is often translated as "the indefinite" (see, for instance, Kirk, Raven, and Schonfield 1983). Others more accurately translate it as "non-limited" (Freeman 1966). Its literal translation is "without boundaries", so a close translation might be "boundless".

[6] It seems that the term "civilisation", which implied from its very origins a contrast between "civilised" and "barbarian", has never completely freed itself from this original connotation of the "superiority" of the "civilised" (Fisch 1992: 688, 785). Recent theories about the multiplicity of civilisations can thus be read as the (later) recognition that there is a plurality of "civilised peoples".

the conceptual structure employed by the Ionic physicians and that employed by Hesiod's cosmogony. In the first place, Hesiod had already presented the creation of the world by referring to characters such as Chaos, the Earth, the Sky, which, as their names point out, can be interpreted in purely naturalistic terms. Even more: the conceptual apparatus of Hesiod's cosmogony and the view of the world put forward by the Ionic philosophers seem to correspond in the details. In both cases, the origin of the world is seen in terms of: chaos at the beginning; the separation of pairs of opposites such as hot and cold, dry and wet, and so on, out of the primordial unity; and the reunification and interaction between the opposites (Vernant 2006: 372ff.; Cornford 1952).

Surprisingly, however, Vernant himself also argues that the birth of philosophy still represents such a deep change in mentality (*changement de mentalité*) that we can, nevertheless, see in it the "act of baptism of Western man, the emergence of the true spirit, with the values that we can recognise in this term" (Vernant 2006: 15; trans. modified). In other words, the birth of philosophy represents in his view the beginning of rational and positive thought.

According to Vernant, such a change consisted in the fact that, with the so-called naturalist philosophers, the *explanans* assumed, for the first time, the form of an abstract quality instead of personified agents – as is underlined by the new use of the article *to* in expressions such as "the humid" or "the hot". In other words, these thinkers were looking for "the hot", a reality defined by the positive action of warming up, and not by some mythical power such as Hephaestus, or any other mythical figure. For this reason, Vernant argues, their theorising represents the moment when positivity invaded being and led to the consequent dismissal of myth: "With the physicists, a certain positivity suddenly invaded the totality of being, including man and the gods. There was nothing real that was not nature" (Vernant 2006: 377).

According to his famous thesis, this separation at the level of mental forms between "thinking", on the one hand, and "physical reality", on the other, corresponds to the separation between society and nature realised by the city at the level of the social forms (Vernant 2006: 386ff.). Here lies the greatest break with the world of myth: whereas myth, according to Vernant, distinguished, but also confused different levels of reality, philosophy clearly juxtaposes physical reality to thinking, much as the *polis*, at the level of social forms, juxtaposes nature to society.[7]

In Vernant's view, we can conclude, it is not the presumed "superiority" of the "Greek man's intelligence" that produced philosophy, but the superiority of an entire political, economic and mental world – a world that resulted from the changes that took place in the Ionia of the seventh century BC. According to this line of reasoning, human beings would have been unable to distinguish between different levels of reality until the rise of philosophy, or, at least, they would have been unable to do so in a coherent manner, whereas, after this change of mentality, thought finds itself quite cut off *(comme à la hache)* from physical reality (2006: 396). Reason, on the one hand, and physical reality, on the other: here were the beginnings of positive thinking, the act of "baptism of Western man" (2006: 15).[8]

It is very difficult to evaluate this and similar accounts of the birth of philosophy. The sources upon which they rest are very few and completely dependent on what successive interpreters decided was worth handing down. We do not even possess fragments of their own texts. Indeed, the "fragments of the Presocratics" are either "*testimonia*", comments made by successive authors on their theories, or "direct quotations", namely, quotations made by subsequent ancient authors. Therefore, doubts over a linear account of the "birth of philosophy" seem to be legitimate.

In the first place, it is very difficult to see how the alleged separation *comme à la hache* between thinking and reality could ever be attributed to the so-called first naturalist philosophers. For instance, we have many indications that the separation of the *logos*, understood as

---

[7] A more recent version of the argument can be found in Castoriadis 2004. In his reconstruction, the philosophical mode of thought is compatible with an enduring presence of myth. All the same, he sees in the birth of philosophy, together with the birth of democracy, the beginning of a tradition of autonomy, the first historical example of a society that is able to radically question its own imaginary institutions. In this, his reconstruction is also misleading because it hides the fundamental fact that the autonomy of a minority of the population, that of the male active citizens, was constructed upon the heteronomy of its majority.

[8] The view here analysed belongs to Vernant's earliest writings. As an anonymous referee pointed out, his conception of the transformation in question becomes more complex in his later work. In this context, I am not, however, interested in reconstructing the evolution of Vernant's thought, but in discussing a given view, as it emerges from the sources quoted, independent of its later developments.

"thinking", and what Vernant calls "physical reality" was unknown even to subsequent philosophers. Indeed, such a separation, with which we are now so familiar, seems to be alien to ancient thought, since the term *logos* indicates both a being and a thought at the same time (Abbagnano 1971: 547). I will return to this point later. If we look at the other side of Vernant's presumed separation of "thinking" and "physical reality", the problematic character of such a separation is even more manifest. The Greeks did not even have a word to designate what Vernant called "physical reality", their corresponding terms being *ousia* and *physis*. *Physis*, however, indicates nature in the most general sense: the term is derived from the verb *phyein* "to rise", which is, in its turn, etymologically linked to *phainesthai* "to show itself". *Physis* is, therefore, literally "what shows itself", "what comes to light", and indicates a much broader reality than a "physical positive reality". The term *ousia* defines what we call "reality", but in the sense of the "immutable or true reality", that is, reality understood as substance (Liddell, Scott, and Stuart 1968: 1274).[9]

In the second place, it is not difficult to recognise in Vernant's separation *comme à la hache* of the *logos* from "physical reality" the modern separation of knowing subject from known object, which accompanied the birth of modern science. Indeed, what seems to be at work here is a strategy of reappropriation of the past in order to provide an identity for a cultural enterprise that occurred much later. As Vernant himself recognises, what is at stake in the debate over the "birth of philosophy" is primarily the search for the official identity papers of Western rationality (Vernant 2006: 379).

The emphasis given to the birth of philosophy as the greatest rupture in the passage from *mythos* to *logos* is linked to the fact that, over the centuries, this moment worked as a powerful means for the self-identification of Western rationality. The idea of "the birth" of philosophy has been used to provide Western rationality with an identity. This is clear in Husserl's *The Crisis of the European Sciences*: it is when faced with the European crisis that he moves back to the Greek nation of the seventh and sixth centuries BC, presenting it as the birthplace of the spiritual shape of Europe (Husserl 1954: 269–99). In Husserl's

---

[9] To bypass this difficulty, Vernant has to postulate a presumed split within the concept of *physis* (Vernant 2006: 378ff.).

view, the new "theoretical" attitude, to which the earliest Greek philosophy gave rise, not only helps us to identify the "distinctive European spiritual shape", but is also aimed at finding a possible cure for the crisis that this spiritual shape is facing. This interpretation of the past not only provides an identity to the "European sciences", it also gives orientation for acting in the present.

In this way, Husserl followed a long-lasting strategy of self-definition through a reappropriation of the past. But what are the bases for saying that it is with the Ionian physicians that philosophy began? As we have seen, the sources that we possess for the reconstruction of the thinking of the so-called presocratic philosophers depend on subsequent testimonies. Among the latter, Plato and Aristotle played a primary role. Plato is, however, very vague in his quotations: he is much more interested in the dialectic confutation of the arguments exposed and, consequently, he often does not even quote the author. In contrast, Aristotle undoubtedly paid greater attention to his predecessors, but the price we pay for this is that his reconstruction is strongly shaped by his reception of these philosophers as steps towards his own philosophy.[10]

Indeed, it was Aristotle himself who first spoke of Thales and the Ionians as the "first philosophers" and as the "naturalist philosophers". This interpretation is developed at the beginning of his *Metaphysics*, where he puts forward his own view of the specific activity that would be called "philosophy" thereafter. After having described philosophy as the search for the first principles and causes (*Met.* 982a–b), he presents the conceptions of Thales, Anaximenes and Anaximander as the first steps in this search, and thus he presents them as the "first natural philosophers".

In particular, Aristotle's reconstruction of the birth of philosophy has the clear function of preparing the presentation of his own doctrine of the four causes. His doctrine is presented as the final result of the previous speculation, and, in particular, of that of the first naturalist philosophers, so that it becomes very difficult to judge where their alleged theories end and Aristotle's theory begins. The influence

---

[10] On this point, see, for instance, Adorno 1961a, and Colli 1975, 1977, 1978a, 1978b. In his works on the presocratics, Colli sharply questions any naïve reliance on Aristotle's testimony.

of Aristotle's authority on this point can hardly be overestimated. He played a major role not only in the interpretation of the work of the first "natural philosophers", but also in the presentation of the whole cultural enterprise that goes under the heading of "Western philosophy". For centuries, Aristotle's words represented the act of baptism of the specific discipline defined as "philosophy", and, for many, they also represented a crucial, if not *the* crucial, moment for the self-identification of the West.[11]

However, some doubts can be raised regarding this narrative as a whole. First, some scepticism seems legitimate because, as we have seen, the sources upon which this narrative rests are narratives whose authority is highly dependent on those, particularly Aristotle, who first formulated them, and who were most often more interested in putting forward their own views of philosophy than in reconstructing the thinking of the Ionians. Second, since we know nothing about the silence surrounding the very few sources upon which this narrative rests, it might well be that there were some "philosophers" who did not fit into Aristotle's reconstruction or into Aristotle's definition of what it means "to be a philosopher", and that they were simply ignored. In particular, even if one assumes, along with Aristotle, that philosophy means an attempt at providing a rational explanation of the world, it is very unlikely that anybody else had already "philosophised" about the world apart from Aristotle's "first naturalist philosophers". To take Vernant's example, it is very unlikely that human beings were all making recourse to Hephaestus in order to explain the phenomenon of "the hot". And, for this reason, we should question the very idea of a possible "birth" of philosophy – unless we mean by philosophy something different from an attempt to provide a rational explanation of the world.

Third, even in the case of the "philosophers" presented by Aristotle, there are good reasons for questioning his reconstruction. For instance, in the case of Thales' thinking, there is a fragment that suggests an alternative interpretation to the traditional one. According

[11] Husserl's approach, as we have seen, is paradigmatic from this point of view (Husserl 1954). More recently, for instance, the narrative of the "birth of philosophy" has entered the debate about European identity. According to some commentators, "the birth of philosophy" is precisely what characterizes the specific "spiritual shape" of Europe. For a general reconstruction of this debate, see Friese and Wagner 2002.

to this fragment, Thales said that "all things are full of gods" (*panta plera theon einai*) (Diels and Kranz 1951, Frag. 22; Kirk, Raven and Schonfield 1983: 95). This fragment seems to refer to a view that comes close to what Vernant called a "mythical conception of reality", that is, one in which different levels of reality are fused together. Despite the obscurity of the formulation and the consequent difficulty in providing any univocal interpretation of this fragment, it seems clear that we are a long way away from the image of the positivist natural philosopher.

Finally, as has recently been pointed out, the idea of the "birth of philosophy" as an "exit from myth" is in contrast with the fact that even in later sources *mythos* can never be said to be totally irrational, and no philosophy is totally deprived of mythical elements (Morgan 2000). Not only, as we have seen, were the conceptual tools of the so-called first philosophers not very dissimilar from, let us say, those of Hesiod's, but – furthermore – the very fact that later philosophers often referred to myths in their writings is a sign that the boundaries between myth and philosophy were far from clearly delineated (Morgan 2000).

The fact that philosophers themselves make recourse to mythical narratives when dealing with philosophical issues should not come as a surprise. The presocratics were considered *sophoi*. The *sophos* was a figure in between poet and shaman: more precisely, he was some-one who excelled in knowledge (see Colli 1975; 1977; 1978a; 1978b). Both their contemporaries and Plato called the presocratic philoso-phers *sophoi*, so that, instead of speaking of "presocratic philosophy", we should speak of "Greek wisdom" (Colli 1977; 1978a; 1978b). The *sophoi* did not write textbooks on physics, or philosophical texts in the sense of the literary genre initiated by Plato and Aristotle. They wrote poems *peri physeos* (on nature) that were destined for oral transmis-sion and diffusion. And, as we have seen, the *physis* that is the object of their poems is not our "physical reality": rather, it is nature in its most general sense, the sphere of the totality of being that literally comes to light.

The dynamic interpenetration of myth and philosophy is also reflected in the semantic proximity of the two terms *mythos* and *logos*. No sharp dichotomy between *mythos* versus *logos* was stated, at least not before the fourth century BC (Morgan 2000). Herodotus, for instance, uses *mythos* only twice, but, as has been observed, he uses the term *logos* in a way that corresponds to what we would call "myth" today (K. Morgan, 2000: 19ff.). When narrating two different versions of Helen's arrival in Troy, he calls them both *logoi* – even the version that he does not believe to be true (*Historiae* II, 116). Thucydides, who, by condemning the *mythodes*, the "mythical element" (*Peloponnesian War* I, 22), also started a new phase of more ostentatiously scientific historiography, did not make any definitive association between *mythos* and false speech, or even with what today we would call "myth" (K. Morgan 2000: 20). Thus, to conclude, not only is the very idea of a possible "birth" of philosophy problematic in itself, but, even if one accepted this idea, it still remains that such a "birth" did not generate any opposition between *mythos* and *logos*.

The association between *mythos* and false speech is, at best, the result of the successive self-presentation of intellectuals who were willing to distance themselves from the world of myth. An important role was probably played here by the movement of the so-called sophists. With sophistry, a new process of professionalising philosophy began. The sophists aspired to be recognised as professional teachers of the technique of reasoning (*dialektike techne*), the importance of which increased notably in Athens in the fifth century. According to Plato, the sophists labelled as philosophy the rhetorical, dialectical and literary education that they were teaching to young politicians (*Symposium* I, 5). Indeed, it was with the centralisation of cultural life in Athens and with the political climate of the middle of the fifth century that dialectics strongly entered the political arena, and it was then that the *sapientia* of the old *sophoi* came into competition with the dialectics of sophists such as Gorgias and Protagoras.

In their effort to present themselves as new professional figures, the sophists attempted to distance themselves from the world of the traditional poets such as Homer and Hesiod. According to the Platonic dialogues, it was at this time that *mythos*, along with its general meaning of tales, took on the further connotation of fable, or fictitious narrative (see, for instance, Plato's *Gorg.* 527a.5; *Phil.* 14a.4; *Phaedr.* 60c.2; *Soph.* 242c.8, d.6; *Resp.* II, 377a.4, b.6, d.5, 379a.4). However, no sharp opposition between *mythos* and *logos* was yet part of the common meaning of the term. Even for the sophists the old tales (*mythoi*) were part of a reservoir of traditional material to which they themselves did not disdain to make recourse in their art of constructing discourses.

According to Plato's testimony, learning to express one's arguments in the form of the *logos* and the *mythos* was part of the basic training in the rhetorical-dialectical curriculum: on the one hand, there was the demonstration of truth based on rational argumentation, and, on the other, its narration through figurative expressions. For instance, Protagoras, who represents the professional sophist in the homonymous Platonic dialogue, asks Socrates whether he wants an argument to be delivered in the form of the *mythos* or of the *logos* (*Protag.* 320c.3, 320c.7; but also 324d.6 and 328c.3). In many Platonic dialogues, indeed, we are given the impression of a double track of the arguments: discursive arguments on the one hand, and mythical narratives on the other. The *Phaedo* is paradigmatic from this point of view, because for every block of dialectic arguments, there is a corresponding group of mythical narratives (*Phaedo* 80b.ff; 107c.ff).[12]

This confirms the fact that the further connotation of untruthfulness entailed by myths was not yet part of the primary meaning of the term. There has been no "birth of philosophy" as a linear road "from *mythos* to *logos*". If one looks more closely at the sources upon which such a narrative rests, one finds not only that the very few fragments may reflect Aristotle's conception of philosophy more than that of the Presocratics, but that even subsequent sources suggest quite a different path: far from being in opposition to each other, a proximity between the two is suggested up to the fourth century BC – at least. Indeed, if Plato can continually move in his dialogues from rational argument to the narration of myths, this is because the question of the "truth" or "reality" of myth had not yet been posed: the *mythos* was generally juxtaposed to the *logos* simply as a different way by which to express a similar content, and the difference between the two was held to be on the level of their different protreptical impact, and not of their respective truth or reality.

Plato's constant recourse to myth is perhaps the most conspicuous scandal from the point of new of the narrative of the "birth of philosophy" as the exit from myth. Different strategies have, however, been employed in order to reconcile them: Platonic myths have been read both as the containers for a kind of truth that is superior to that entailed by the *logos*, and as a primitive way of expressing a

[12] On this point, see Reale 1991: 74, 124.

truth that was to be superseded by the *logos* itself. An example of
the first approach can be found in Joseph Pieper, who conceives of
Platonic myths as a message from a divine source – an analogy with
the idea of the original revelation that would later be developed by
Christendom (Pieper 1965). The second approach is more common
and sees Hegel among its supporters. According to Hegel, Platonic
myths are beautiful representations to which Plato made recourse
simply for pedagogical purposes or because he could not give more
pure representations of thought. Myths are thus said to be a form
of pollution of thinking through sensitive images (*Verunreinigung des
Gedankens durch sinnliche Gestalt*), which would have been avoided by
Plato when he had to express the crucial parts of his argument (Hegel
1995: 20).

Many objections can be raised against both these interpretations.
It is, for instance, quite difficult to see how Pieper's interpretation
could suit a myth such as that of the cave, which is used by Plato
to describe his conception of the different levels of knowledge and
the role of philosophers in society (*Resp.* 514A–521C). The human
condition can be described, according to this myth, as that of people
in a cavern who are fettered in such a way that they can only see the
bottom of this cave. Having always been imprisoned in this way, they
believe that what they see at the bottom, the shadows produced by
statues outside the cave, are the things themselves. Philosophers can
be seen as people who, having liberated themselves from these fetters,
are given the opportunity not only to see the statues directly but also
to see the sun itself, the idea of good (*Resp.* 517c). Having been given the
opportunity to contemplate the idea of good, which is the source of
being, in Plato's view, philosophers must go back to the cave in order
to help their fellows to free themselves, even if they take a great risk in
doing so, because their fellows, imprisoned as they are by appearances,
may not believe in them (*Resp.* 519c.ff.).

This myth, like many others in Plato's writings, is presented as a figurative description of a philosophical theory, rather than as a "revealed
truth", which is impossible to express in rational terms. The myth of
the cave also suggests, contrary to Hegel's interpretation, that Plato
commits not only marginal or introductory themes to myth, but also
very crucial parts of his conception. This holds for the myth of the cave,
which is introduced by Plato to explain his theory of knowledge and

his conception of the role of philosophers in society, and also for the myth of races, the myth of Er in the *Republic*, the myth of the chariot in *Phaedrus*, and many others (*Thaet.* 156c.4, 164e.3; *Laws* I, 645b.1; *Tim.* 69b1).

Furthermore, Hegel's view seems to contrast with what Plato says in the *Seventh letter*, that the most important part of his own philosophy is not contained in his dialogues (341c).[13] This statement has been widely debated, but most interpreters agree in relating it to the criticism that Plato raised on many occasions against the "written word" (*Protagoras* 329a; *Phaedo* 276c, 277a, 277e, *Phaedrus* 274c–278e). In an epoch in which Greek culture was still moving from an oral to a literary one, Plato proposed considering the practice of writing only as a "medicine for the memory", which should never substitute for the art of dialogue (*Phaedrus* 274c–278e). In his opinion, the written word is "dead" because it is unable to give answers if you interrogate it, whereas the "discourse written in the soul of the disciple" is alive, because the disciple is able to defend himself and to distinguish the appropriate moment for speaking or being silent (*Phaedr.* 276a).

In this line of interpretation, the myth – as a figurative expression – could be held to entail a surplus of meanings, and therefore acts as a *stimulans* to thinking, and could be considered as a way of overcoming some of the shortcomings of the practice of writing. Rather than providing an inferior means of argument, Platonic myths could be seen as ways of expressing a conceptual content which is superior to rational argument, because once the argument is translated into a single written form it is dead, whereas myths are open to a proliferation of meaning that can always generate further discussion.[14]

---

[13] Some commentators read this passage in connection with Aristotle's testimony on Plato's "unwritten doctrines" (*agrapha dogmata*). See, in particular, the work of the so-called *Tübinger Schule*, whose major representatives, in their attempt to reevaluate the indirect Platonic tradition as fundamental for an accurate image of Plato, strongly emphasise Plato's scepticism towards the practice of writing (Krämer 1982, 1995; Geiser 1963; Reale 1986).

[14] The extent to which literacy influenced the rise of philosophy is still very controversial. Among those emphasising the importance of literacy for the rise of abstract rational thought, see Goody and Watt 1968; Goody 1977, 1986; Havelock 1986; and Vernant 2006; among the critics, see Cornford 1952, who focuses on the link between traditional religion and the origin of philosophy, and Finnegan 1988, and Thomas 1992, who emphasise that literacy is, in the end, what a specific culture makes of it, i.e., that it can have very different outcomes and consequences in different cultures.

Furthermore, both Pieper's and Hegel's interpretations seem to reflect subsequent worldviews too closely. Piper's view is clearly linked to the Christian conception of revelation, while Hegel's approach is a good example of the typically modern attempts to rationalise myth. In both cases, *mythos* is placed on a heterogeneous level with respect to *logos* – standing either above or below it. In both interpretations, *mythos* and *logos* are considered as counterpoised, whereas, as we have seen, by the time of Plato, myth was most probably seen as a means to express a content that could also be developed through rational argument.

Indeed, it is only by considering rational argument and mythical narrations as two different dialectical techniques (*dialektike techne*) that one can come to terms with Plato's usage of the term *mythos.* Plato sometimes uses the term in the sense of what we would call "fables" (*Gorg.* 523a.2, 527a.5; *Phil.* 14a; *Phaedr.* 6oc.2; *Resp.* II, 377a.4, b.6, c.1, d.5; *Soph.* 242c.8), most often in the sense of "tale" without any further connotations (*Resp.* I 350e.3, III 391e.12, X 621b.8; *Thaet.* 164d.9; *Phaedr.* 237a.9, 241e.8; *Protag.* 320c.3, 320c.7, 324d.6, 328c.3; *Alc.* I 123a.1; *Laws* III 682a.8; IV 713a.6; VIII 841 c.6; *Gorg.* 505c.10), but sometimes also in the expression *ton eikota mython,* which defines a form of common or probable knowledge (*Tim.* 29d.2; 59c.6; 68d.2), and, finally, sometimes in the sense of discourse that contains a rational theory (in particular, *Thaet.* 156c.4, 164e.3; *Resp.* 376 d.9; *Laws* I, 645b5; *Tim.* 69b.1). Thus, not only are images such as *Phedros'* chariot said to be *mythoi,* but also *Timaeus'* speech about the constitution of the world and Socrates 'discourse about the education of the guardians in the *Republic* (*Tim.* 69b.1; *Resp.* II, 376d.9).[15]

Plato, as a philosopher, that is as an intellectual willing to claim the specific role that philosophy has to play, had to criticise the mythological narratives provided by poets such as Homer and Hesiod. It is not by chance that it is in the *Republic*, where he presents the education that should be given to rulers-philosophers, that we find the term *mythos* systematically used in the sense of "fable", of "untrue narrative": rulers must be philosophers, not poets (*Resp.* II 374a–III 417b; and also *Resp.* II 377a). However, it is not for their fictitiousness that the tales told by

---

[15] See the entry for *myth** in the *Thesaurus Linguae Graecae*; see also Brandwood's *A Word Index to Plato* (1976: 593).

Homer and Hesiod are condemned (*Resp.* II, 377d–378e; III, 386a–392c). It is because the religious and ethical models that are transmitted through them could be morally deceptive (*Resp.*, II, 378e–379b; III, 392 a–c).

The Platonic condemnation of poetry must therefore be understood as a proposed moral emendation of traditional material, as a critique made according to a moral criterion. Otherwise, one cannot understand why, after such a condemnation, Plato himself could possibly make such extensive use of traditional myths in the same book. Not only does Plato recognise the importance of mythical narratives for the transmission of moral models, as is shown by the fact that he recommends myths to the rulers as a helpful means to promote social cohesion (*Resp.* III, 414c, 415d), but he also uses myths as an important medium for discussing crucial philosophical issues.

According to this reconstruction, one can still contend that, if it was not with the presocratic or with Plato, then it was with Aristotle that the definitive passage from *mythos* to *logos* occurred, and the consequent association of myth with a distorted reproduction of reality took place. Whereas up to that time, a *sophos* like Parmenides could still start his philosophical poem with an invocation to the Muses, with Aristotle philosophy seems to have acquired a distinguished epistemological status: philosophy became the science of first causes and principles, whose results are ultimately guaranteed by logic. While Plato could still intermingle dialectical argument and mythical narratives, Aristotle, by starting his theorising with the statement of the formal conditions of discourse, and by identifying a type of reasoning – the syllogism – meant to guarantee the correctness of discourses, thereby provided philosophy with a method (*organon*) that set it definitively apart from the stories told by myths.

All the same, not even in Aristotle is there a definitive association of myths with untrue tales.[16] Aristotle explicitly claimed a specific status

---

[16] It should be remembered here that, whereas we only possess Plato's exoteric writings, in the case of Aristotle we possess only his esoteric writings, basically notes he used for teaching. However, we know from testimonies that he wrote "Platonic dialogues", all of which have been lost and which would probably reveal a more complex image of his thinking and its relationship with myth. Still, it is significant that what Aristotle himself wanted to publish were precisely those "Platonic" dialogues, whereas the writings known as *corpus aristotelicum* were the doctrines that he – as the old

for philosophy. It is therefore no coincidence that, while Plato was the first to define his activity as "philo-sophia", namely love of *sophia* (Colli 1975: 13), Aristotle provided philosophy with a place and date of birth, a history, and – most importantly – a specific task. The problem then becomes to establish what precisely distinguishes philosophy from myth; that is, exactly where they depart from each other. Let us return for a moment to the passage of *Metaphysics* where Aristotle presents his view of the presocratics: this should provide us, if not with an accurate reconstruction of their thinking, at least with some clues about what he considers as specific to philosophy itself.

In this passage, Aristotle observes that in saying that water is the principle (*arche*) of everything, Thales was stating something that was already contained in many myths of the origins (*Met.* 983b). From the point of view of content, Thales' theory does not contain any radical novelty. The problem, then, becomes to understand why we should consider such a statement as the beginning of the specific discipline that is philosophy.

Aristotle does not provide any explicit answer to this question, but in the passage about water he continues by saying that Thales derived his theory from the observation that the nourishment of everything is wet and that even heat comes from humidity and lives in it (*Met.* 983b, 30). Here, there is – at least in Aristotle's perspective – a novelty, and this concerns the method employed: no longer mythical narratives, but direct observation. Again, what was new in Thales' statement is not the content, but the form of argument: whereas aquatic *mythoi* were narratives, this statement was presented by these thinkers – according to Aristotle's testimony – as the result of observations.

Thus, it seems as if in Aristotle, as already in Plato, *mythos* and *logos* were considered to differ only from the point of view of their form and not of their true or false content. However, Aristotle seems to go further. He does not simply present myth as false, but also seems to recognise its link with philosophy. In the *Metaphysics*, a few passages before those regarding water, we read that both myth and philosophy

sophoi – communicated orally to his disciples. In fact, we cannot even say that we possess the texts of his esoteric lessons: the actual shape of the *corpus aristotelicum* derives from the edition of these notes made by Andronicus Rhodius, a later disciple of the Peripatetic who probably gave to the *corpus* a division that reflects more the cultural view of the first century AD than Aristotle's intentions (Adorno 1961b: 287).

stem from wonder (*to thaumazein*) (*Met.* 982b). Indeed – so continues
the passage – the person who doubts and wonders shows thereby that
he or she does not know, and this is the reason why we can say that
a person who loves the myth (*o philomythos*) is also a philosopher (*o
philosophos*) (*Met.* 982b).

Aristotle's statement that the *philomythos* is a philosopher is very
significant. We have seen to what extent myth and philosophy differ
for him. How could he say that the *philomythos* is also a philosopher
precisely where he states that philosophy concerns the knowledge of
principles and causes? One possible answer requires a further clarifi-
cation of Aristotle's view of causes (*aitiai*) themselves. This is a point
that is hard for a modern mind to catch – used as it is to conceiving
causes in terms of an abstract relationship between events. However,
such a view of causality only began with modern science; antiquity
understood it according to what I would call a model of production.[17]

Indeed, both the noun *aitia* (cause) and the corresponding nominalised adjective *aition* are derived from the adjective *aitios*, which
means "responsible of, guilty of", even in the juridical sense. In the
first place, therefore, *aitia* means responsibility (Liddell, Scott, and
Stuart 1968: 44). It is not by chance that in order to understand Aristotle's distinction between the four types of causes – formal, material,
efficient, and final – we must make recourse to the image of the artistic creation that Aristotle himself suggests in his *Physics*. Aristotle does
not develop the concept of cause in terms of abstract relationships
between events, but rather through the description of artistic production. In the creation of a sculpture, the formal cause is the idea of the
statue, the material cause is the marble itself, the efficient cause is the
artist himself, and the final cause is the ultimate result of the artistic
creation (*Physics* II, 194b).

Since, for Aristotle, "to know" means to know why things are like
this, that is to know their causes (*Met.* 983a), one must conclude that,
for Aristotle, mythological narratives are also a form of knowledge.
Inasmuch as they tell us where things come from or who has made
them, they also aim to identify causes in the sense of the Greek *aitiai*.
This does not mean that there are no differences between myth and

---

[17] A similar point is made by Abbagnano in the entry "*Causalità*" of his *Dizionario di
filosofia* (1971: 118), and by Pellegrin in his recent *Le vocabulaire d'Aristote* (2001: 12).

philosophy for Aristotle. It only means that he recognises that, stemming as they both do from wonder, they aim to provide some kind of explanation of why things are a certain way and not another.

Once we have recognised that myths, too, are a form of knowledge, the next task is to establish what kind of knowledge we are dealing with. Even a very quick look at a list of the Aristotelean concordances for the entry "*myth**" reveals that, if one wants to find out the specificity of myth, it is in the ambit of *poiesis* that we have to search.[18] Indeed, it is in the so-called *Poetic* that the term *mythos* most often appears, and there are reasons to suspect that it is here that a more systematic use of the concept is made. In the very first paragraph of the *Poetic*, we read that the aim of the book is to examine the poetic technique (*techne*), that is the way in which *mythoi* should be composed. Therefore, from the very first sentence, we know that *mythoi* – understood as tales and plots without any further qualification – are the constitutive elements of poetry (1447a.ff.).

A few paragraphs later, while explaining the difference between poetry and history, Aristotle affirms that *poiesis* is a more philosophical and elevated (*philosophoteron kai spoudaiteron*) subject than history (1451b.6). As a consequence, far from associating myth with untrue speech, Aristotle places it close to philosophy, since he attributes to it a capacity to catch the universal that is superior to that of history.

Indeed, for Aristotle, given that the historian has to deal with the particular, that is, with unrelated and dispersed facts, the historian is further from the truth than the poets. While the historian tells facts as they happened, the poet tells them as "they could have happened according to likelihood and necessity" (*kata to eikos e to anagkaion*) (1451b). In this sense, poetry deals with something closer to the universal, and is therefore a much more elevated and philosophical subject than history.[19]

However, the universal entailed by poetry is not the same as philosophy. At this point in the argument, one might object that, however

---

[18] While in the *Metaphysics* we have only two examples of the word *mythos* (Delatte et al. 1984: 260), in the *Poetics*, we have 50 (Denooz 1988: 61). See also the entry for *myth** in the *Thesaurus Linguae Graecae*.

[19] On this point, see also the beginning of the *Metaphysics* and the distinction between *empeira* (knowledge of the particular) and *techne* (knowledge of the universal) (*Met.* 980ba).

important, the role of myth is still limited to the ambit of *poiesis*. *Poiesis*, according to a possible reading of the passages where this distinction is made,[20] differs from *theoresis* because it "creates" its objects. This, however, does not necessarily imply that the ambit of *mythos* is that of arbitrariness, and, as such, that it must be counterpoised to that of the *logos* – as we often tend to assume when talking about poetic creation. To say that poetry creates its objects does not mean that these are fictitious or that they exist only in the poet's mind.

Let us return to the passages in question. In both *Metaphysics* and in *Topica* the expression used by Aristotle to state the difference between *theoresis* and *poiesis* is not "to create its objects" but "to have or not to have in itself the principle of movement" (*e arche tes kineseos*) (*Topica* VI, 145a15; *Met.* VI, 1025, XI, 1064a). According to these passages, both *praxis* and *poiesis* differ from *theoresis* because only the latter deals with substances that have the principle of movement in themselves. In contrast, the *arche* of *poiesis* is found in the person who produces and not in the things produced (*Met.* 1025b 22). Similarly, in the ambit of the *praxis*, the *arche* of actions is not in the things "acted", but in the agent (*Met.* 1025b 22). In order to understand the kind of universality with which poetry deals, it is at the subject of *poiesis*, or better *poietes*, that we must look.

From these passages it also clearly emerges that poetry, for Aristotle, is far from being "imaginary" and "fanciful". As we read in *Poetics*, the essence of poetry is the *mimesis*,[21] the representation of reality (*Poetics* 1447a 20). This is not understood as the reproduction of an empirically conceived "objective" reality, but as the *mimesis* of human beings who act. *Mimesis* is not the reproduction of what has actually happened, but rather of what could have happened according to the "likelihood and necessity" that is intrinsic to the different human characters (*Poetics* 1448a).

In the following passage, Aristotle continues by saying that, from childhood, human beings have a genuine instinct for *mimesis* and that

---

[20] See, in particular, *Topica* VI, 6, 145a15, and *Met.* VI, 1, 1025, and XI, 7, 1064 a.

[21] The translation of the term "*mimesis*" has always been a problem, because its meaning ranges from the semantic area of the term "imitation" to that of "representation". I will use the original Greek term, as far as possible.

this is the way in which they first learn their lessons (*ta matheseis*) about the world: this learning (*manthanein*) gives pleasure not only to philosophers, but also to all human beings, because it is in this way that we learn and infer (*syllogithesthai*) what each thing is (*Poetics* 1448b). *Mythoi* display a kind of knowledge that is fundamentally a knowledge about human beings, about the "likelihood and necessity" intrinsic to their nature.

To conclude, not even in Aristotle is there an association of myth with untrue tale. On the contrary, *mythoi* are in his view the constitutive elements of *poiesis* and thus entail a knowledge that is more "philosophical" and elevated than history. *Mythoi* deal with the universality that resides in knowledge about different human characters; and, in this sense, they display what we can call a plural universality.

However, as Auerbach has shown in his analysis of the Western evolution of the concept of *mimesis*, it is precisely this plurality that got lost in the passage from antiquity to modernity. While both Plato and Aristotle conceived of different levels of *mimesis* of reality, this plurality went through a process of *reductio ad unum*, the result of which is modern realism (Auerbach 1953). When we talk of "realism" in art we mean the closeness to an empirically conceived reality, whereas, for antiquity, there were different levels of "reality" to be reproduced – and it was not assumed that the proximity to *empeiria* was the criterion for what is "more real".

Indeed, it is precisely the *plurality* of Greek myths that is a scandal for us. We cannot but keep asking ourselves "Did Greeks really believe in their myths?" (Veyne 1988); and this is because we cannot come to terms with the fact that Greeks accepted a plurality of contrasting variants, which simply coexist: to our minds, this plurality should have undermined their faith in the truth. What lies behind this different attitude towards truth?

The ancient Greek word that comes closest to our word "truth" is *aletheia*, which, in contrast to "truth", is a privative word. *Aletheia*, according to its etymology, is "what is not hidden", "what is not forgotten". The term is composed of the privative prefix "alpha" plus the root *lath-*that forms the verb *lanthano*, "to remain hidden" and the composite *epilanthanomai*, "to forget" as well as the substantive *lethe*, "forgetfulness". As Martin Heidegger first pointed out, according to its original meaning, the semantic area expressed by the Greek term *aletheia* is therefore that of the "unhiddenness" or "unforgetfulness" (Heidegger 2002b).

Many interpreters have noticed that the world of myth, linked as it is to the ancient culture of orality, was defined by *aletheia*. This was conceived of not as the opposite of non-correspondence, but as the opposite of forgetfulness: truth is what is worth preserving from oblivion (Detienne 1967; Cole 1983). The poet is the person who preserves things from oblivion. On this basis, Hesiod can claim to be a vehicle of *aletheia*. At the beginning of his *Theogony*, he celebrates the Muses who have inspired in him the voice to disclose progressively the *aletheia*, that is "the things that shall be and that were aforetime" (*Theogony* vv. 1–32). Yet, in the same passage the Muses are said to be the vehicle of an *aletheia* that is plural and even goes hand in hand with falsity, as "they know how to speak many false things as though they were true; but they know, when they will, to utter true things" (*Theogony* vv. 1–32).

The archaic world of Hesiod was no longer the world of Plato and Aristotle. These latter still conceived of *aletheia* as the result of a process, but the road to it was no longer shown by the Muses. In Plato's dialogues, *aletheia* is the result of the dialogue of the soul with itself (*Thaet.* 189e–190a; *Sophis.* 263a, 264b). Plato states that the discourse that speaks of things as they are is true (*alethes*), whereas the discourse that speaks of things as they are not is false (*Crat.* 385b). Similarly, according to Aristotle, "the false" negates what is and affirms what is not, whereas the *alethes* affirms what is and negates what is not (*Met.* IV, 7, 1011b 26).

From this and similar passages, it seems that both Plato and Aristotle conceived of *aletheia* as correspondence to reality.[22] In this sense, their views seem to be closer to the modern ones. However, even if they conceive of truth as correspondence to reality, the crucial point is the way in which they conceive of reality itself.

The ancient Greeks did not even have a word that corresponded to our term "reality". We, children of the Cartesian revolution, conceive of what is "real" as fundamentally opposed to what is "ideal". In contrast, for the ancient Greeks, there were only *ta onta*, the things that are, or *to on*, the being as expressed by the nominalised participle of the

---

[22] For Plato's view of *aletheia*, see also *Soph.* 262e and *Phil.* 37c, while for Aristotle, see *Met.* V, 1024b5.

verb to be (*einai*). While all these words come from the verb "to be" (*einai*), the word "reality" comes from (*res*), an altogether different root. And this different root is the sign of a different approach to the definition of "reality". The Greek *ta onta* are only things insofar as they are already conceptually clear, whereas individual things that are just given in experience are simply *ta pragmata*. The things that fall under the umbrella of *ta onta* include the things that reveal themselves for what they are: *einai* does not simply mean to exist, but designates a certain mode of existence.[23] In other words, the things that can be described as *ta onta* are only those entities that have already revealed themselves to the understanding, whereas *ta pragmata* refers to things that remain to be determined. In this sense, *ta onta* are more true and more real than *ta pragmata*.

This does not mean that *ta pragmata* are not "real". It simply means that they are less "real", or – even better – that they are less *alethes*. Plato conceived of the real as constituted by different degrees of being (Vlastos 1965). According to his theory of ideas, ideas are being that truly is.[24] Ideas constitute the maximum form of reality, because they present being in its clearest form. Compared with them, sensitive reality is just a pale imitation. Thus, if we want to talk – anachronistically – of Plato's conception of "reality", reality must be understood as the opposite of appearance, because ideas are being that remains in the instability of becoming, and, in this sense, ideas themselves must account for appearances (Moravcsik 1992).[25] Ideas themselves, far from being purely mental content, as we, from the time of Descartes, have started to understand them, are at the same time thought and reality.[26]

---

[23] The term *ousia*, too, far from designating what we mean by "reality", indicated being in the sense of the substance – also in the sense of material substances (Liddell, Scott, and Stuart 1968: 1274).

[24] On Plato's theory of ideas, see Ross 1951. On the Platonic idea of different levels of reality see Vlastos 1965. On the way in which, according to Plato, "reality", in this sense, accounts for appearances, see Moravcsik 1992.

[25] This view of "reality" as opposed to "appearances" went on to become extremely influential in subsequent philosophical thinking. Examples of this view can still be found today. See, for instance, Audi's *Cambridge Dictionary of Philosophy*: "Reality: in standard philosophical usage, how things are, in contrast to their mere appearance" (1999: 775).

[26] See the entry "*Idee*" in the *Historisches Wörterbuch der Philosophie* (Neumann 1972: 56) and also "*Idea*" in Abbagnano's *Dizionario di filosofia* (1971: 450).

Aristotle does follow his master Plato in both his view of the truth and in the idea of "different degrees of reality". Aristotle also states that *aletheia* and falsity pertain to the ambit of unification and separation (*Met.* IV, 1011b26, V, 1024b25; *De Interpretatione* 16a9). Moreover, he also conceived of what we call "reality" in terms of different degrees. He even states an explicit correspondence between the degrees of reality and the degrees of truth, because in his view each thing possesses as much being as it has truth (*Met.* 993b).

Aristotle, unlike Plato, conceived of being as a *synolon* of matter (*ule*) and ideas-forms (*eidos-morphe*) and he conceived of becoming as the actualisation (*entelecheia*) of a being, which possesses the being in *potency* (*dynamis*) (see, in particular, *Physics* II). The two theories are also combined for, while *matter* is the material cause of *becoming* and its *potency*, form is the formal and final cause as well as the principle of actualisation (*entelecheia*). Now, given that what is in potency can become actual only under the effect of something which is already actual, this made it necessary for Aristotle to postulate the existence of a being that is already actual and, following the chain of *dynamis* and *entelecheia*, we thus arrive at the postulation of a being that is always, that is, God himself (*Met.* XII).

The Greek term *entelecheia* comes from the adjective *enteles* which means "complete, perfect". *Entelecheia*, properly speaking, defines a "full, complete reality" as opposed to what has only potential reality (Liddell, Scott, and Stuart 1968: 575). The Latin term *realitas* was first used as a synonym of "perfection" (Courtine 1992a, 1992b) – a view that can only be understood by using, as the starting point, the ancient idea of the different degrees of "what is real".

Thus, it is only within such views of being and truth that the pluralistic Greek myth was possible. As Veyne maintains, a plurality of programs of truth existed for the ancient Greeks: it is because of this plurality that one could believe in both the legendary world of myth and the truth of everyday "reality" (Veyne 1988). What appears to us as an untenable contradiction between a plurality of narratives was no problem for them – and not even for Aristotle, the father of the principle of non-contradiction. Indeed, when stating this principle, Aristotle added an extremely important qualification: "It is impossible for the same attribute at once (*hama*) to belong and not to belong to the same thing and in the same relation (*kai kata to hauto*)" (*Met.* IV, 1005b).

The importance of this apparently insignificant adverb *hama* can never be sufficiently emphasised.

Let me conclude here with a story. The Ethiopic people of Dorzés believe that leopards are Christian animals and that, as a result, leopards respect the precepts of the Coptic Church and, in particular, will fast on Wednesdays and Fridays (Messeri 1997: 1). All the same, as leopards are very dangerous for their livestock, the Dorzés watch over their animals even on Wednesdays and Fridays. They see no contradiction between the two beliefs, that the leopards fast on those days, and that they might attack their livestock during them. On the one hand, it is the truth of their tradition that is at stake; on the other, it is what they have learned through experience. Clearly, for them, it is a different truth that is at stake each time. The emergence of the idea of myth as a "purely fictitious, untrue tale" is a sign that this plurality has now been lost.

2

The *Biblos* and the Dialectic of the Sacred *Logos*

While it was still possible in the Hellenistic epoch to produce an intellectual and artistic movement such as that of aetiology, this would have been impossible in the Christian epoch. The aim of aetiological poetry was to narrate the origins of things by re-elaborating mythological material. It was not only a manifestation of the Alexandrian taste for erudition, willing to recover ancient traditions, but also an expression of the desire to provide a meaning to features and aspects of ordinary life – a need that became particularly acute as the system of the *polis* declined. Aetiological poetry, as represented by Callimachus' *Aitia*, aimed to overcome the sense of displacement produced by such a decline, and it did so by re-elaborating the contingency of reality through the identification of its origins – understood in the sense of the Greek *aitia*.[1] This approach entails a relationship with myth and its plurality that is impossible in a Christian worldview. But why is this impossible?

In order to understand what happened to the concept of myth, we have to look at the transformation of the other side of the dichotomy: the *logos*. With Christianity *mythos* and *logos* were given completely new

---

[1] *Aitia* is the title of Callimachus' collection of elegies. The object of these elegies was the narration of tales that explain the origins of rituals, festivals and institutions. The text of the *Aitia* was lost during the Middle Ages. We possess only a small number of papyruses, which originate from Greek-Roman Egypt, and from which it has been possible to reconstruct the original plan together with part of the text (Callimachus 1958).

meaning. The genealogy of myth begins with the term *logos*, which originally simply meant "word", or "discourse", and was therefore almost a
synonym of *mythos.* Around the fifth century BC, the term *logos* began to
occupy the semantic space of *mythos*, adding the connotation implied
by the verb *legein*, "to say", but also "to count" and "to enumerate", to
it. While *mythos* began to be used in the sense of "popular tale", the
term *logos* acquired further connotations, such as "measure", "esteem",
"proportion", "explanation" and "definition". All these meanings were,
nevertheless, still part of the primary meaning of the term: "calculus",
"discourse" and "reasoning". In this sense *logos* did not, however, define
a "mere discourse" as we understand it; it meant both "discourse over"
and "structure of reality". It was used in this way by Heraklitus (Diels
and Kranz 1951: Frag. 114) and, through Plato (see, for instance, *Thaet.*
206d) and the stoics, it reached the Neoplatonists (Abbagnano 1971:
547).

With Christianity, the term acquired a completely new meaning, one
that, apparently in continuity with the past, in fact had a revolutionary
impact:

In the beginning there was the Word [*logos*], and the Word [*logos*] was with
God, and the Word [*logos*] was God. (John I: 1)

The overwhelming power of the transformation brought about by
Christianity is inscribed in this beginning of the Gospel according to
John. Here the *logos* is not only the structure of being: *logos* is the
Word of God, a Word which has been written in the will of God since
the origin of time. And when the *logos* became the word of God, a
word that is *written*, and is written in a definitive form because it is the
Sacred Will of God, there tends to be no space for the recognition of
myth.

Logos is the term used by Hellenist Jews in their translation of the Old
Testament to render the Hebraic term *dabhar*, the scriptural name for
the creative word of God.[2] By comparing the beginning of the *Biblos*

---

[2] Jews did not accept the so-called Bible of the Seventy, that is, the Greek translation
of the Old Testament made around the second century BC in Alexandria by some
Hellenised Jews of the Diaspora. This text, encompassing both writings excluded by the
canon of the Jews and others directly written in Greek, reflects the attempt by Hellenist
Jews to reconcile Judaism with the Greek tradition. However, after the destruction of
the temple of Jerusalem (70 AD), Jews felt there was a strong incompatibility between

with Hesiod's *Theogony*, which systematised ancient Greek mythical material, three levels of rupture can be observed.

In the beginning, God created the heavens and the earth. (Genesis I: 1)

At the origins of the world, according to Hesiod, there was *chaos* (*Theogony*, 116), which was only later mitigated by the division of power among different gods (110). In Genesis, the world presents itself as a *cosmos* from the very beginning. While the Greek gods divided a world, which already existed, among them, the world of the Christians is a world *created* by God himself.

And God said, Let there be light: and there was light. God saw the light, that it was good: and God divided the light from the darkness. God called the light Day, and the darkness he called Night. And the evening and the morning were the first day. (Genesis, I: 3–5)

The text goes on to describe the way in which all things were created, and the model is always the same: it was by naming things through his word (*logos*) that God created them. The break could not be greater. While the conception of a creation *ex nihilo* was completely alien to Hesiod's polytheistic universe, the world of Genesis is created *ex nihilo*, and it can be so because it is the world of an omnipotent God.

The omnipotence of the unique God is the omnipotence of his Word (*logos*) – in the singular. The world of Genesis is not only created *ex nihilo*: it is created through the Word. Here, the Greek *logos*, the discourse and structure of a polytheistic world, became the Creative Word of a unique God. If Hesiod's mythical universe reflects the human need to have a world ordered through a plurality of narratives that corresponds to a plurality of gods, in a Christian worldview there is no need – but also no space – for any further narratives besides that of the Sacred Word of God: everything is potentially provided with a meaning from its very beginning. In the idea of the Sacred History, there is, therefore, an absolute claim: no further narrative is needed because the *logos* was there from the beginning, so that, from their very coming into being, all things were endowed with a meaning.

Judaism and the Greek-Roman culture. Although they returned to the original source of the Jewish tradition and therefore rejected the Bible of the Seventy, this Bible became the basis of the Christian Faith's Old Testament.

We move here to another point – the different conceptions of time expressed in the Old Testament and in Greek myth. The Christian conception of history is an eminently linear conception, whereas Greek myth does not allow a view of time understood as a linear sequence with a beginning and a *telos.* Properly speaking, there is no "history" (in singular) in myth, but only "stories" (plural). In contrast to this pluralistic view of time, all the three monotheist religions share a linear view of history. For each of them, the world is created, it is created by God, and, at the very same moment, it is situated in a linear flux of time. The *telos* of this flux corresponds to the day of the final judgement: the coming of the Messiah for Judaism, the return of the judging Christ for Christianity, and the *yawm ad-deen,* literally "the day of the religion", for Islam. Notwithstanding the huge differences among them, the three great world monotheisms share a threefold schema: creation – revelation – final judgement.

In particular, for Christians, the coming of Christ represents the first great eschatological event, because it marks the first defeat of sin and death. Through the mystery of the incarnation, the passion and the resurrection of Christ, time is given a further connotation. The coming of Christ represents the beginning of time in a more human sense, because it is only after liberation from original sin that time – understood as a sequence of occasions for the exercise of human freedom – began. Notwithstanding the endless theological disputes on this issue, Christianity will never go beyond the eschatological schema of the Old Testament and the omnipotence of God that it exhibits.

As emphasised by Blumenberg in his *Work on Myth,* the difference between Greek antiquity and Christianity is also reflected in their attitudes towards chronology. In Greek myths, there is no proper chronology, but a series of sequences, whereas Christianity is obsessed by chronology. Inasmuch as time was divinised, it also acquired a completely new meaning. And this is why negligence in chronologising is unforgivable in dogmatic observance (Blumenberg 1985: 100ff.).

If the *logos* defines the beginning and the end of time, then the kind of truth that the *logos* itself embodies must and can be situated in a linear flux of time. Hesiod's stories are thus replaced by a single History. We are moving here to a third level of rupture. While one feature of myth is its continual retransmission and retelling, the "truth revealed" in the Holy History presents itself as unique. Once the truth is revealed, and it is revealed in a Holy History, there is only the need to interpret it. The biblical saying "so it is written" represents the funeral epitaph of ancient myth, whose essence was the possibility of a plurality of stories.

Indeed, there is something in the idea of a "religion of the Book" that is fundamentally hostile to myth (Gadamer 1993b). And this can be found precisely in the fact that when the written word became the means through which God revealed himself and revealed himself as Unique God, the *biblos* became the bearer of an absolute claim to truth that was alien to myth. We have already seen that the Greek word for the truth was *aletheia*, which points to the progressive uncovering of being; in contrast, the idea of a religion with Sacred Scriptures implies that truth is revealed and that it is revealed in the definitive form of uniqueness.

All three of the monotheistic religions are religions of the "Book", and they all reflect this absolute claim to truth. They all share the commandment in Exodus: "Thou shalt have no other gods before me" (Exodus 20: 3).[3] The *sacred logos* is not only the creative Word of God, but is also, at the same time, the Word through which God reveals his Will: the *logos* is also the *Law*. Even if certain forms of monotheism have accentuated the aspect of the Law more than others, this absolute claim still represents a revolution that is common to the three monotheistic religions.

There is a clear symmetry between this God, the absolute creator and lawgiver, and the political systems under which these religions came to be. Recently, the idea of a political theology has been advanced in order to emphasise this link (Assmann 2000). According to Assmann, the belief in God as absolute lawgiver is a form of political theology, in which the relationship between the religious and the political order should not be read as dualism or as the subordination of one to the other, but as a relationship of representation (*Repräsentation*) (Assmann 2000: 28). By reversing the thesis of Schmitt,[4] Assman

---

[3] Monotheism was already present in other religious experiences. For instance, the attempt by Amenophy IV in the Egypt of the eighteenth dynasty (*ca* XIV sec BC) to reform the Egyptian religion in a monotheistic sense is a famous example.

[4] According to Schmitt, "all significant concepts of modern theory of the state are secularised theological concepts not only because of their historical development – in which they were transferred from theology to the theory of the state, whereby, for

has shown how the religious concepts developed in Ancient Egypt, Israel and Europe were originally political concepts. The connection between domination (*Herrschaft*) and the sacred (*das Heil*) not only goes in the direction of the instrumental use of the sacred in order to uphold political domination, but also works the other way round: it is the political institutions that, by shaping the contexts, help to create certain attitudes towards the world.[5] The sacred not only produces domination, but is, at the same time, its result.

As Hegel would have it, only in the unhappy times of generalised fear and serfdom could monotheism have established and asserted itself (Hegel 1931: 251–67). The religious consciousness of mono-theism is a fundamentally unhappy consciousness (*Unglückliches Bewusstsein*), because it alienates all freedom from itself by projecting it into a transcendent immutable (*Unwandelbare*) and thus remains entrapped in its self-created serfdom. The world of the unique omnipotent God is therefore the religious counterpart of political alienation. The omnipotence of the *dominus* is the impotence of its *servi*. The struggle between the *dominus* and its *servi* takes the form of a division within the consciousness itself *(die Verdopplung des Selbstbewusstseins in sich selbst)*, in which the essence (*das Wesen*) is projected into the im-mutable (*das Unwandelbare*), while what remains for the consciousness is only what is inessential (*Das Unwesentliche*) (Hegel 1931: 251–67).

Clearly, such a process of emptying the world in favour of a transcen-dent being, the bearer of an absolute claim, is fundamentally hostile to the polytheism of myth. In the world of the Unique God, myths could not but be perceived as blasphemy. *Mythoi*, originally simply "words, or tales", have been relegated to the idea of "fanciful", "imaginary" tales which, far from containing any kind of truth, are deceitful and dan-gerous for the salvation of the soul. Given that all the claims to truth were advanced by the *sacred logos*, the Word of God, no space was left

example, the omnipotent God became the omnipotent law-giver – but also because of the systematic structure" (Schmitt 1985b: 36). Schmitt's preferred examples are thus the parallel between God and the absolute law-giver and the idea of exception that he sees as analogous in jurisprudence to the miracle in theology (Schmitt 1985b: 36ff.).

5 It should be added that for Assmann, the Jewish conception of God as sovereign lawgiver is essentially a negation of sacred kingship in its most extreme form, the Egyptian (Assmann 2000).

for myth. It was then that the negative connotation of "myth" was first established: myth became all that the *sacred logos*, the Unique Truth, is not – the enemy to defy, the pagan to be converted.

Unquestionably, the revealed Word of God must also be interpreted. Both a Jew and – to some extent – a Protestant would agree, for instance, that, as interpretations of the Sacred Scriptures are endless, the Sacred Scriptures admit of a plurality within themselves.[6] However, even if one agrees on the openness of possible interpretations, it still remains that this plurality is only admitted as that of mere interpretations. As Castoriadis pointed out, "interpretations" and "commentaries" are the means employed by world religions in order to process and assimilate the new: once a closure of meaning has been operated, "interpretations" become the means through which the new can be subjected to a fictitious, but efficient, *reductio* and a closure of meaning thus perpetuated while apparently accepting the new (Castoriadis 1991: 153).

In other words, interpretations are provided within a general plot that is already given because it is *presented* as the revealed and unique sacred truth. The absoluteness of the claim to truth already defines the range of possibilities. In contrast, the plurality of myth is not only a plurality of interpretations, it is also a plurality of gods. First, it is a plurality of variants within a *mythologem*, in which each variant presents itself as legitimate in its own right: there is no possible contradiction among the different variants of a myth because no superior criterion is given. Instead, each variant finds within itself its own *ratio essendi*. Second, the plurality entailed by myth is also a plurality of *mythologems*, that is, a plurality of different narrative cores. Each *mythologem* is legitimate in its own right because each god has his myth and none of these gods aspires to become a unique God.[7]

---

[6] The creative force of Judaism is expressed by the fact that the biblical comment (*midrash*) is composed of both *halakhah*, which is the part that interprets the Torah by actualising its precepts, and the *haggadah*, the exegetic tradition of tales inspired by the biblical text and aimed to clarify its meaning.

[7] On the polytheism of myth, see Schmitt (1988), and also Chapter 10. In his analysis of the myth of Prometheus, Blumenberg speaks of a conflict between different gods (Blumenberg 1985). The idea of the polytheism of myth was further developed by Marquard, who, in the context of the divided Germany of the 1970s, contrasted the concept of the polytheism of myth with the "monomythie" of the great narrative of emancipation (Marquard 1979).

Indeed, the idea of myth implies the recognition of a plurality of truths that was denied by the idea of a Holy History. A comparison between Hesiod's *Theogony* and Exodus can further clarify the point. As we have seen, in the introduction to his *Theogony*, Hesiod starts with an invocation to the Muses, who are said to have breathed a divine voice into the poet in order to celebrate things that shall be and things that have been (*Theogony*, 30ff.). At the same time the Muses present themselves as those who know how to speak many false things as though they were true, but who also know, when they will, how to utter true things (*Theogony*, 26). Therefore Muses are introduced as the source of a divine knowledge, but, at the same time, this knowledge is intrinsically plural not only because the Muses are many, but also because they tell "true things" as well as "false things as though they were true".

In contrast, the God of monotheism is a God who could never tell false things, because this would contradict his absolute claim to truth. Thus, whereas Hesiod's Muses appear to the poet saying who they are, the God of Exodus presents himself to Moses with a tautology: "I am who I am" (Exodus, 3: 14). The claim to truth can be absolute only because it is based on a tautology: God is not defined by any other Word than his own. God is *causa sui* and therefore has no other *ratio essendi* than himself. It is precisely because it is tautological that the *logos* needs no other Word or words and can be unique. This is, finally, the foundation for the Commandment: "thou shalt have no other gods before me" (Exodus, 20: 3).

And the *Euangelion* does not mitigate this absoluteness either. On the contrary, the new alliance announced by the Gospel (*Euangelion*) reinforced this absolute claim to truth by adding a new dimension. Now the *logos* is not only the creative Word of God and the word with which God reveals his Will (the Law), but has also become the living Christ, the God that became flesh. The beginning of John's Gospel continues: "And the Word (*logos*) was made flesh, and dwelt among us (and we beheld this glory, the glory as of the only begotten Father) full of grace and truth" (John I: 14). Thus, Christianity legitimises itself as the fullest revelation of the nature of the *logos*: while the Old Testament had already known the creative Word of God (Genesis I: 3ff.; Isaiah 40: 8; 44: 24–28; 48: 13; Psalms 33: 6) and his revealing mission (Psalms 107: 20; 147: 15–18), it is the task of the *Euangelion* to complete the revelation by announcing the *personal* nature of the Sacred Word (*logos*).

The words of Christ, "I am the way, the truth and the life" (John XIV: 6), closed the circle that had been opened by the creation-revelation in the Old Testament. As such they justify a process of theologisation of the truth. It is to these words that Saint Augustine referred when he stated that the truth is God himself. Truth for Augustine coincides with God, because the "truth" is the source that we must necessarily admit in order to understand the condition of true things: the truth is the measure, so that the true thing is true because it is measured by it (*Confessiones* VII: 10–11; 17).

God as the measure of truth is also the measure of what is real. God himself is the *ens realissimum*, the presupposition necessary in order to explain the existence of reality. In what sense is God the *ens realissimum*? To what "reality" are we referring? We have seen that ancient Greeks did not have a word that corresponded to our word "reality". Indeed, it was not until the Latin Middle Ages that the word *realitas* was first coined. The first attested occurrence of the term appeared in late scholasticism (Courtine 1992a). However, the term *realitas* at this stage refers primarily to the substantive *res* in its widest meaning and defines what makes a *res* what it is, namely its *essentia*, or, even better, the *essentialitas* of each *res* (Courtine 1992a, 1992b).

In this sense, *realitas* is identified with the *formalitas*, and *realismus* was said to be the view according to which these *formalitates* exist as universals *in re*. This view was then opposed to *nominalismus*, that is, the view that asserts that universals only exist *in voce*. The term *realismus* originally meant a concept that is almost the opposite of what it came to mean in modern philosophical usage, at least after Kant. While Kant understood "realism" to be the opposite of "idealism", the original medieval term *realismus* defined a position that is, in fact, closer to what Kant would call "idealism" (Hoffmann et al. 1992).[8]

The term *realitas* thus designated a semantic area that is close to what we call "perfection" – where "*perfectio*" must be understood in its etymological meaning of a "complete being". We are now used to a completely different meaning and have forgotten that, in medieval

[8] On this point, see Abbagnano 1971: 732.

sources, the word *realitas* meant something else (Courtine 1992a, 1992b). Traces of this use, however, can still be found in the works of modern philosophers. Descartes, for instance, used the expression *realitas sive perfectio in aliqua re* (1984: 24–36), and Spinoza explicitly stated in the second part of his *Ethics* that *per realitatem et perfectionem idem intelligo* (Spinoza 1985: 447).

We must take this identification of the *realitas* with the *perfectio* seriously. This does not mean that those who used this expression did not believe in the reality of this world – which is certainly not perfect. It simply indicated that they conceived of this world as one of the possible levels of "reality". In scholasticism, the concept associated with it was that of "analogy". The being of the creature is neither identical with the being of God nor completely alien to it: it is *analogical*, that is, similar, but different. As Thomas Aquinas put it, only God has being as his essence, whereas creatures have being only for participation; in this, they are similar to God, who is the first principle of being, but, for the same reason, God is incommensurable with them, and can therefore be the subject of only an analogical predication (*Summa theologiae*, I, q. 4, a.3).[9]

The concept of *realitas* as *perfectio* suggests a view of "reality" which, like the Greek *to on*, contemplates different degrees of reality, but within this view, in contrast to the Greek one, God himself, the *ens perfectissimum* by definition, works as the ordering ontological criterion. The omnipotent God, creator of being and measure of truth, is also the *ens realissimum* and thus a measure of what is "real". According to this view, the closer to God things are, the more real they are.

Traces of this approach to truth and reality can still be found in some fragments of the medieval imaginary.[10] Cosmology was particularly crucial from this point of view, since it conveyed images of the universe that were echoed in the numerous astrological and magical handbooks and practices as well as in the representations of the afterlife used in sermons and for the saving of souls.

---

[9] When Duns Scotus criticised this view by saying that *omne ens habet aliquod esse proprium,* he aimed to reconstruct the unity of being as common to all that exists. He did this because he thought that it would have been impossible otherwise to know the true nature of God, but by recognising the autonomy of each individual being he opened a way that went beyond the typically medieval view.

[10] On the notion of imaginary, see in particular Castoriadis 1987 and Chapter 10.

As Duhem observed, commentaries on Genesis, which functioned as the basis for early medieval cosmology, were not writings directed towards specialists: they addressed their views to the Christian masses, who were expected to progress not in the studying of astronomy, but on the road to salvation (Duhem 1965: 396). While some of these commentaries, following Origen, tried to reconcile the scriptures with previous cosmological speculation, others proposed an approach that was characterised by a strict adhesion to the text of the Sacred Scriptures. These were also considered to contain all the truths regarding the constitution of the natural world. The world was perceived as a second "book written by God" and was therefore interpreted as *sacramentum salutaris allegoriae* and then read through the biblical exegesis itself (Duhem 1965: 396ff.).

For instance, in the sixth century, Cosmas Indicopleustes, a pious Christian, wrote the very influential *Christian Topography of the Universe, Demonstrated Through the Sacred Scriptures and Whose Truth Christians Cannot Question* (Cosmas 1897). By mixing the ancient doctrines retold by fathers of the Church and the more recent biblical exegesis, Cosmas affirmed that the right model for the universe was the tabernacle constructed by Moses. The earth was flat and the stars were carried by angels. This was the universe depicted in churches, books and representations of the afterlife for a long time. Around the eleventh century, however, a new series of previously unknown Greek and Arabic classical texts were translated into Latin. The Platonic *Timaeus*, known in its first part and accompanied by a commentary by Calcidius (fourth century), together with Ptolemy, translated from the Arabic, generated a new view that, on the basis of a rediscovered Aristotle's *Physics*,[11] went on to prevail for centuries.

The Aristotelean-Ptolemaic world was a qualitative world. Indeed, Aristotle conceived of the world in *purely qualitative* terms, that is, he

---

[11] Plato was known to the Middle Ages essentially through the testimony of Augustine, while Aristotle was know only through Boetius' translation and comments on his *De interpretatione* and *Categoriae*. The physical and metaphysical writings were translated only in the twelfth century (the ethical, political and rhetorical even later). Initially viewed with suspicion for their idea of natural necessity (which was considered as a possible threat to the dogma of God's omnipotence), Aristotle's writings were later reconciled with Christianity particularly thanks to the thinking of Thomas Aquinas, who made Aristotle's natural necessity into an instrument to demonstrate the truth of faith.

divided the universe into several parts constituted by different qualities corresponding to different degrees of perfection. In this universe there was the sub-lunar world, whose elements, earth, water, air and fire, moved according to a linear movement, which was imperfect. Beyond the sky of the moon, there were the skies, conceived as spheres, of the sun and the other planets, which were made by an incorruptible substance (ether), and which moved in a circular motion, which was perfect. Beyond the sphere of the fixed stars, which was the limit of the Aristotelean universe, there was the first immovable motor, the first principle of everything, which was non-material, because matter is subject to corruption, pure thought of thought. With imperfection on one side, and all the perfection culminating in an immovable motor on the other, the Church liked this cosmology. And its agreement with the dogmas of faith certainly helps to explain its persistence.

Supported by the authority of the Church, the Aristotelean-Ptolemaic cosmology dominated for centuries. People were exposed to this image of the universe: they saw such a world in churches, in the paintings adorning them, in astrological and magical handbooks, in sermons, and in the various representations of the afterlife. This was a world constructed according to a multilevel scheme, in which the higher the level, the higher was the grade of perfection. The culminating point was obviously the being always in act, God, the perfect being, or *ens realissimum.* This is not to say that people did not believe in what we can call the "external empirical reality", but only that this was thought of as only one level of reality and, possibly, as the level with the lowest degree of perfection.[12]

Medieval figurative art is quite often characterised as "non-realist", meaning that medieval painters did not paint bodies and objects as they are "in reality", that is, as we perceive them through our senses. However, the point is not that these paintings are not "realistic", it is that *realitas* was itself perceived differently. It is not that medieval painters could not see that their paintings did not reflect the way in which things appear through the senses. The way in which things

---

[12] Criticism of this view was raised within the mendicant orders in particular. According to Saint Francis, for instance, every single creature, having been created by God himself, carries signs of perfection. However, this was the view of a minority only, and it was opposed for a long time for its political implications.

appear to our senses was not so important for medieval painters. There was no point in depicting bodies and objects in this way for them. Only with a new *Weltanschauung*, where the human being, not God, was the measure of everything, would the way in which things appear to our senses be given a new centrality (Geertz 1983: 94ff.).

At first sight, the attitude of Christianity towards the mythological heritage might appear to be ambiguous rather than totally hostile, because to a great extent Christianity itself made recourse to that heritage. However, this ambiguity reflects a fundamentally negative attitude, which transpired even when previous mythological narratives were apparently "admitted". Myths were indeed "Christianised", through both the *reductio ad unum* of their truth and the conversion of their content. In other words, they were not recognised in their own right; even when apparently recovered, their plurality was denied. Ancient myths were either deleted by material oblivion or, whenever possible, read as *involucra, integumenta* of the revealed truth, that is, read as an anticipation of it.

Among the hermeneutical devices that led to this *reductio ad unum*, two were particularly efficient. Both of them had their origins in the biblical exegesis. One of the fundamental problems for the first Christians was how to interpret the stories of the Old Testament. Among the fathers of the Church, two fundamental approaches were, in particular, elaborated. The first, recommended by Origen, was more spiritualist and proposed interpreting these stories as allegories, that is as stories or images that refer to some hidden and remote meaning that was different from the literal one. In this approach, the literal meaning was dissolved into a spiritual one.

The second, more realistic approach was proposed by Tertullian and is constructed around the notion of *figura futurorum*.[13] Tertullian pointed to the historical truth of the tales of the Old Testament – which was completely ignored by the allegorical reading of them. In Tertullian's view, Moses actually went through the desert, and this was a historical truth that must be preserved in the exegesis. At the same time, Moses leading the Jews out of the desert is read as the *figura* or "real prophecy" of the coming of Christ and the liberation of souls from sin. Both are historical events, Moses' exodus and Christ's coming, but

[13] See, in particular, Auerbach 1944.

the first is a *figura futurorum*, an *umbra* or *imago*, that finds its realisation in the future coming of Christ, which is, in fact, its *veritas*.

Figural interpretation was very influential in the Latin Middle Ages, above all, as a consequence of Augustine's authority. As Auerbach pointed out, it was Augustine who most emphatically recommended its use in sermons and in the mission of evangelisation; indeed, he gave examples of how to develop it further: Noah's ark is *prefiguratio Ecclesiae* (*De Civ.* 15, 27); Moses is in different ways *figura Christi* (*De Civ.* 10, 6 or 18, 11); Aaron's *sacerdotium* is *umbra et figura aeterni sacerdotii* (*De Civ.* 17, 6), and so on (Auerbach 1944).

The two hermeneutical devices, allegorical and figural reading, enabled the whole history to be read as a history of salvation: each event, each narrative could be read as being either an allegorical *involucra* of the superior truth of salvation or as its "real prophecy", which, in a chain of successive *figurae futurorum*, will find its final truth at the end of time and at the final triumph of the judging God. The figural interpretation could thus be used as the basis for the interpretation of all history: if the world is a *liber*, a book created by the Word of God, then it is natural to interpret it with the same means used to interpret the Sacred Scriptures.

Through these hermeneutical devices, the pagan world of myth, even when apparently appropriated, was in fact reduced to a unique truth and thus denied its pluralistic nature. Noteworthy examples of this can be seen in Dante's *Divine Comedy*. This *summa* of both the ideological and imaginative medieval apparatus is full of figures taken from the pagan world. This seems to be the obvious consequence of the fact that the object of this sacred poem (*Paradiso* XXV, 1) is the description of Dante's voyage in the afterlife and his *visio* of the *status animarum post mortem* (*Lettera a Cangrande della Scala*).[14] Pagans often appear among the damned. But Dante's guide, Virgil is also a pagan. This fact has always been explained by referring to an allegorical reading of Virgil as a symbol of human reason: Virgil, who cannot accompany Dante

---

[14] Here, just as when he compares his voyage in the afterlife with those of Aeneas and Saint Paul (*Inferno* II, 32), it is clear that Dante conceived of it as "real". The reality of Saint Paul's *descensus* is guaranteed by the Sacred Scriptures – an authority that such a deeply Christian mind as Dante's would never have questioned. For the reality of Aeneas' journey, the authority is Virgil, an authority that Dante fully accepts (*Inferno* II, 13–15).

to Paradise, would then be the allegory of the impossibility of human reason to go beyond certain limits, much as Beatrice, who comes to Dante's aid, would be the allegory of divine grace. But what about other pagan figures, for example Cato or Ulysses?

Cato, pagan and guilty of suicide, one of the most horrible sins for Christians (*Purgatorio* I, 70–5), is nothing less than the guardian of Purgatory, the realm where souls can gain freedom from their sins. This is possible because the historical Cato, who committed suicide for the sake of political freedom, is read as the *figura* of the Cato that is presented here as guardian of Purgatory (Auerbach 1944). Only inasmuch as the political freedom, for the sake of which he committed suicide, can be read as the *umbra futurorum* of Christian freedom, can Cato represent the guardian of Purgatory, of the place where the soul can free itself from the serfdom of sin.

Dante's recovery of the myth of Ulysses should be interpreted in a similar vein. The story of the Ulysses, burnt with Diomede in *Canto* XXVII of *Inferno*, is conceived by Dante as the fullest realisation of the Homeric Ulysses: the pagan Ulysses is only a *figura* or *umbra* of its fullest Christian truth. The Ulysses who is burning here is not only condemned to be burnt eternally for the fraud of the Trojan horse, but, in Dante's account of this myth, he is swallowed up by the sea for having dared to navigate beyond Hercules' Columns. Thus, Dante's Ulysses is neither a recovery of Homer's mythical character nor one of the possible variants of a variously reinterpreted myth: it is its fullest truth, the *figura* of human reason and its incapacity to go beyond the limits imposed by God.

The point is not that Dante rejected Homer's version of the story of Ulysses, or that he denied the historical truth of Cato's story. It is that these events are subordinated in their fullest realisation to the coming of Christ. Analogously, it is not that Christianity altogether refuses to admit mythological stories, but that these stories were reinterpreted as the *involucra* of a superior truth and thus reduced to a unique History.

The History is unique because it is the History of salvation. And the Church, as the material incarnation of this History of salvation, was the authority that claimed to be destined by God to interpret his truth. On this basis, the Church claimed its right to determine the criteria for the figural interpretation. The struggle for authority thus became the struggle for the right to interpret.

Martin Luther's principle of an individual reading of the Sacred Scriptures (*sola Scriptura*) was the most tangible sign of a rejection of the authority of the Catholic Church. Luther strongly opposed allegorism in biblical exegesis. The Lutheran hermeneutical principle of *sola Scriptura* was fundamentally contrary to an allegorical and figural reading, because the privileging of the literal over the allegorical meaning was also in opposition to the Catholic Church's authority to fix the codes of interpretation.

But, with the Reformation, once the principle of free interpretation is admitted, a new process begins at the end of which the *sacred logos* cannot but find itself as a plurality again. Here the dialectic nexus of myth and the *sacred logos* fully emerges: the *logos*, the Word that presents itself as the uniqueness of a tautological truth ("I am who I am") and constitutes itself as Holy History precisely by condemning the polytheism of myth, must find itself as a plurality once more. It is at this point that Holy History, which was presented as a History in the singular precisely because it was unique, in contrast to the plurality of myth, is shown to be nothing more than one of the many possible stories.

The first reaction to the rediscovery of the plurality of histories is to try to recompose the unity on a different level. Protestant liberal theology, a result of the application of the philological method to the Sacred Scriptures, which resulted in a claim for its "demythologisation" (*Entmythologisierung*), can be read as an attempt to recompose the dialectics of theological truth. In his programmatic conference of the 1941 *New Testament and Mythology*, Bultmann denounced the mythical elements in the Sacred Scriptures (1984). It is to their presence, in his view, that all the inconsistencies of the text are due. He observed that we could no longer believe in the stories of the Gospels, because stories about the Resurrection and Assumption could no longer appeal to modern ears and must be considered as nothing more than mere "myths". Hence, the proposal for a new hermeneutical method for the interpretation of the Sacred Scriptures: "demythologisation" – a hermeneutical tool for assessing the content of the reality (*Wirklichkeitsgehalt*) of mythological texts (Bultmann 1962: 19).

The debate on the demythologisation moves from the recognition, within Christianity, of the plurality that defines myth. All the same – so Bultmann argued – this plurality is simply a contingent plurality, that is, it is the plurality of antiquated representations *added* to by primitive catechism; as such, it must be kept separated from the *kerygma*, the unique, always living Christian message. Thus, while the stories in the New Testament are recognised as plural but then said to be antiquated, the *kerygma* is said to be the always living and real unique message of salvation (Bultmann 1962: 33). In this way, the demythologisation recognised a plurality of stories on the one hand, while aiming to neutralise it by recomposing a new unity at the level of the *kerygma* on the other.

In his debate with Bultmann, Jaspers pointed out that, for Christians, the demythologisation is a road full of traps since it can lead to the denial of the sacred character of the Scriptures. "Demythologisation" – Jaspers wrote to Bultmann – "is almost a blasphemous word" (Bultmann and Jaspers 1954: 19, trans. mine). Jaspers' response to Bultmann's proposal was not just an attempt to rehabilitate the mythical elements that were present in the *Biblos*.[15] It was also the recognition that once the mythical nature of the sacred *logos* has been recognised, its range cannot be limited.

As a result, demythologisation is blasphemous because it amounts to a denunciation of the dialectic of the sacred *logos*. Indeed, once the mythical nature of God's Word has been recognised, it clearly becomes arbitrary to determine what the borderline is between the "mythical side" and the "*kerygmatic* core" of the sacred *logos*. And this arbitrariness cannot but reveal the tautological emptiness of the sacred *logos* itself. Therefore, Jaspers' reply was not so much an attempt to rehabilitate the mythical element as an attempt to save the sacredness of the *logos*, that is to re-establish the opposition between "sacred *logos*" and "myth" upon which the Exodus Commandment ultimately rests.

Ecumenical movements can be seen as the last of the attempts to re-establish the uniqueness of the sacred *logos* at another level. When commenting on the concept of demythologisation, the theologian of inter-religious dialogue, Panikkar, has observed that it is in the inevitable encounter of Christianity with other religions that the problem of demythologisation is exacerbated: the attempt to demythologise becomes inevitable precisely because of the inevitable

---

[15] This is, for instance, the interpretation by Jamme, who saw a simple attempt to rehabilitate myth in Jaspers' reply (Jamme 1991: 107).

confrontation of Christianity with other world religions (Panikkar 1962: 243). On the other hand, Panikkar observed, what renders the dialogue of Christianity with other religions impossible is precisely the claim to exclusivity that is typical of Christianity. Indeed, a Hindu might well recognise one avatar in the Christ, that is, one of the possible manifestations of God in space and time, and even recognise his absoluteness, given that any religion aims to be absolute, but a Hindu could never come to terms with Christianity's assumption of uniqueness and exclusivity (Panikkar 1962: 262).

According to Anglican theologian Hick, the *Euangelion* of the salvation in Christ must therefore be recognised as a myth in itself, that is, as "the myth of the incarnate God" (Hick 1977). The Holy History of the Christ is now said to be nothing but a myth, simply one among many possible stories. However, even now that Christianity is recognised as a myth next to many others, a new *reductio ad unum* is predicated on a different level. In Hick's view, the recognition that Christ represents only a myth, should lead to the abandonment of the model constructed on the Christ and to the adoption of a new model depending only on God. The different names of God are now said to be only different historical incarnations of the unique divine truth, historical incarnations of the unique sacred *logos*. Once again, then, it is through the *logos* that a claim to uniqueness is advanced, because it is the *logos* itself that is said to be the promise of salvation that is common to all religions (Hick 1982; Panikkar 1964).

To conclude, notwithstanding the efforts to go beyond the dialectic of a sacred *logos* that condemns myth as deceitful, hiding thus its own mythical nature, new attempts towards recomposing this dialectic are emerging. The final page of this process is still to be written. At the same time, another battle is under way. This consists in the dialectic of an Enlightenment that constitutes itself by condemning myth as unreal and it is to the reconstruction of this that the next chapter will be devoted.

3

Scientific Rationality and the Dialectic
of the Enlightenment

Pierre Bayle, the author of the monumental *Historical and Critical Dictionary* (1740), the "real arsenal of all the Enlightenment philosophers" (Cassirer 1951: 167), establishes himself as *philosophe* with an earlier book, first published in 1682, *Various Thoughts on the Occasion of a Comet* (2000). This book was written following the appearance of a comet, held to be a divine presage of great misfortunes according to a widespread belief of the time. The event gave priests and theologians on all sides the opportunity for a lively discussion.

Various Thoughts was first published anonymously, as a series of letters written to a theologian of the Sorbonne (Bayle 2000: 3ff.). By disguising his identity, Bayle was able to put forward a sharp criticism of the beliefs in divine presages, using the language of theologians. Thus, for instance, as we read in the preface, he could claim that the merit of these spontaneous letters written to a friend was in the fact that their "unknown author is willing to use, against the presage of comets, the same weapons belonging to piety and religion that have been used until now in favour of these presages" (Bayle 2000: 5).

Through this cover, Bayle was able to put forward the most revolutionary statements, such as his famous argument in favour of a society of atheists.[1] Through the typical *escamotage* of commenting on an event of the past, Bayle was also able to explain why he had to make recourse to all these precautions. Discussing Plutarch, he wrote that, in Nicias'

---

[1] On this point, see, in particular, Chapter 7.

time, one did not dare to explain lunar eclipses in terms of natural causes except with one's own best friend, and only after taking all sorts of precautions (Bayle 2000: 141). This was so, he said, because when events are reduced to their natural causes, they no longer predict anything, which deprives people of an infinite number of "vain imaginings" on which they would otherwise feast. This, Bayle added, also deprives diviners of their employment (Bayle 2000: 141).

The political implications of these religious beliefs are manifest. Indeed, a political critique seems to be the very rationale of Bayle's critique of the belief in comets as presages and of his appeal, against them, to the enlightenment of philosophy. Again, in an apparently insignificant passage, Bayle observed that in all times politicians have had a major interest in fomenting the beliefs surrounding comets, because there is no more powerful way of keeping populaces in check. As Bayle explicitly says, "however unruly and inconstant [populaces] may be, if their minds are once struck by a vain image of religion, they will obey the diviners better than their chiefs" (Bayle 2000: 99).

In order to criticise this use of religious beliefs, Bayle found himself putting forward a critique of the reliance on "vain images and tales" in general. In this, it is not only the authority of theologians that he criticises, but also that of poets. In addressing the issue with his interlocutor, the anonymous writer of the letter made explicit the approach that he expected from him: we should "nourish our minds only with an *altogether pure reason*" since "it is not possible to have a more miserable foundation than the authority of the poets" (Bayle 2000: 18; emphasis mine).

In the name of "the enlightenment of philosophy" (*les lumières de la philosophie*), a criticism of all the "traditional tales" is put forward. "Pure reason" tells us that comets are natural events and can therefore be explained in terms of their purely natural causes; once this explanation has been put forward, there is nothing else in comets that can link their occurrence with fortunes and misfortunes. But why should this view bring with it a condemnation of poets' tales?

We have seen that *sacred logos* condemned ancient myths because of their plurality. Here, the condemnation is on a new ground: they are judged to be deceptive because they are "vain" and "imaginary", and thus "unreal", or, in other words, because they are mere myths (Bayle 2000: 18ff.). But what kind of "reality" is Bayle talking about? As we have seen, the Greeks did not even have a word for our "reality", and scholasticism conceived of *realitas* primarily in reference to the *essentia* of each *res*, so that *realitas* was used as a synonym of perfection.[2] Clearly, it is to another view of the "real" that Bayle is referring. Here, the "real" is not opposed to what is "imperfect", but to what is merely "imaginary" or "ideal" (Hoffmann et al., 1992).

Descartes was a turning point for the emergence of this "real" versus "ideal" dichotomy. He was the first to inaugurate the modern use of the term "idea" in the sense of a "mental content", whereas, as we have seen, the Ancient Greeks conceived of an idea as a being and a thought at the same time.[3] Descartes was one of the founding fathers of the scientific revolution and was thus one of the first philosophers to establish the typically modern problem of the separation of the knowing subject from the object of knowledge. It was because of this separation that the problem of the existence of an external world was first formulated. Notwithstanding the fact that Descartes used the word *realitas* in the old sense of perfection,[4] he formulated the set of problems that went on to give rise to the contraposition between "real" and "ideal" that later was fully developed by Kant (Hoffmann et al. 1992).

Let us dwell briefly on the lines of reasoning presented in Descartes' *Discourse on the Method* and his *Meditations on First Philosophy*. They delineate an approach that was to become the model for successive enquiries into the possibility of knowledge. The starting point is one of methodical doubt: in order to test the certainty of knowledge, Descartes starts by casting doubts over whatever is liable to doubting. In this way, he finds that all the truths he had received from his personal experience and education – ranging from scholastic metaphysics to sensitive certainty, and to mathematical knowledge – can be doubted.

Even in the case of mathematical thinking (the kind of knowledge entailing, in his view, the highest level of certainty), Descartes admits the possibility of mistakes. This happens through the hypothesis of a malicious demon, which makes him believe, for instance, that "two

[2] As we have seen, this conception reached modern philosophers such as Spinoza 1985: 447 and Descartes 1984: 24–36.

[3] See Chapter 1. For an analysis of the history of the term idea, see Abbagnano 1971: 450 and Neumann 1972.

[4] As we have seen, in the *Meditations*, one can still find expressions such as *realitas sive perfectio in aliqua re* (Descartes 1984: 24–36).

plus two equals four". Thus, we arrive at the hyperbolic doubt in which there seems to be no more truth, but only doubts. The way out of this is to claim that this is the truth itself: the only truth that cannot be questioned is precisely the fact that when one is in the process of doubting, and even if one is deceived, at that moment one will nonetheless be *thinking*. From this, therefore, one can draw the certainty that one exists – at least as a *res cogitans*. This is the meaning of the Cartesian *cogito ergo sum*: the first certainty that human beings can reach is the fact of their existence as a *res cogitans*, that is, the certainty of their existence as a knowing subject.[5]

As a consequence, the problem, to which Descartes devoted his thinking until his death, became that of the relationship between the *res cogitans* and the *res extensa*, that is, how to move from the certainty of the knowing subject to that of the existence and knowability of the external world. The solution proposed by modern science was to consider the external world as intelligible by the knowing subject only because of its being formed by matter and movement, and therefore being expressible in mathematical language. Thus, the multilayered and complex world of the medieval cosmology was transformed into the simple world, made of matter and movement, of modern mechanicism. Only by virtue of this simplicity could the world be read by the knowing subject.

The rise of a scientific view of the world brought with it a new critical stance towards myth. In Galilei's terms, for instance, the universe is a book that is readable because it is written in a mathematical language. This is what sets the *scientific logos* definitively apart from the "mythical" and the "imaginary". In his *The Assayer* – a book that, while discussing the nature of comets, delineates this new scientific method – Galilei strongly defends the "new philosophy", meaning science, and he does so precisely by juxtaposing science to what is described as a mere "human fantasy" (Galilei 2005: 631).

Our philosophy, Galilei argues in this book, is not, like the Iliad, the product of human fantasy precisely because

philosophy is written in this vast book that is continually open before our eyes, i.e. in the universe; but this book cannot be understood without learning the language and the characters in which it is written. The book of the universe

---

[5] See, in particular, the *Second Meditation* (Descartes 1984: 16ff.).

is written in a mathematical language, and its characters are triangles, circles and other geometrical figures, without which it is impossible for humans to understand a single word; without these, it would be like wandering around a dark labyrinth in vain (*e' un aggirarsi vanamente per un oscuro laberinto*). (Galilei 2005: 631–2; trans. mine)

The universe is in front of us: we simply have to read it. However, it is possible to read the universe only by learning to understand its mathematical language. If we don't learn this language, we are wandering in the dark. Experience, the same experience to which Bayle would refer as the only authority recognised by the "enlightenment of philosophy" (Bayle 2000: 4), is the *trait d'union*, the point of contact between the knowing enlightened subject and the object of the universe. However, as the Galilean expression "sensory experience and certain demonstrations" (*sensata esperienza e certe dimostrazioni*) suggests, it was not all sensory experience that played such a role (Galilei 2005: 525ff.). If the world is written in purely quantitative terms, in order to read it we have to dismiss everything that has to do with qualities, that is, all that is "merely subjective". Galilei was also the first thinker to formulate the distinction between what would be called "primary and secondary properties": while figures, weight, and movement are necessarily attached to any object of our experience and cannot be separated from that object, other qualities, such as colour, taste, and so on, are not necessarily attached to an object and are therefore simply secondary. As he puts it:

For this reason, I started thinking that, in virtue of the part of the subject in which they lie, all these tastes, odours, colours, etc. are nothing but pure names that reside in the sensitive body, so that, once the animal is taken away, they are also annihilated. (Galilei 2005: 778; trans. mine)

In these words a boundary is drawn between what can be subjected to scientific enquiry and what cannot, because it resides in the "animal part" of the subject. Seventy years later, John Locke was to write in his *Essay Concerning Human Understanding* that primary qualities are the only "*real properties*" because only they "really exist" in bodies (Locke 1997: 135ff.). In contrast, colours, smells, tastes, sounds, and the other qualities perceived through the senses, "whatever reality by mistake we attribute to them, are in truth nothing in the object themselves": they derive from "a power of the subject to produce various sensations in us, whose real existence, though, depends on those other qualities such as bulk, figures, texture and motion that are primary because they are the *real* ones" (Locke 1997: 136; my emphasis).

Learning to read the book of the universe thus required a process of learning how to distinguish between "primary" and "secondary" properties. These latter, properly speaking, are "not real" and one must therefore leave them out of consideration in a scientific enquiry. In Galilei's words, we must get rid of the "animal", so that once we have "taken away ears, tongues, and noses, there would remain only figures, numbers and movements" (Galilei 2005: 778; trans. mine). All that cannot be reduced to figures, numbers and movement is the merely *subjective*, and thus, in Locke's terms, the *unreal*.

As a result, myths – which cannot be reduced to a mathematical language – were also said to be "unreal". As Horkheimer and Adorno pointed out, even if Bacon had not yet understood the crucial role of mathematics, his philosophy best represents the attitude of science towards myth (Adorno and Horkheimer 1997). In Bacon's view, the construction of a true science should be preceded by a critique of all the false conceptions, or *idola*, in which human beings are immersed because of their subjective experience – be it the experience they derive from their nature or from their culture and education (Bacon 1963). The subject conducting the scientific enquiry has to deprive himself of every residue of myth since nature can only be mastered by "pure reason".

Bacon distinguishes four types of *idola* that must be removed in order to construct a new method of scientific enquiry: 1) the *idola tribus*, which are derived from the innate characteristics of the human mind, such as the mind's tendency to look for uniformities and to anticipate; 2) the *idola specus*, or the prejudices that human beings derive from their own "cave", that is, according to the homonymous myth of Plato, from the fact that human beings usually live in the darkness and can only contemplate the shadow of things; 3) the *idola fori*, or the mistakes that are derived from the use of language in social life; and, finally, 4) the *idola theatri*, that is, the mistakes that are derived from a belief in the authority of traditions and ancient theories.

Bacon thus identifies the four types of *idola* as sources of prejudice, ambiguity and incomprehension. Notwithstanding the fact that these *idola* are rooted in the very nature of the human mind, language and social life, the pure subject of scientific enquiry must rid itself of them. The *idola theatri* are, in a sense, the most significant, because they reveal what is at stake in this process of removal. Why, one could ask, should human beings engage in such a costly enterprise and not remain in their *idola* if these are rooted in the nature of human mind and social life? The answer leads us to the core of the project of the Enlightenment: human beings had to rid themselves of the *idola* because otherwise they would remain prey to the authority and influence of others. The struggle for liberation from the *idola* is the struggle for individual autonomy.

It is no coincidence, then, that the modern scientific revolution took place through a discussion about the nature of comets and other astronomic phenomena. The new scientific method was developed in order to uphold an astronomic revolution, and cannot be separated from it: the battle for modern science was a battle for a new conception of the cosmos and for the place that human beings occupy within it.[6] When Galilei, using his self-made telescope, observed that, according to the "certainty given by eyes" (*certezza che è data dagli occhi*), the lunar landscape is similar to ours and that there is no single centre of the universe, he was undermining both the traditional view of the universe and the human position within it. (Galilei 2005: 271ff.)

This "traditional" image of the universe, against which the "new philosophy" was constructed, was built around two pillars: the division between the lunar and sublunar worlds, and the idea of a closed universe in which the earth was at the centre. In 1600, Giordano Bruno was burnt as a heretic in Campo dei Fiori for having questioned these two pillars by asserting the infinity of the universe. Subsequently, in 1616, Galilei was ordered to abandon his Copernican view, and then, in 1633, he was condemned for holding it.

The reason for the condemnations was not only because all the teachings of the Church were enmeshed in the geocentric view, which was supported by some passages in the Bible, but also because the new philosophy entailed a revolutionary change in the concept both of

---

[6] Many authors have underlined this point: see, in particular, Blumenberg 1983. It is no coincidence that both Galilei and Bayle put forward their theories while discussing the nature of the comets (Galilei 2005: 595ff; Bayle 2000).

the world and of the place of human beings within it. As a result of this revolution, which operated on the basis of the "certainty given by eyes", the closed universe of the Aristotelean tradition, divided into two spheres – perfection on one side, and imperfection on the other – became an infinite homogeneous universe made of matter and movement, where human beings were no longer relegated to imperfection. While in the old multilayered world human beings were teleologically assigned by God to the sub-lunar world, with the new philosophy they found themselves projected into an infinite and homogeneous universe where no distinction, in terms of greater or lesser degrees of perfection, could be made (Koyré 1957).

The battle for the new science was thus also a battle for human self-legitimacy against theological absolutism (Blumenberg 1983). Among the chief means by which this absolutism ruled was the traditional image of the universe as a closed and teleologically assigned multilayered scheme. The process of self-legitimating involved the destruction of this image of the world and the criticism of the authorities that supported it. Thus, the battle of the *scientific logos* for its self-legitimacy coincided with the project for human autonomy.

Kant defined the Enlightenment (*Aufklärung*) as the exit from a condition of self-imposed immaturity, where immaturity is the inability to use one's own understanding without the guidance of another, and where it is self-imposed because it derives not from a lack of understanding, but from a lack of courage to use it. The motto of the Enlightenment, according to the Kantian formulation, is therefore "*sapere aude*", to have the courage to use one's own reason, that is, to be autonomous (Kant 1991a: 54–60).

However, whatever form it may have assumed at different times, the Enlightenment, which identifies autonomy with pure reason, also threatens in turn to become a form of mythology. As Horkheimer and Adorno pointed out in their *Dialectic of Enlightenment*, reason is not opposed to myth, as the Enlightenment expects, so that the Enlightenment's celebration of the pureness of reason runs the risk of remaining entrapped in a dialectic movement at the end of which the pureness of reason can turn into a mythology of its own (Adorno and Horkheimer 1997). In its search for self-legitimacy, the Enlightenment tends to exacerbate its contrast with myth and thus hides the fact that myth is already a form of enlightenment; however, in this way, the

Enlightenment itself risks falling into a mythology, that is, the mythology of an absolute pure reason.

By criticising myth as being subjective and thus unreal, the Enlightenment strengthens itself, for it thus asserts the possible and necessary separation of the knowing subject from reality – a separation that, as we have seen, is at the very basis of the existence of scientific rationality as such. In this way, the Enlightenment hides the fact that the myth is already enlightenment because myth is already a form of explanation (*Erklärung*). But, on the other hand, the pureness of reason that the Enlightenment celebrates can become a myth in its own turn, because once a pure reason has unified the whole world within its pure relationships and thus completely dominates it, what it finds outside is no longer the world, but its totalitarian abstract categories (Adorno and Horkheimer 1997). This *Dialectic of Enlightenment* is the trap into which any sort of absolutism of pure reason always risks falling.[7]

In fact, the role of myth is already to explain (*erklären*) insofar as it concerns telling, naming and discovering the origins of things. For instance, if, together with Aristotle, we understand "causes" in the sense of the Greek *aitiai*, then we should also conclude with him that myth is the knowledge of causes. Instead, the Enlightenment denies that myth is already a form of knowledge, and derives this from a strict adhesion to the conception of causes that was developed by modern science. According to this view, causes are not the production of something, but are rather the objective connections between events.[8]

The difference between this view and Aristotle's view is best captured by comparing the image of artistic creation through which Aristotle explains his view of the *aitiai* and the typically modern metaphor of the billiard balls. This is the image used by Hume in his discussion of the problem of causality. Here, we no longer have the production of something, responsibility, as was the case for Aristotle, but

---

[7] When writing their *Dialectic of Enlightenment*, Adorno and Horkheimer were faced with the positivism of the first half of the twentieth century. Here, the idea of "dialectic of Enlightenment" refers, however, more to a category of the spirit, to an ever-open trap into which the absolutism of pure reason can fall, rather than to a historically given form of Enlightenment.

[8] On the distinction between the Greek concept of *aitiai* and the modern view of causes, see Chapter 1 and Abbagnano 1971: 118.

two events where one is the cause of the other: ball A touching ball B, and ball B moving from a status of stillness to movement. To say "the movement of A is the cause of the movement of B" is to affirm that there is an objective, necessary connection between the two. But what is the basis of this objective connection? Hume maintained that there was no basis for such a connection other than mere habit (Hume 1985: 57ff. I). Kant agreed with him that connection is not objective, but subjective, although he described this subjectivity as "transcendental".

Facing the sceptical objection raised by Hume over the possibility of grounding the connection between two events on something more than mere habits, Kant's answer was to admit that we cannot attain things as they are in themselves (*noumena*), but, precisely because of this, that is, precisely because every possible knowledge is a *phenomenal* one, it is the subject, the transcendental subject, which becomes the criterion of truth itself. It is a "subject", then, albeit, in Kant's view, a transcendental subject, because it is the bearer of the a priori categories of experience, that is, the categories (space, time, causality, etc.) without which experience itself cannot exist (Kant 1998).

If the external world has to be presupposed as the matter of knowledge, but is only capable of being a formless substratum of experience, then once reason has reached the whole world, what it finds outside is nothing more than its own categories. As Adorno and Horkheimer point out, by following Kant's line of thought, one must conclude that philosophy knows nothing because it merely repeats what reason itself has placed in the object (Adorno and Horkheimer 1997: 13ff.). "Reality" is thus nothing but what reason, disguised as objective *empeiria*, puts into it. In his *Transcendental Analytic* of experience, in the section of the *Critique of Pure Reason* aimed at determining the a priori intellectual categories of experience, we read that "possible" is whatever agrees with the "formal conditions of experience", whereas "real" (*wirklich*) is that which is connected (*zusammenhängt*) with the "material conditions of experience" (Kant 1998: 321).

Kant's treatment of imagination is perhaps the most conspicuous sign of the Enlightenment's embarrassment with regard to myth. From the point of view of a genealogy of myth, this is perhaps the best way to show how the "mythical" that is constituted via its exclusion from "rationality" is, in fact, often intermingled with rationality itself. In the first edition of the *Critique*, Kant emphasised the central role played by imagination for the possibility of knowledge itself (1998: 229–30), while, in the second edition, he retreated from this discovery and relegated imagination to a secondary role (1998: 273–4).[9]

In the first edition of the *Critique*, when looking for the source of that pure transcendental synthesis understood as the condition of possibility of all experience, Kant identified it with imagination itself and came close, therefore, to admitting a sort of primacy of imagination (Arnason 1994: 160). As we read in a crucial passage of the 1781 edition:

If we can demonstrate that even our purest *a priori* intuitions provide no cognition except insofar as they contain the sort of combination of the manifold that makes possible a thoroughgoing synthesis or reproduction, then this synthesis of the imagination would be grounded even prior to all experience on *a priori* principles, and one must assume a pure transcendental synthesis of this power, which grounds even the possibility of all experience. (Kant 1998: 230).

Imagination, as the active capacity for the synthesis of the manifold, is said to be the condition for bringing the plurality of intuitions into single images and thus also the transcendental condition of all knowledge. As has been observed, imagination, insofar as it is the faculty that loosens mankind's relation to and reliance on wholly empirical conditions, can be said to be the truly transcendental faculty and therefore also the paradoxically concealed, yet "real" condition of all knowledge (Rundell 1994a, 1994b). Reason without imagination is dead reason.

However, in the second edition of his *Critique*, Kant retreats from this perspective and relegates imagination to a more subordinated and intermediary role between intellect and intuition. Section A95–A130 of the *Critique* is replaced by a new section (B129–B169). In this, Kant distinguishes between what he now calls the figurative synthesis of imagination from its intellectual counterpart, the transcendental schematism, which remains today one of the most obscure concepts in the *Critique* (Kant 1998: 257, 273ff.):

This schematism of our understanding with regard to appearances and their mere form is a hidden art in the depths of the human soul, whose true

---

[9] Among those who have recently insisted on this point as a crucial step in order to rethink the faculty of imagination, see Arnason 1994, Castoriadis 1994, Rundell 1994.

operations we can divine from nature and lay unveiled before our eyes only with difficulty. We can only say this much: the image is a product of the empirical faculty of productive imagination, [...] the schema of a pure concept of the understanding, on the contrary, is something that can never be brought to an image at all, but is rather pure synthesis. (1998: 273–4)

Although the Kant of the first edition of the *Critique* seems to hold that imagination is the truly transcendental faculty of synthesis and thus the very condition for the possibility of knowledge, a few years later he draws back from this discovery. By reducing his previous claim over the formative power of the imagination and its crucial role in the process of knowledge, he restates a more conventional division between reason and imagination, science and art, and thus also, as we will see, between critique and creativity: in this way, critique collapses into cognitivism and the imagination is treated either mediately or aesthetically (Rundell 1994a).

Imagination, which Bayle had condemned as "vain", was progressively associated with the ambit of aesthetics. Correspondingly, the Aristotelean term for imagination, *phantasia*, was moved to the realm of the unreal (Friese 2001). While Aristotle recognised a crucial role for fantasy in the process of knowledge, both because it preserves what has made an imprint on memory (*reproductive phantasia*) and because it belabours the *phantasmata* of knowledge (*productive phantasia*) (Friese 2001),[10] Galilei, as we have seen, considered *fantasia* as the ambit of poetic "fantasy" and thus as the opposite of scientific knowledge (Galilei 2005: 631). "Imagination", as the modern correspondent to Aristotle's *phantasia*, was excluded from the ambit of knowledge and became the faculty of poetry *par excellence* (Vattimo 1999b).

This process corresponds to what Gadamer has called the subjectification of aesthetics (Gadamer 1988: 39ff.). "Art" as an autonomous domain grounded on the notion of taste is, indeed, a creature of modernity. Before modern times, the term art (*ars*) covered a very wide meaning, including everything that had to do with the application of general principles to a certain domain, so that, for instance, in the middle ages, *artes* included the dialectic (that is, philosophy itself) together with grammar, rhetoric, arithmetic, geometry, astronomy, and

---

[10] For an analysis of the differences between Aristotle's and the modern view of fantasy, see Friese 2001, and Castoriadis 1994.

music. Subsequently the meaning of the term has been restricted to
that of the fine arts.[11]

Thus, while the category of *beauty* was initially dealt with in the
treatises of metaphysics, it has now become the object of a specific discipline whose autonomy is guaranteed by the concept of taste (Vattimo
1999a). In particular, Kant's third *Critique* (2000) was a turning point.
In the preface of this book, Kant labelled as aesthetical the judgement
concerning the beautiful and the sublime (2000: 55–8). The judgement of taste is defined by a contraposition with cognitive judgement:
while the latter operates by subsuming the particular into a general
rule, the former is the kind of judgement in which a universal is looked
for in the particular. Even if these judgements rest on a spontaneous
agreement with a subjective sentiment of pleasure-displeasure and, at
the same time, are expected to have some kind of universality because
they are linked to a sort of "aesthetical common sense" (2000: 123),
they do not contribute in any way to the advancement of knowledge.[12]

The process of the subjectification of aesthetics went hand in hand
with its autonomisation. Morals went through an analogous process.
In other words, if "possible" and "real" came to mean what respectively
"agrees" and is "connected" with the conditions of experience, namely,
the intuition of space and time and the categories of understanding,
for a reason caught in the dialectic of Enlightenment (*Aufklärung*), the
problem arises of what to do with everything that does not fall within
these conditions. Are we destined to wander in the dark as Galilei
suggested?

The answer given by Romanticism to the autonomisation of different spheres (knowledge, art, morals) was to call for a "new mythology"
(Frank 1982). In *Das älteste Systemprogramm des deutschen Idealismus* (*The
Oldest Program for a System of German Idealism*), a text attributed to the
three disciples of the Tübinger Stift – Hegel, Hölderlin and Schelling –
the restoration of myth took the form of an appeal to a new mythology presented as the only way by which to overcome the mechanisation

---

[11] A trace of the medieval use of the term "art" can still be found in institutional labels
such as "Faculty of Arts" or the titles "Bachelor of Arts" or "Master of Arts".
[12] Kant set the judgement of taste apart from knowledge and, at the same time, by
referring to the notion of "common taste", that is, a way of feeling shared by a
human community, he laid the ground for the connection between aesthetics and
the philosophy of history that is characteristic of romanticism (Vattimo 1999a).

operated by the Enlightenment (Hegel, Hölderlin and Schelling 1971; trans. mine). In this text, myth appears to encompass all that pure reason is not. However, as we will see, the appeal for a "new mythology" ends up reproducing the Enlightenment's view of myth by simply inverting its axiological connotation, instead of radically questioning it.

According to this text, the programme of a new mythology should encompass ethics, politics, aesthetics, and religion. The document starts with an invocation of ethics understood in a Kantian fashion as a system of all the ideas or postulates of reason – first of all, the postulate of the self (*Ich*) as the absolute free essence (Hegel, Hölderlin and Schelling 1971: 234). With the idea of a free essence, the idea of nature understood as the world for a moral essence also emerges. From this, we move to the realm of the human products (*Menschenwerke*). Here, the claim is advanced that all the human products that are incompatible with the idea of human freedom should be overcome (*aufgehoben*); in particular, the political form of the state, which always implies something mechanical (*etwas Mechanisches*), since it treats human beings as clockworks (*Räderwerke*), rather than as free beings, should disappear (*aufhören*). The programme of a new mythology was therefore also a radical political programme for the demolition of the state. As they openly put it: "we must abolish the state!" (Hegel, Hölderlin and Schelling 1971: 234; trans. mine).

From this radicalisation of the Kantian idea of freedom, the document moves on to the idea of beauty, presented in the Platonic sense of supreme idea. Beauty is seen as the culminating point of the programme since it unifies all other ideas (freedom, truth and goodness) within itself. According to the young authors of the text, "the philosophy of spirit is an aesthetic philosophy". The philosopher is required to exhibit the aesthetic sense (*ästhetische Sinne*) of a poet: those who do not possess this sense are "*Buchstabenphilosophen*", that is "calculating philosophers". The *Buchstabenphilosophen*, the ultimate products of the Enlightenment, are those who can work only with numbers and the abstract categories of intellect, and they are completely lost "when it comes to going beyond tables and registers" (Hegel, Hölderlin and Schelling 1971: 235; trans. mine).

Thus, in the text, a dichotomy is drawn between the *Buchstabenphilosophie*, a product of the Enlightenment with its clockwork universe, and, on the other hand, a philosophy of the spirit that unifies within itself all that is seen as left out by the former: the idea of human beings as free essence, grounding the possibility of a moral and political realm of absolute freedom, the aesthetical sense, with its unification of truth, freedom and goodness, and, finally, also a new form of religion. Paradoxically the programme for a new mythology, which moves from a radicalisation of the Kantian idea of autonomy to the extreme result of an anarchic programme, ends with an appeal for a religion:

> The great masses, so they wrote, need a material religion of the senses [*eine sinnliche Religion*]. Not only the great masses, but also the philosopher needs it. Monotheism of reason and heart, polytheism of the imagination and art, this is what we need.... We must have a new mythology, but this mythology must be at the service of ideas. It must be a mythology of reason.... Then perpetual unity will triumph among us. (Hegel, Hölderlin and Schelling 1971: 235; trans. mine)

While in the mind of the young architects of the programme the claim for autonomy should have led to a reign of absolute freedom where even the state, seen as something mechanical (*etwas Mechanisches*), should have disappeared in the name of individual freedom, the romantic appeal for a new mythology tends to be resolved into the sole appeal for myth, which is understood as the totality. In this way, myth and religion, which were assimilated by the Enlightenment's critique of all the vain imaginings (Bayle) or human fantasies (Galilei), are unified once more, so that Romanticism simply reproduced the Enlightenment's view of myth. But once the appeal to myth is resolved into religion, the risk is that this will restore the heteronomy of a divine revelation against which Enlightenment had developed its project for individual autonomy.

Schelling's intellectual trajectory is paradigmatic from this point of view. In his later writings, he identified mythology as the place of the divine revelation of God as person (Schelling 1856–1861: 567ff.). Here, myth became the ambit of the immediate intuition, in which the God of monotheism reveals himself. In this way, the new philosophy of mythology resulted in an attempt to "restore" myth, that is, into an appeal for myth as it had been conceived by the Enlightenment itself. Indeed, as has been observed, Schelling's philosophy of mythology does not deal with the new, but with the oldest of the mythologies (Marquard 1979: 50).

However, as has been observed, Schelling subordinated the content of truth of myth to that of the *logos* (Volkmann-Schluck 1969: 111 ff.). For this reason, his philosophy of mythology is not a theory of myth (Lotito 2002: xl). Indeed, once the *logos*, understood as the word of a God revealing himself, is proposed as the *telos* of myth, there is no longer space for myth with its plurality, but only for a final great myth. In this sense, as Blumenberg has pointed out, Schelling's philosophy of mythology is an attempt to bring myth to an end (Blumenberg 1985: 263).

Blumenberg extends his interpretation of Schelling's philosophy to the whole of German idealism. However, he only suggests, and does not fully develop his interpretation. Nevertheless, his few remarks on the topic suggest a possible interpretive perspective on German idealism. For instance, reading Hegel's philosophy as a reply to the programme of a "new mythology" could perhaps be a very productive heuristic strategy.[13] And further, whatever Hegel's role in the writing of *The Oldest Program for a System of the German Idealism*, the idea of a philosophy of spirit as an "aesthetical philosophy", that is, as a combination of the "monotheism of reason" with the "polytheism of imagination", may perhaps throw some light on the interpretation of his *Phenomenology of Mind* (Hegel 1931).

Nevertheless, it seems as if it is the aspect of "monotheism of reason" that prevails in the later developments of Hegel's thinking. Here, myth became an earlier stage in the unfolding of the spirit understood as freedom, precisely the stage where it does not yet know itself as free, and therefore needs the pollution of sensitive images (*Verunreinigung des Gedankens durch sinnliche Gestalt*) (Hegel 1995: 20, A). At the same time, the Kantian idea of autonomy, which, according to the young students of the Stift, should have led to the overthrow of the state in the name of freedom, is here replaced by adherence to a real (*wirklich*) that is said to be rational (*vernünftig*) in itself (Hegel 1991: 20).

---

[13] This is a point that deserves to be pursued. To my knowledge, Blumenberg's suggestion has not yet been taken up systematically. Apart from Blumenberg's remarks (Blumenberg 1985:263ff.), helpful insights towards this direction can be found in Frank 1982.

The young Hölderlin also aimed to recover the ancient world of myth as a tool for the critique. In his first lyrics poems, he presented the mythological figures of ancient Greece as symbols of a natural harmony, seen as having been lost under modern conditions (Hölderlin 1966). He revisited Greek mythology as a symbol of the harmony that rules a pantheistically conceived nature. Myth here was the medium for an aesthetic experience in which the union of the subject and the object could once more be achieved ("Hyperion", in Hölderlin 1966: 78–9).[14]

Through a trajectory similar to that of Schelling, Hölderlin's conception progressively assumed the connotation of a religious experience: in his last poems, myth was said to be the dress of God (*Gott an hat ein Gewand*), the medium of a superior religious experience in which the Lutheran *Deus Nudus* reveals himself as *Deus Vestitus* ("Griechenland", in Hölderlin 1966: 564–5). The God that appears in the later lyric poems is, indeed, the God of monotheism: the recurring figure of Christ, who is syncretistically accompanied by Heracles and Dionysius, is now celebrated as the only universal God ("Patmos", and "Der Einzige", in Hölderlin 1966: 446–64).

However, once again, this view of myth as a totality that assimilates myth and religion does not question, but simply inverts, the axiological connotation of the view of the Enlightenment. When myth is considered as the ambit of immediate intuition, through which only the true revelation, that is, the manifestation of God as a person, can take place (Schelling), or as the dress of God, the medium of a superior aesthetical experience that embodies the ethical experience of a people (Hölderlin), the presuppositions of the Enlightenment are not rejected but instead reinforced.[15]

In contrast, it is by radically questioning these presuppositions that we must start. First, we must revisit the identification of the project of

[14] On Hölderlin's recovery of myth as the medium of a superior aesthetical experience realising the union of the subject and object, see Hübner 1985.
[15] Here I am not talking about Romanticism as a historical process. I have tried to isolate a certain view of myth from the sources analysed, drawing from them a sort of ideal-type. In my understanding of a genealogy as critique, this should serve as a warning about the consequences of a series of conceptual manoeuvres that are always possible, and not as the depiction of a historical phenomenon that would be in any case too complex to be reconstructed within the limits of this work.

autonomy with the project of a "pure reason". Not all that is not "pure reason" is heteronomy. Myth, in particular, does not always coincide with religious revelation in general, and even less with the revelation of God as a person of Christianity. Rather, as the dialectic of the *sacred logos* shows, the plurality of myth can be fundamentally hostile to theological absolutism.

Second, following a crucial insight of early Romanticism, we must recognise that myth is itself a possible means for the project of auton-omy. Only by identifying – together with Kant – "autonomy" with the "pureness of reason" can one possibly deny this fundamental fact. How-ever, if one understands autonomy literally as the possibility of giving oneself one's law, one must also recognise that autonomy means inter-rogation of what exists. As a consequence, imagination can also be one of the means for questioning what is given, and thus of critique.[16] In other words, we should recognise that imagination is as central as reason to modernity (Arnason 1994).

Together with the repetitive imagination, one should also recognise the existence of what Castoriadis has called the radical imagination (Castoriadis 1987). Imagination is radical because, as Kant discovered in the first edition of the *Critique*, it is at the basis of the possibility of knowledge itself, and also because it creates *ex nihilo* – which means not *in nihilo* or *cum nihilo*. Imagination operates with pre-existing material, but it can also always create *ex nihilo* because it can potentially always question its own products (Castoriadis 1997).

While a great deal of philosophical work has been done on the con-cept of reason and its possible contribution to the project of auton-omy, nothing similar has been done on the concept of imagination. In comparison to reason, imagination has remained a marginal topic in recent philosophical debates. In particular, while the move from a philosophy of subject to a new emphasis on context has led from a theory of "reason" to one of "rationality", we need a parallel develop-ment from a theory of "imagination" to a theory of the "imaginary" (Arnason 1994). Undoubtedly, some steps have been taken in this direction – Castoriadis' work on the imaginary institution of society being the major recent example (Castoriadis 1987). But the disparity

---

[16] For more on myth, the project of autonomy and the possibility of critique, see Chap-ter 7.

with the amount of work done on the concept of rationality remains overwhelming.

In addition, we now seem to dispose of the theoretical means for going beyond the opposition between an enlightened and a romantic view of myth. In particular, starting with Wittgenstein's philosophy, alternative views of meaning and language have been developed. Now that the linguistic turn has given rise to a new emphasis on the different routes for the construction of reality, and that the virtual, the imaginary par excellence, has, in a sense, become the most real, there is a chance for further steps forward.

In conclusion, we have seen how the Enlightenment brought with it a critical stance towards the world of myth, relegating it to the ambit of the "imaginary" and the "unreal". Nevertheless, if one questions the very identification of the project for autonomy with a pure reason, it becomes possible to recognise that myth itself can be a means for critique and thus for autonomy. This, however, must be done by avoiding the romantic temptation to restore a myth understood as divine revelation.

II

THE NEED FOR MYTH

The genealogy of myth must not be understood as an invitation to return to the "origins of myth". It would be wrong to conclude from a genealogy of myth that "myth" is simply "word" because *mythos* was "word" to Homer. This reasoning rests on a sort of fallacy of origins, that is, on the idea that what happened at the beginning was good simply because it was at the beginning. Indeed, such reasoning, if not further justified, can easily turn into an empty tautology.

Even if this tautology is avoided, doubts may still arise over the feasibility of a hermeneutical jump backwards. The world in which we live is much more complex than that of Homer, and even if we go back to the Homeric uses of *mythos*, it would be impossible to return to such simplicity. This is the reason why Nietzsche's appeal for a return to myth could not be other than a call for an impossible restoration.

In contrast, the proposed genealogy of myth is not a call for a restoration of myth, but an attempt to recall the conceptual movement that gave birth to the view of myth as "untruth" and "unreal". Once the forces at work in this process are identified, there is hope that we can go beyond the view that they have shaped. In particular, once it is discovered that the "untruth" and "unreality" of myth are consequences of the dialectics of the *sacred* and of the *scientific logos* respectively, we can attempt to escape them.

Contemporary thinking seems to provide the means for doing so. If the genealogy of myth shows that to stigmatise myth as "untrue" and "unreal" means to approach it from the point of view of a unique truth (sacred *logos*) and of an absolutism of reason (Enlightenment), then Chapter 4, following Wittgenstein's insights, is meant to point out that any approach to myth in terms of truth is essentially flawed. This is, indeed, a crucial step because contemporary theories of political myth, despite the fact that they do not stigmatise myth as being necessarily false, still define it in terms of its claims to truth (Lincoln 1989, Flood 1996). By reconstructing Wittgenstein's critique of Frazer's view of myths as mistakes and by drawing from Wittgenstein's concept of language games, the chapter proposes to understand meaning as an act of doing and not simply as an act of saying.

Subsequently, moving from Wittgenstein's characterisation of human beings as "ceremonious animals", Chapters 5 and 6 delineate an interrelational and phenomenological approach to myth understood as one of the forms in which the ceremonious activity of human beings takes place. If Wittgenstein's few remarks unify different phenomena, such as myths, rituals, and religious beliefs, Blumenberg's reflections provide crucial insights on the specificity of myth understood as work on myth. While discussing some of the most important theories of myth, Chapter 5 focuses on four crucial features of myth. Chapter 6 further discusses this view, arguing that human beings not only need meaning in order to orient themselves in the world, but they also need significance in order to live in a world that is less indifferent to them.

4

Myth and Meaning

In 1890 the first two volumes of a monumental anthropological work on magic and religion were published: Frazer's *Golden Bough*. In this work, later republished in twelve volumes (Frazer 1922), Fraser collected an enormous amount of material concerning traditional beliefs and social practices of different societies. By classifying the material according to the criteria of evolutionary comparative method, he attempted to develop an explanation of "magic behaviour". Magic, he argued, is based on the belief of a correspondence between entities that are separated in space and time, but are, nevertheless, linked to one another. This link, according to Fraser, can be interpreted in two different ways: either as the relationship between part and whole, so that by acting on one part, an influence on the whole can be realised, or as an imitation, so that by fictitiously reproducing an object or an act, its effective realisation can be expected actually to occur (Frazer 1922).

According to Frazer, magic is based on the application of beliefs that are inaccurate per se, but are nevertheless applied in a way that can be defined as rational and coherent. In his view, when analysing the myths of "ruder ages and races, we shall do well to look with leniency upon their errors as inevitable slips made in the search for truth, and to give them the benefit of that indulgence which we ourselves may one day stand in need of" (Frazer 1922: 264). As he openly put it:

their errors were not wilful extravagances or the ravings of insanity, but simply hypotheses, justifiable as such at the time when they were propounded, but which a fuller experience has proved to be inadequate. It is only by the successive testing of hypotheses and the rejection of the false that truth is at last elicited. After all, what we call truth is only the hypothesis which is found to work best. (Fraser 1922: 264).

Myths, according to this view, are thus read as a sort of prototype, however mistaken, of the inductive and deductive procedures of science. One of the strongest critics of this concept was Ludwig Wittgenstein. In his *Remarks on Frazer's Golden Bough*, he points out that the major weakness of Frazer's account is that it makes magical and religious notions appear as *mistakes* (Wittgenstein 1979: 1e). Even if Frazer seems to be indulgent towards the notions and practices that he analyses, he does so by adopting a point of view that is fundamentally flawed because he looks at these practices as if they were supported by certain "hypotheses" about the constitution of the world, and, therefore, as if they could be found to be "true" or "false", "right" or "wrong".

As we will see, these kinds of judgements are not only deemed to fail to capture the nature of social beliefs and practices, but, moreover, they are based on a limited view of what language and meanings are about. Judging magical and religious notions as mistakes means bringing these notions onto a terrain that is not their own and interrogating them from the standpoint of an overtly limited view of language. After having pointed out the weaknesses of Frazer's account, Wittgenstein provocatively asks:

Was Augustine mistaken, then, when he called on God on every page of the Confessions?
    Well – one might say – if he was not mistaken, then the Buddhist holy man, or some other whose religion expresses quite different notions, surely was. But *none* of them was making a mistake except where he was putting forward a theory. (Wittgenstein 1979: 1e)

According to Wittgenstein, one cannot come to terms with myth, magic and religious notions by interrogating them over their truth value. As the dialectic of *myth* and *logos* also shows, there must be a claim to "truth"– understood as "unique" or as "objective" – in order to have a "mistake". In magic and religious notions, however, no mistakes can ever exist, inasfar as they do not aim at advancing any theory. Indeed, as Wittgenstein points out, there is a whole set of meanings and actions that human beings carry out in their everyday life and these meanings and actions do not rest on any expectation of truth, and do not therefore presuppose any theory. As he argues, by using two persuasive examples:

Burning in effigy. Kissing the picture of a loved one. This is obviously *not* based on a belief that it will have a definite effect on the object which the picture represents. It aims at some satisfaction and it achieves it. Or rather, it does not *aim* at anything; we act in this way and then feel satisfied. (Wittgenstein 1979: 4e)

There are actions that do not aim at anything, but, rather, are ful-filled simply by their performance. The meaning of "kissing the picture of a loved one" must not be looked at as something different from the action of "kissing the picture of a loved one" itself. As an action, it expresses a desire and fulfils it at the same time; as a meaning, it is all present in itself. It is in this context that Wittgenstein puts forward his provocative thesis of "human beings as ceremonious animals":

We could almost say, man is a ceremonious animal. This is partly false and partly non-sensical but there is something in it.

In other words, one might begin a book on anthropology in this way: When we watch the life and behaviour of men all over the earth, we see that apart from what we might call animal activities, taking food etc. etc, men also carry out actions that bear a peculiar character and might be called ritualistic.

But then it is nonsense if we go on to say that the characteristic of these actions is that they spring from wrong ideas about the physics of things (this is what Frazer does when he says magic is really false physics, or as the case may be, false medicine, technology, etc.).

What makes the character of ritual action is not any view or opinion, either right or wrong, although an opinion – a belief – itself can be ritualistic, or belong to a rite. (Wittgenstein 1979: 7e)[1]

Frazer's view of myth and rituals as "mistaken" is derived from a misunderstanding about the nature of these notions and practices. Indeed, only by assuming that the aim of these notions is to describe facts – which only can be either "true" or "false" – can one consider these notions as "diseases of language". This is the famous expression coined by Max Müller to underline the fact that the stories told by myths are intrinsically "untruthful" and "unreal". By starting from the

---

[1] On Wittgenstein's idea of human beings as ceremonious animals and its relationship with anthropology, see in particular, Bouveresse 1982. On Wittgenstein and anthropology, see Bouveresse 1982, Das 1998, and Clack 1999.

assumption that the fundamental business of language is to describe facts, Müller was led to conclude that ancient myths were derived from the misunderstanding of names, especially those attached to celestial objects (Kirk 1974: 43).

Paradoxically, Frazer's view of myth is based on a conception of language to which the young Wittgenstein had made a fundamental contribution. Simply put, one might state that this is the paradigm that has dominated the philosophy of language over the last century (Marconi 1999: 15). It was Gottlob Frege who first elaborated its fundamental theses. However, it was the writings of Russell and the young Wittgenstein – in particular, the *Tractatus Logico-philosophicus* (1961) – that filled out the fundamental contours of this paradigm.

The paradigm can be briefly summarised as the combination of three theses. The first asserts that the meaning of a proposition is given by its "truth conditions", that is, by the specification of the circumstances in which a proposition is true. This theory of meaning is a theory of propositions, and assertive propositions are the privileged units of interest. Second, the meaning of a complex expression is considered to be functionally dependent on the meaning of its smallest basic parts, so that, for instance, the meaning of any single unit of a proposition is given by its contribution to the meaning of the proposition. This is the thesis known as logical atomism and points to the composite nature of meaning. The third thesis asserts that, given that the meaning of an expression is provided by the combination of the first two theses, any psychological consideration over the mental processes associated with the linguistic expressions is irrelevant for a theory of meaning.

In this view, sentences are pictures of facts, the meanings of complex expressions are given by the combination of their constitutive parts, and everything that cannot be reduced to this belongs to the category of the "mystical", and, properly speaking, is deprived of meaning (Wittgenstein 1961: 73). As Wittgenstein concludes his *Tractatus*,

> The correct method in philosophy would really be the following: to say nothing except what can be said, i.e. propositions of natural sciences – i.e. something that has nothing to do with philosophy – and then when someone wanted to say something metaphysical, to demonstrate to him that he had failed to give a meaning to a certain sign in his propositions. (Wittgenstein 1961: 73)

Even from such a brief picture, it should be clear that within such a view of language there cannot be much place for a philosophical treatment of myth. Scepticism would be twofold: towards myth as an object and towards philosophy as a suitable method of enquiry. In other words, if "the essential business of language is to assert or to deny facts" (Russell 1922: 10), and assertive propositions are consequently the atoms of any meaningful expression, then either we can reduce myths to these assertive propositions, or we have to conclude, with Max Müller, that myths are "diseases of language". This seems to be the position of the early Wittgenstein: only *how* things are in this world can be said, the rest being "mystical" (Wittgenstein 1961: 73).

Philosophy is reserved no better place within this paradigm. No philosophical enquiry has ever limited itself to a collection of assertive propositions and thus no place seems to be left for it in the field of meaningful enquires. On the other hand, the limitation to assertive propositions is self-defeating in the long run, for not only is the assertion of the meaninglessness of philosophical enquiry self-contradictory, given that any such assertion is itself philosophical, but it also entails a view of language that is too limited.

When Herbert Marcuse criticised the fact that philosophy had been reduced to the analysis of sentences such as "the broom is in the corner", he was not just pointing to the dangers of political conformism that such one-dimensional thinking implies (Marcuse 1991: 170ff.). He was also pointing to the fact that what is analysed is not the language that we actually use in our lives, with all its complexities, but desegregated atoms of language. These – he observed – are, in the best case, baby talk: sentences such as "he saw a robin", or "I had a hat" are far from being representative of our language (Marcuse 1991: 175). Yet, much of contemporary analytic philosophy is still devoted to this kind of analysis. The problem here is not only that by taking fragments of common language as a guide to the research there is a great risk of remaining trapped in the positive acceptance and reification of single historical forms; it is also that these fragments represent such a limited part of our language that to take them as unique objects of enquiry cannot but be misleading for an understanding of what human language is about.

Wittgenstein's self-critique is perhaps the best way of distancing ourselves from these views. The insights that can be drawn from his later writings opened up a completely different perspective on the nature of language and meaning – and this is the perspective that can best support a philosophy of political myth.

Wittgenstein's *Philosophical Investigations* start with a critique of the view of meaning that we have been analysing here. He now puts this view under the name of Augustine and his major criticism is that such a "philosophical concept of meaning has its place in a *primitive* idea of the way language functions. But one can also say that it is the idea of a language more *primitive* than ours" (Wittgenstein 1975: 3e emphasis mine).

Wittgenstein now moves from the assumption that the essential business of language is not to describe facts, but instead that we do a number of things with language, and these things cannot be judged according to their truth or falsehood. When we give an order, provide a suggestion, make a joke, ask for something, thank someone for something, beg someone, tell a story, or even construct a scientific hypothesis – just to give a few examples – it is not by the criterion of their truth that we expect them to be judged. Wittgenstein's major point now is that we play all sorts of language-games through language (Wittgenstein 1976). Meanings are not the pictures of facts, but the result of language-games, that is, of indissoluble wholes made of both language and actions (Wittgenstein 1976: 5e).

The concept of "game" is meant to stress that the rules embodied in the wholes made of language and actions are constitutive of meaning. This does not mean that language is the domain of the arbitrary. Indeed, rules govern our use of language, as is shown, for instance, by the fact that we do not learn a language by learning sentence after sentence. We construct sentences by putting words together according to certain rules – no matter whether we have learnt these rules intentionally, as when we learn a foreign language, or we have internalised them by imitation, as children do.

When Wittgenstein elaborated the concept of the language-game, he probably had precisely the *constitutive* role of the rules of games in mind. When one does not follow a rule in the game of chess, one is not simply doing something wrong: one is playing another game. At the same time, the idea of a game also points to the fact that it is our *acting* that lies at the bottom of the language (Wittgenstein 1969: 66e). A meaning is both an act of saying and an act of doing.

In other words, the grammar of a language, that is, the eliciting of the rules governing certain linguistic expressions, is not sufficient to reconstruct their meaning. Wittgenstein does not provide a definitive answer on this point, and, for instance, in the *Philosophical Grammar*, there is a passage in which he seems to suggest the opposite, that the meaning of a word is given by its place within the grammar (Wittgenstein 1974: 59). The problem seems to be to understand what Wittgenstein meant by "grammar" – a point on which he always remained ambiguous.

Moreover, it seems that, towards the end of his life, he became increasingly sceptical about the possibility of even describing the rules of language-games. These rules are always changing and are much too varied to provide a definitive grammar. All these perplexities emerge particularly in the remarks published under the title *On Certainty*. As we read here: "Am I not getting closer and closer to saying that, in the end, logic cannot be described? You must look at the practice of language, then you will see it" (Wittgenstein 1969: 66).

Whatever is the right interpretation of Wittgenstein, a couple of crucial points can be drawn from this discussion. One of these is that grammar – understood as a compilation of rules – is a necessary but not yet sufficient condition for understanding the meaning of a sentence. In the first place, this is because sometimes a fully descriptive rule cannot be formed. In these cases, there is simply not enough generality to extrapolate a rule from usage. Those who have some experience in learning a foreign language know that there are sometimes no rules for the employment of certain expressions. They are simply *used*, and are used in a way that does not allow for generalisation or for the eliciting of rules.

Here, it becomes clear that, as Wittgenstein persuasively put forward, the *meaning* of an expression derives from its *use*. And the term "use" must be understood here in its widest meaning – as encompassing both the possibility of extrapolating *rules* and the dimension of *action* (Wittgenstein 1976, 20e).[2] In other words, the meaning of an

---

[2] Wittgenstein states that "For a large class of cases – though not for all – in which we employ the word 'meaning' it can be defined thus: the meaning of a word is its use in

expression is not merely given by the rule that emerges from our use of that expression in our action. It is also the continuously changing context against which this rule must be seen that contributes to the meaning of an expression. To make a slogan of it, we might say: "no meaning without use, and no use without a context". Indeed, it is also the context, that is, the background against which we see actions, that is crucial to our understanding of the meaning of a word (Wittgenstein 1967: 98).

Let me illustrate the point with an example. Take the sentence "Close the door". Clearly, this expression can acquire very different meanings according to the different contexts in which it is applied: it could be an order, an ironical comment over the failure of an order, the expression of a desire, a reproach and many other things. In all these cases, it will be the context that takes us in the right direction. In particular, the understanding of this expression does not only require the mutual recognition of certain rules, those that govern the place of each single expression as well as those of the use of orders, reproaches, and so on. Apparently meaningless actions such as the tone of the voice or the expression of the face or even the prehistory of a situation will guide us towards a successful understanding. A rule cannot be recognised without some knowledge of the context in which it is applied.

What emerges here is an essentially immanent view of meaning that is at odds not only with the twentieth century paradigm, but also with the prevalent modern view. When Wittgenstein wrote that logic cannot be described, but must be seen through practice (Wittgenstein 1969: 66e), he was not only distancing himself from his previous conception, according to which sentences are pictures of facts or states of affairs. He was implicitly criticising the modern view, according to which meanings are something that can be "transferred" from one mind to another.[3]

---

the language" (Wittgenstein 1976, 20e). Again, he seems to mean here that meaning is defined by the place in language. For an interpretation that puts more emphasis on action, see Schneider 1999.

[3] The Fregean paradigm described here also distances itself from the typically modern view of the "transfer" of meanings, but, as we have seen, it does so either by dismissing the issue as meaningless, or, in the best case, by leaving it to psychology.

In the third book of his *Essay Concerning Human Understanding*, Locke wrote: "To make Words serviceable to the end of Communication, it is necessary that they excite, in the hearer, exactly the same Idea, they stand for in the mind of the speaker. Without this, Men fill one another's heads with noise and sounds, but convey not thereby their Thoughts, and lay not before one another their Ideas, which is the end of Discourse and Language" (Locke 1997: 426). Here, the process of understanding a speaker's utterance is presented as a mental event occurring in the head of the hearer when he derives from the utterance the thoughts that the speaker intended to convey by it. This passage discloses a view of verbal communication that has dominated most of modern philosophy of language (Taylor 1990). Be it viewed as naturalistically grounded or as conventionally imposed, the underlying idea is that the meaning of a word is something that could be transferred from one head to another.

While the first Wittgenstein distanced himself from this view and dismissed the problem as a pseudo-problem, as a problem that concerns only psychology, he later elaborated a view of meaning that took on board the problems that the modern view had addressed and provided an alternative answer. In this new view, meanings are not conveyed by words from one mind to another, but are constructed in language-games. Or, to put it another way, since they are not something that is "added" to the interaction, they are simply there, immanent to any communicative action and context. It is the sharing of these that provides the guarantee of a mutual understanding.

This does not mean, though, that Wittgenstein adopts an "expressivist understanding of language". In his *Philosophical Arguments*, Charles Taylor distinguishes between two fundamental paradigms of language: the first is best represented by Locke and is mainly concerned with language as an instrument for the construction of our picture of the world, with its proper use and abuse, whereas the second moves from a romantic critique of this view and has Herder as its key exponent (Taylor 1995: ix). According to Taylor's reading, Wittgenstein would be an exponent of this second paradigm (Taylor 1995: ix, and, in particular, 66). In fact, it can be shown that Wittgenstein's reflections on language are part of a linguistic turn which, by going beyond the presuppositions of modern philosophy of consciousness, has also gone well beyond the expressivist paradigm. In a way, it can be argued that Wittgenstein's philosophy of language points to the uselessness, if not the impossibility, of even separating the two paradigms.[4]

Undoubtedly, Wittgenstein shares an emphasis on language as a fundamentally social phenomenon with romantic theories such as that elaborated by Herder. And, for this reason, Wittgenstein, perhaps more than any other representative of the linguistic turn, has been widely used within the social sciences.[5] His view of language is a fundamentally social view. By "social view", I do not simply mean that language is a social business, that is, that we need a language, that we learn it, and that we use it because of and in our interactions with other people. Starting from Wittgenstein's insights, one might argue, furthermore, that a human being who had never had contact with other living beings – not just with other humans, and the reason for this will be clear later on – would have no language at all. Such a creature, if she or he could ever exist, would at best produce sounds, not words.

According to Wittgenstein, in order to have words, that is, signs that have a meaning within a language, you need to have a criterion for the correctness of their use. But any measure needs to be independent of the thing that is measured, and thus the use that one single person makes of a word cannot be the criterion for that word's correctness. And it is the *social* element that provides this criterion. With his critique of the possibility of a private language and of the possibility of ostensive definitions, what Wittgenstein does is to open the way for a view of language and meaning that fundamentally departs from the romantic philosophies of consciousness.

It is in this sense that we must also interpret Wittgenstein's argument against the possibility of a "private language" (Wittgenstein 1976: 88e).[6] By "private language", Wittgenstein meant a language that a

---

[4] On Wittgenstein and expressivism, see, in particular, Clack 1999. After analysing Wittgenstein's *Remarks on Frazer* from the point of view of expressivism, Clack suggests that perhaps Wittgenstein's theory would go towards overcoming the distinction between expressivism and instrumentalism (Clack 1999: 129ff.).

[5] Recently, for instance, Wittgenstein's philosophy of language has been used as the basis for developing a social psychology. On this point, see Jost 1995.

[6] On this point, see, in particular, Kenny 1973: 10.

person could use to give expression to his own immediate inner experience without it being possible for another person to understand it. Let us suppose, with Wittgenstein, that I want to keep a diary of the recurrence of a certain sensation and I decide that I will write the sign "S" each time that this sensation recurs (Wittgenstein 1976: 92e). But how can I discern this sensation?

Of course, Wittgenstein replies, I can give an ostensive definition of it: concentrate my attention and point to it inwardly. But what, he goes on to ask, can guarantee that I will recognise it in the future? This is not to say that I cannot have a memory of this sensation. It means that I can have no criteria for the correct association of that sign "S" with this particular sensation, so that whatever association appears as right to me can be defined as "right" (Wittgenstein 1976: 92e). This situation is similar to one in which I say "I know how tall I am", and, by putting my hand on top of my head, I believe that I have proved it (Wittgenstein 1976: 96e). The point is that a measure must be independent of what it is measured by,[7] and therefore it is impossible to control the association of "S" with a certain object if it is not inserted in a public language.

By criticising the idea of a private language, Wittgenstein did not mean to deny the possibility of communicating our inner experience. On the contrary, inasmuch as we are, have been, and will be engaged in language-games in which the expressions of pain, anger, joy, and so on, are at stake, we also learn to express our inner experience. The recognition of a common bodyliness helps this task – so that if someone in front of us is hurt by a heavy object falling on the person's body, we expect a reaction of pain. But the point is that in order to understand the person's expression as a meaningful act, we must have been trained through certain language-games.

A common bodyliness is thus not sufficient to elaborate meanings. If I find myself in India and I want to express my inner disapproval at something by shaking my head, I am simply playing the wrong game in this context, because people will take it as a sign of my approval. To be successful in communicating my feelings in this specific context, I must also have some experience of the context. Similarly, Wittgenstein's point is that, in order to recognise a certain meaning as an expression

---

[7] On this point, see also Wittgenstein 1976: 93e.

of my own pain, I must have gone through a specific language-game training.

This, however, does not mean that, since Wittgenstein puts emphasis on the embeddedness of language, he must be put together with Heidegger and other representatives of the hermeneutical turn within the romantic or expressivist paradigm (Taylor 1995: 61ff.). The point is how the context itself is understood and there are reasons to suspect that Wittgenstein's concept of the language-game entails a concept of the context that is fundamentally at odds with the romantic view.

Wittgenstein's emphasis on context has often been interpreted as an argument for the distinction and even incommensurability between different cultural contexts.[8] If meaning is use and use is the context, then, whenever you leave a given context, you also leave that universe of meanings. But this view reflects too rigid a view of the context, as though it were some sort of self-enclosed unit. And this is the view that Taylor, following Herder, seems to endorse. It is on the basis of this view that Taylor can, for instance, call for a politics of the recognition of different cultures understood as different contexts or horizons of meaning (Taylor 1992).

However, by emphasising the importance of language-games, Wittgenstein distances himself from such an understanding of contexts. Indeed, from my reading of Wittgenstein's approach, to assume a rigid view of contexts appears as the exchange of the egocentric for an ethnocentric point of view. The risk in doing so is a form of solipsism on a larger scale.[9] The concept of language-games implies, on the contrary, the idea of fluid and continuously changing contexts and situations, where even the idea of boundaries can hardly be applied. The difficulty is both diachronic and synchronic. Not only are there many and different language-games taking place at the same time, so that it becomes difficult to identify the boundaries between them, but we ourselves are continuously within a plurality of language-games and

---

[8] Rorty 1989, von Savigny 1991, and Coulter 1999, for instance, advance culturalist interpretations of Wittgenstein.

[9] Taylor ultimately avoids this risk, by recalling the hermeneutic tradition of comparison between cultures (see, for instance, Taylor 1995: 146–64). Other authors, as we will see, have instead held the thesis of incommensurability between cultures. I am grateful to an anonymous reader for suggesting I clarify this point.

thus contexts, so that it becomes difficult even to distinguish between the contexts.

Most of the misunderstandings on this point have been generated by Wittgenstein's few and never fully developed identifications of the language-game with what he calls "forms of life" (Wittgenstein 1976: 8e, 11e, 88e).[10] For instance, he wrote that "the term language-*game* is meant to bring into prominence the fact that the speaking of a language is part of an activity, or of a form of life" (Wittgenstein 1976: 11e). Unfortunately, Wittgenstein never developed the concept of a form of life and it is therefore very difficult to understand what he meant by this. Further this omission has left a great deal of room for speculation, and, consequently, many authors have interpreted this concept in over-culturalist terms.

Culturalist interpretations of the identification of "language-games" with different "forms of life" have also been used as an argument in favour of the incommensurability of different "cultures": if meaning is use, and use is a form of life, then communication between different forms of life is deemed to be problematic, if not impossible.[11] Other passages have also been used to support this interpretation. For instance, at the end of his *Philosophical Investigations*, after saying that one human being can be a complete enigma to another, he continues by saying that "we learn this when we come into a strange country with entirely strange traditions; and what is more, even given a mastery of the country's language. We do not *understand* people (and not because of not knowing what they are saying to themselves). We cannot find our feet with them. If a lion could talk we could not understand him" (Wittgenstein 1976: 223e). Indeed, as we read in *Zettel*: "we do not understand Chinese gestures any more than Chinese sentences" (Wittgenstein 1967: 39).

Together with culturalist interpretations, there have been those who, in the expression "forms of life", prefer to point to the importance of the second term – "life". According to Stanley Cavell, for instance,

---

[10] On the problems raised by the concept of "forms of life" within Wittgenstein's philosophy, see Scheman 1996.

[11] Arguments *à la* Wittgenstein of this sort can also be found quite often in the social sciences: see, for instance, the "ethno-methodological approach" developed in Coulter 1999. For a culturalist interpretation closely based on a reading of Wittgenstein's writings, see von Savigny 1991.

Wittgenstein wanted to point to the fact that it is life – and thus activity – that lies at the bottom of language-games. In this view, one can also point to a biological basis that is common to all human beings (Cavell 1979): this is what would guarantee a common background[12] against which to insert any single language-game. It would be to this background that Wittgenstein was referring when he spoke of a "common behaviour of mankind" (Wittgenstein 1976: 82e).

However, we do not need to solve all the problems that these two opposing interpretations raise. The first impression is, however, that Wittgenstein could not have embraced a radical incommensurability thesis. All the same, the very idea of "forms of life" remains a fundamentally problematic concept that created more problems than it solved. Indeed, it inevitably suggests the idea of some kind of "unity" within each single form of life, that is, something that is also at odds with the idea of putting action at the basis of the concept of the language-game.

Human (inter)action cannot be limited within the spheres of single self-enclosed forms of life – today less than ever. We are able to interact not only with people from other cultures, but even with animals of other species (Churchill, 1989). Clearly, there is no guarantee that upon entering a strange country, we will not have the feeling that it is impossible to find our feet there. However, this is due to our contingent lack of familiarity with these language-games, and not to an ontological incommensurability with them. Here, it is the fact that we can, if trained, learn different language-games that is most important. Maybe we do not, in the present circumstances, understand Chinese gestures any more than I do Chinese sentences, but we can, potentially, learn to understand both of them.

Reversing Wittgenstein's statement, we can, therefore, conclude that, even if a lion cannot talk, we can – and we do – understand it. Anyone who has the experience of having shared an interaction context with an animal for a long time knows quite well that we do understand their language, just as they understand ours, because we

---

[12] On the importance of the concept of background, see also *Zettel* proposition 567, where we read: "How could human behaviour be described? Surely only sketching the actions of a variety of humans, as they are all mixed up together. What determines our judgement, our concepts and reactions is not what one man is doing now, an individual action, but the whole hurly-burly of human actions, the background against which we see any actions" (Wittgenstein 1967: 98)

have been participating in the same language-games. It is simply a matter of creating an interaction context and progressively entering and learning language-games. In other words, meanings are not something we carry around with our identity cards. They are much more the result of what we *do* – than the result of what we *are*.

Not only is Wittgenstein not a representative of the romantic paradigm, but he is also an implicit critic of the very possibility of distinguishing between the two paradigms. Indeed, if meanings are language-games, in which no distinction between the "designative" and the "expressive" functions can be made, then it is meaningless, if not impossible, to distinguish between the two paradigms identified by Taylor.[13]

Going back to Wittgenstein's *Remarks on Frazer*, we should recall here that, according to this text, "a whole mythology is deposited in our language" (Wittgenstein 1979: 10e). This also implies that one cannot approach the meaning of certain practices and notions by looking for what they designate as distinguished from what they express. Ultimately this can be only a fallacious attempt at separating what cannot be separated and it reflects a limited view of both truth and meaning. According to Wittgenstein:

> When we explain, for example, that the king must be killed in his prime because, according to the notions of the savages, his soul would not be kept fresh otherwise, we can only say: where that practice and these views go together, the practice does not spring from the view, but both are there. (Wittgenstein 1979: 1e–2e)

To put it in another way, what we have here are practices and views that are simply there, together and inseparable: one does not define, or express the other. In this view, an act of saying is, intrinsically, an act of doing. As Wittgenstein observes, in the end "we can only *describe* and say, human life is like that" (Wittgenstein 1979: 3e).

Wittgenstein's critique of Frazer and the notion of language-games enables us to develop a concept of meaning that goes beyond the very distinction between a designative and a romantic paradigm as well as beyond any reified view of contexts and cultures. In particular, the idea of language-games, with its emphasis on both language and

[13] A similar point is made by Clack (1999).

action, can provide the conceptual tools to escape the danger of the dialectic of Enlightenment. Indeed, it is on this basis that the next chapters will attempt to delineate an approach to myth that does not raise the question of its "truth" and "reality".

Wittgenstein, indeed, did not go into the description of the mythology that he held to be deposited in our language. He did not write the book of anthropology that might have followed from those first words. As a consequence, his remarks remained sparse and all these notions – myth, magic and religion – remained undifferentiated. The task of the next chapters is to distinguish between them by proposing a concept of myth which insists on its specificity.

5

Approaching Myth

As we have seen, myths as such could not be recognised within a Christian world view because of their deceitful plurality of stories. However, it is precisely this plurality that characterises myth, in contrast to the point of view of a *sacred logos*. This does not simply mean that myths are the objects of different interpretations, but also that, phenomenologically speaking, myths present themselves as a plurality both of variants and of *mythologems*.

To catch the intrinsic plurality of myth one cannot simply analyse single myths, that is, the stories that we can fortuitously collect or find in books. These are only the final products of myth, the reified traces of the work of myth. As Blumenberg pointed out with his idea of myth understood as "work on myth", a myth is best understood as a process that is, at the same time, an act of saying and an act of doing (Blumenberg 1985). This is a process of continually reworking that involves a multiplicity of subjects. There are narrators, on the one hand, and receivers or potential re-narrators, on the other – without there being any possibility of tracing any sharp division between the two.

As Blumenberg put it, it is precisely in the relationship between narrators and receivers that we should look for the specificity of myth: the myth is the "work on myth" (*Arbeit am Mythos*), that is, work *of* myth and *at* myth. The plurality of myth is not only a plurality of *mythologems*, of basic narration patterns centred on a character or an episode, such as the myth of Prometheus or the myth of the foundation of

Athens.[1] Even a single *mythologem* expresses itself through variants, and each single variant presents itself as a story that is legitimate in its own right. This is the difference between the Sacred History and the stories of myth: even if they both present variants, since it is implicit in the act of telling a story that there can be variants, the plurality of myth is both a plurality of variants and a plurality of *mythologems*, all of which are recognised in their own right. In other words, the plurality of myth is the plurality of polytheism, in which there is no single god who can advance a claim to absolute truth.

The idea of work on myth stems precisely from the polytheistic vocation of myth (Blumenberg 1985). As Blumenberg showed by reconstructing the re-elaboration of the myth of Prometheus through the centuries, there is not *one* single myth of Prometheus whose meaning is given once for all. Prometheus can be better defined as a *mythologem*, a basic narration pattern which evolved over time and which acquired new and unexpected meanings with the changing of the historical circumstances (Blumenberg 1985).

Now if the work on myth is constitutive of the concept of myth, then it is only by looking at the relationship between narrators and receivers that the specificity of myth can be caught. I propose to call this an *interrelational*[2] approach to myth. In other words, I will not look at single myths, by focusing on their content and their structures. This would mean reifying myth, making an object out of a relational process. Rather, it is at the actual life of myth that I will look, namely at the whole *work on myth*, the work *at* and *of* myth.

This is clearly only one of the innumerable possible approaches to myth.[3] In the face of the variety of the possible theories of myths, it is useful to recall Cassirer's parallel between myth and the enchanted

---

[1] In this perspective, my approach differs from those who consider the definitions of myth as story and of myth as *mythologem* as alternative (see, for instance, Henry 2000 and 2001). In my approach, it is implicit in the very concept of myth as story that there can be more variants of it.

[2] The term "interrelational", in contrast to "intersubjective", puts the emphasis on the contexts, instead of on the "subjects". As such, it points to the fact that it is in the relationships between narrators-receivers that one should look for the specificity myth. As we will see, the work on myth is such that it becomes difficult even to separate the narrators from the receivers of myth.

[3] Particularly helpful overviews of the different approaches to myth from a philosophical perspective are: Bohrer 1983, Jamme 1991; 1999, and Poser 1979.

glass in which Goethe's Faust thought he was seeing a beautiful woman that was, in fact, his own image (Cassirer 1973: 5). In the enchanted glass of myth, linguists have found a world of signs and names, philosophers have found a "primitive philosophy", and psychologists have found a product of the unconscious. In other words, scholars have found in it those objects with which each was most familiar. When faced with such an enchanted mirror, one should better look at oneself, reconstruct one's own genealogy and then situate it within the spectrum of other possible approaches.

The starting point of an interrelational approach does not, for instance, coincide with that of Freud. This means that, although psychoanalytical considerations are not excluded by an interrelational approach, they do not exhaust it. To simplify things, one can say that, whereas Freud, who was mainly interested in the general understanding of the human mind, aims to identify myth's general features, an interrelational approach points in the opposite direction. Its aim is to search for the specificity of myth, in order to understand what differentiates it from other kinds of human expressions.

If no other modern thinker has perhaps made such extensive use of mythological narratives as Freud, given that the ubiquity of the Oedipus complex can be read as the ubiquity of a myth, it still remains that he has done so from the perspective of an etiological reductionism aimed at eliciting the universals of the human mind. The Oedipus complex works as a platform for explaining all the manifestations of the human mind – from religion to society, morals and art (Freud 1937; 1950). Now, this reductionism might be helpful – and even fundamental – but it does not say much about the specificity of myth, which is the primary object of this enquiry.

Furthermore, Freud's etiological reductionism also seems to bring with it the corollary of the primitivism of myth. In particular, Freud's parallels between the mythical constructions of animism, neurotic symptoms, and the process of secondary elaboration of dreams reduces myth to a primitive phenomenon that only concerns the savage mind, and that is destined to be swept away by the development of abstract intellectual language (Freud 1950). In this view, while primitives, like neurotics, overestimate their own thoughts over reality, civilised people, full of conscious perceptions, can separate what is "real" from what is not. Behind the contrast between the "civilised" and the "savage"

mind we again find the separation between "thinking" and "reality",
which is one of the fundamental presuppositions of the Enlightenment, and which should therefore be overcome if one does not want
to risk falling once more into the dialectic of the Enlightenment.

Freud's analysis of mass psychology is also shaped by his general
etiological reductionism. In particular, the analogy he put forward
between the neurotic's overestimation of his own mind in relation to
reality and the savage mind of primitive peoples reflects the attempt
to analyse the problems of a psychology of peoples with the tools of
the psychology of the individual. This is recognised as problematic
by Freud himself, for it presupposes a sort of collective mind which
creates more problems that it seems to solve (Freud 1950: 195).

When Freud deals extensively with the issue in his *Group Psychology and the Analysis of the Ego* (1959), he points out that psychoanalysis is already a social psychology insofar as it cannot analyse individual minds without taking into consideration their relation to others
(Freud 1959: 3). However, as he points out later on, the others that
are taken into account are those encompassed in the pre-given and
limited plot of the individual's complex (Freud 1959: 35), whereas
mass psychology considers the way in which being the member of a
mass – a race, a people, a social group or class – affects an individual's
behaviour. Freud moves to this ground through the analogy "mass"
equals "undisciplined infant" equals "passionate savage", which suggests a reified view of social groups as homogeneous entities. But the
concrete unity of the infant's mind is fundamentally different from
the supposed unity of a mass.[4] This parallel is particularly problematic
from our point of view, because we want to find out precisely what
kind of relationship (unity or difference) is entailed in the narrators-
receivers relationship, and we cannot therefore assume it as being
given from the beginning.[5]

[4] For a critique of the analogy between personal identity and the identity of social
groups, see Chapter 11. On the concept of group identity as a "problematique", see
Wagner 2002.
[5] The approach adopted here also differs from other psychoanalytical approaches to
myth. For instance, it differs from Gustav Jung's approach: here, the focus of an
interrelational approach is the specificity of myth as a relational process, and not the
universal truths of the archetypes expressed in all kinds of human expression – poetry,
rituals, totemic practice, etc. – as described by Jung. (see, for instance, Jung 1981)

As a result, the interrelational approach also differs from structuralist theories of myth. As Claude Lévi-Strauss made clear at many points in his work, the aim of structuralism is no different to that of the "hard sciences", since both are moved by the "quest for the invariant".[6] In Lévi-Strauss' view, structuralism overcomes the contrast between the scientific positivism and the historical particularism of the cultural anthropology precisely by individuating the *systematic relationships* between different cultural systems. By recovering Jakobson's linguistics, which emphasised the structural system of differences occurring between the terms of each language, Lévi-Strauss held that these "structures of the human spirit" can be found not only in verbal utterances, but in all sorts of symbolic systems, such as totems, masks, and rituals, and all other kinds of cultural expressions (Lévi-Strauss 1968; 1987).

If we consider that Lévi-Strauss's theory of myth was also concerned with outlining the universal structures of the human mind rather than with defining the specificity of myth, it comes as no surprise that he maintained that there was a close "similarity" and "contiguity" between myth and music – a theory for which he was strongly criticised. By similarity he meant the closeness of structure between the two, and by contiguity the fact that the point at which myth decreased in significance in Western thinking – that is, during the Renaissance and the seventeenth century – corresponded to the emergence of the great musical styles (Lévi-Strauss 1964; 1990). With regard to similarity, one may object that the fact that he was able to identify the same structural invariants in such different fields might well be the result of the fact that the same invariants can be found everywhere, because they are the product of the same mind that now tries to "discover" them. What he treats as objects are, in fact, human products, namely the products of the same mind that is now trying to analyse them as if they were not its own product.[7]

---

[6] See, for instance, his 1977 interview, where he clearly asserts that structuralism in the field of linguistics, or anthropology and the like, is nothing other than a very pale imitation of what the "hard sciences" have been doing all the time (Lévi-Strauss 1978: 9).

[7] It might be helpful to note here that "object", from the Latin *obicio*, literally means something that is thrown before or against us (see Simpson and Weiner 1989: X, vol. 641).

With regard to the contiguity between myth and music, this view also reflects the same dichotomies that we have seen in Freud, and, as with Freud, aims at classifying myth as a product of the "savage mind" destined to be overcome by scientific rationality. Lévi-Strauss sometimes seems to push the dichotomy as far as to "naturalise" it through the argument of the mutually exclusive capabilities of the human mind. In one significant passage, he suggests that "primitive thinking" and "the civilised mind" rely on two different sorts of mental capacities, and that these capacities cannot be developed by the same mind at the same time. This is, in his view, a necessary consequence of the fact that humans are able to use only a small sector of their mental capacities, and that, consequently, each culture and each stage of human evolution has to develop its own sector (Lévi-Strauss 1978: 19).[8]

However, such a dichotomist approach is unable to explain why myth has survived over time despite and next to scientific rationality. How can we explain this? Lévi-Strauss' approach seems unable to handle the issue because he approached myth from the perspective of its having to be overcome by the same forces of scientific rationality through which he himself tries to catch the invariants of myth. In this sense, he too remained entrapped in a dichotomy that risks leading into the dialectic of the *scientific logos*.[9]

The only way to avoid the dialectic of the Enlightenment is to leave open the issue of the reality of myth. This does not mean that myth is real and objective; it means taking some distance from the "enlightened" view of myth as fanciful stories and, consequently, leaving the issue of the "reality of myth" in parentheses.

---

[8] For criticism of Lévi-Strauss' ethnocentrism, see, in particular, Geertz's "*The Uses of Diversity*" in Geertz 2000. As Geertz observes, the problem with ethnocentrism is not that it commits us to our own "cultural" commitments, but that it impedes us from discovering at what sort of angle we stand to the world. In particular, it obscures the fact that foreignness does not start at the water's edge but at the skin's (Geertz 2000: 76).

[9] It should be pointed out that in Lévi-Strauss' view, the savage mind has a cognitive potential which translated into the momentous success of the Neolithic revolution. The point is that in his view modern science has been able to reach another level of reality, transcending the *science du concret*, and therefore gaining a new mastery over nature (Lévi-Strauss 1962). In this sense, modern science remains the *terminus ad quem* of his approach to the savage mind.

Thus, an *interrelational* approach to myth is also a *phenomenological* approach. What characterised the phenomenological method, as first elaborated by Husserl,[10] was precisely this intention to put the question of realism in parentheses. Since we do not have the means to determine whether our representations of the world correspond to the world as it is "in itself" (if this expression has a meaning), phenomenology chooses to leave this question aside and to examine the way in which our consciousness relates to the phenomenological world – independently of whether the latter corresponds to a supposed world in itself or not.

In this sense, phenomenology was defined as a "return to the things themselves", by which Husserl meant that these are phenomena, understood not as appearances counterpoised to hypothetical things in themselves, but as the original disclosing of "reality" in the consciousness (Husserl 2001). The aim of the phenomenological method is to describe phenomena as they are given in the consciousness in order to grasp their pure form or idea (*eidos*). It therefore requires a preliminary reduction through which all common judgements are suspended, which is what Husserl called the *phenomenological epoché*. This means that all theories – ranging from scientific theories to judgements of common sense – are placed in parentheses. Among these theories, Husserl includes naïve realism, which is a belief in the existence of an external world that should be faithfully reproduced by our consciousness (Husserl 1992).

Adopting a phenomenological approach to myth means, fundamentally, to start from an *epoché* regarding the question of the "reality of myth". In other words, one should not consider the relationship between myth and reality as being constitutive of myth. By raising the issue of the reality of myth, one risks adopting a pre-given conception of reality. In contrast, it is a phenomenological starting point that should be combined with an interrelational approach. This primarily means that the emphasis is placed on relationships, and thus on contexts, rather than on consciousness.

---

[10] Reference is made here to the phenomenological method developed by the early Husserl (1992; 2001). Insights are drawn from his early writings and not from his later writings with their idealistic turn, which is particularly clear in the series of lectures given in Paris in 1929, published only after his death (Husserl 1973).

What is a myth, then? Moving from this interrelational and phenomenological approach, there are at least three features of myth that can be emphasised. The most general is that the work on myth takes place within a network of symbols. In a sense, then, a myth is a symbol or, to be more precise, it involves a network of symbols. But while all myths employ symbols, not all symbols are myths. Indeed, although symbols are everywhere, at least wherever there is language and communication, myths are not. We need more than a symbol in order to have a myth.

Keeping the two categories of myth and symbols analytically distinct is crucial. In avoiding the Scylla of neglecting myth, we must not fall into the Charybdis of mythologizing everything. To distinguish myth from symbols is necessary in order to distinguish myth from all the other forms of symbolism. For instance, both rationality and myth rely on symbols, but they do so in a different way. Indeed – and here we approach the first feature of myth – a myth differs from rational argumentation because, despite the fact that both operate with symbols, myths operate with figurative means. A myth is made of images, figures and characters.

This does not, however, mean that, following the self-presentation of the Enlightenment, we must understand myth and rationality as being mutually exclusive. It simply means that the two categories must be analytically distinct if we want to capture the specificity of myth. Myth is not incompatible with rationality, but, at the same time, it does not coincide with it. Indeed, a string of numbers in a mathematical proportion is a series of symbols, but nobody – or at least only a very few – would argue that it is a myth. As a consequence, it is not in the category of symbol that we must look if we want to find the specificity of myth.

The conflation between myth and symbol stems, perhaps, from a further conflation between two different mainstream meanings of the term "symbol". In a broad sense, a symbol is simply a sign for something else. This is the original meaning of the Greek word *synbolon*, which stems from the verb *synballo*, "to put together". It originally defined the two halves of a broken object that can be recomposed only by putting these halves together: in this way, each half is a sign referring to something else. However, the term acquired a further meaning over time. In a more restricted sense, a symbol is a special kind of sign, that is, a sign that is indeterminate, referring to some hidden or remote reality. In this sense, we can say, for instance, that a symbol is a sign with an equivocal meaning.

The concept of symbol has been the subject of much philosophical speculation. The first philosopher to take symbol, and not some other related concept such as "sign" or "meaning", as the key concept of a philosophical system was Cassirer. According to him, symbols are the transcendental conditions of human thinking, because they are the only means through which meanings are possible. As we read in the Introduction to his *Philosophy of Symbolic Forms*, the symbolic function is the fundamental function of our consciousness, the function through which only the activity of human consciousness is possible. Consciousness, according to Cassirer, is nothing but a pure form of referring. This means that each single content of the consciousness is interwoven in a net of relationships, and it is through this net that a content, in its simple being, implies reference to other contents (Cassirer 1977: vol I, 41ff). Symbols are the products of this original activity of consciousness.

In Cassirer's view, therefore, every significant realisation is a symbol. In a symbol, the sensory element – a written sign, a sound, an image, and so on – presents itself, simply on account of its being, as both differentiation and materialisation, that is, as the manifestation and incarnation of a meaning (Cassirer 1977: vol. III, 108ff.). It is therefore unnecessary for the two elements, the sign and the object referred to by the sign, to be already known as separated in order to have a symbol. On the contrary, according to Cassirer, it is precisely through conceiving of the image and the object as separate that the "expressive" function can be distinguished from the "conceptual" function. While in the pure phenomena of expression, there is no "skin" or "core", no "one" or "other", because even if the expression is an exteriorisation, we are still in the interiority in this exteriorising, with conceptual knowledge both the representation and the object of the representation are seen as clearly distinct.

These are, in Cassirer's view, the two fundamental forms of consciousness, to the analysis of which he devoted most of his thinking. He also went further in this and identified the *expressive* form as the basis of the lower formations of the consciousness, or mythical consciousness, and the *conceptual* form as the basis of scientific consciousness. Myth, in his view, is a form of the expressive experience that is primitive precisely because the consciousness is completely absorbed here by the object of its representation, without it being possible to distinguish clearly the sign from the object defined by it (Cassirer 1977).

As has already been observed, this approach to myth somehow presupposes scientific rationality as a *terminus ad quem*.[11] Myth is characterised as being inferior precisely because it is assumed that it *must* be superseded by scientific rationality, with which, in Cassirer's view, only a clear distinction between the representation of consciousness and its objects can be realised. However, as we have seen, the separation between the object and the subject of representations is the result of a self-presentation of the *scientific logos*, which risks falling into the dialectic of the Enlightenment.

The only way to try to escape this dialectic is to analyse myth autonomously. Suggestions in this direction can be drawn from Vico, the first modern thinker to dedicate systematic thinking to myths. In his polemic against Descartes' rationalism, Vico supported the rights of fantasy and rhetoric, and contested the idea of a unique scientific method. By appealing to the principle that we can only know the truth of that of which we, ourselves, are the authors (*verum ipsum factum*), he claimed the need for a "new science" of human history. It was to this project that he dedicated his life and his major work, the *New Science* (Vico 1999). In Vico's view, the new science is the science of the human world, a world that is constructed by human beings and whose knowledge is therefore assured by the very fact that the subject of knowledge is also at the same time the maker of this world. As a consequence, it is in the human mind itself that the principles of this new science can be found. And the human mind, in Vico's view, is characterised by the great part played by fantasy (*fantasia*), or imagination, understood as an autonomous faculty, and upon which, in its turn, the autonomy of the poetic wisdom rests.

Two prejudices, Vico argues, have prevented human beings from recognising this autonomy: the conceit of scholars (*boria dei dotti*) (Vico 1999: 47–8, 77) and the conceit of nations (*boria delle nazioni*) (45, 76). On the one hand, there is the conceit of the nations, all of them claiming they were the very first to invent the comforts of human life (76)

---

[11] See, in particular, Blumenberg 1985: 3ff.

and, thus, tracing the origins of all that they hold as valuable in human life back to some remote epoch of their past. The narrative of the birth of philosophy as the act of baptism of Western man is a very good example of this conceit. Vico's argument against the conceit of nations can also be used, therefore, as an argument against enlightened readings of myth, such as that developed by Cassirer. As Vico argued, myth must be analysed in its autonomy and not in the perspective of rationality as *terminus ad quem*.

The second prejudice hindering an autonomous understanding of myth is the conceit of scholars "who assert that what they know is as old as the world" (Vico 1999: 77). According to Vico, even those who have not rejected the rights of myth and fantasy against rationality have often fallen into the opposite prejudice, that of presenting myths as the fount of some remote and ancient *sapientia* of which they themselves are the heirs. Here, Vico's polemic was directed against all the Neoplatonist readings that, by means of allegory, aimed to recover some sort of hidden wisdom from ancient myths.

Vico's criticism towards the conceit of scholars can also be used as an argument against the continually recurring romantic approaches to myth. Indeed, the romantics who presented myths as the deposit of a lost past were not recognising the autonomy of myth, which is the autonomy, as Vico taught us, of a continuously operating faculty of the human mind. To conclude, two dangers must be avoided if we want to recognise the autonomy of the poetic wisdom (*sapienza poetica*): the rationalistic disdain for what preceded the rise of scientific rationality, and the nostalgic attempt to rediscover the origins of a supposed lost wisdom.

It is for this attitude towards a new science that Vico's criticism against his time still provides crucial insights for an understanding of myth. Vico, who spent all his life in the Naples of the eighteenth century, lived at the margins, both temporal and spatial, of modernity and thus perhaps was in the best position to perceive its limits. However, he still remains a product of his time and, therefore, even if he criticised the claims of the emerging scientific method, he did so while accepting at least some of the terms in which the Enlightenment itself had posed the question.

In a sense, Vico's theory of poetic wisdom also reflects an enlightened attitude towards myth. In particular, his theory of the three epochs of world history through which all the nations must pass – the ages of gods, heroes, and men – reflects a teleological scheme where myth, which corresponds to the age of heroes, also appears in the perspective of rationality as the *terminus ad quem*. This course (*corso*) of human history reflects a truth that Vico derives from what he takes to be the course of the development of the human mind. The theory of the three stages of the development of humanity is constructed via an analogy with the development of the human mind: "People first feel things without noticing them, then notice them with inner distress and disturbance, and finally reflect on them with a clear mind" (Vico 1999: 94). The development of the human mind is characterised by the fact that reason is the last faculty to be developed, after the senses (*senso*) and fantasy (*fantasia*). The poetic wisdom corresponds therefore to an early stage of the development both of the human mind and of the historical course (*corso storico*).

In other words, Vico vindicated the rights of myth and poetry against those of science, but, in doing so, remained entrapped in a dichotomic approach of myth versus rationality, which is the very presupposition of the Enlightenment itself. Vico claimed the rights of myth and, consequently, the necessity of a poetic logic (*logica poetica*). Not only did he conceive of poetry and myth[12] as the origins of the language,[13] but he also claimed the truth of myth. Vico seems to have pushed his claim to the point of vindicating, through an audacious etymology, the idea that myth is the "*vera narratio,* or true narration" (Vico 1999: 157). However, he did so from the point of view of a truth that must be recovered against rationality, and, thereby, he accepted the self-presentation of scientific rationality.

Notwithstanding this, both Vico and Cassirer remain the starting point for any reflection on myth, since both captured the first and perhaps most basic feature of myth. Myth, they argued, is a form of poetic expression. Myth, like poetry, relies on figurative tools and this is what primarily distinguishes it from other symbolic forms. All the same, we must not draw from this the conclusion that myth and reason

---

[12] Vico, as Cantelli has pointed out, sometimes used the terms "myth" and "poetry" as synonymous (Cantelli 1986: 15ff).

[13] The point is raised in many passages of the *New Science* and is based on an analysis of the way in which the human mind develops. For instance, see Vico 1999: 24.

constitute two mutually incompatible faculties, one of which precedes the other. This is only to say that a myth, in contrast, for instance, to rationality, evokes images and figures.

It does not mean that a myth necessarily implies heroism either. In constrast to Vico, who identifies myth with the language spoken in the age of heroes and defines it as a language that uses "heroic emblems – such as similes, comparisons, images, metaphors, and descriptions of nature" (Vico 1999: 22), we should not reduce myth to the narration of heroic undertakings (*imprese eroiche*). If we do not accept the tele-ological scheme implicit in Vico's theory of the three ages, there is no reason why we should identify myth with the stories of heroes and heroines.[14]

On the contrary, the history of myth shows that everything can be the object of a mythical narrative. We do not need princesses to be saved or dragons to be killed in order to have a myth. This is its second crucial feature: the work on myth can operate with extremely different types of content. This means that no particular kind of content can be considered as defining myth. Myths are not just stories of imaginary gods, heroes and undertakings – as an enlightened approach would expect. The content of mythological narratives has changed continu-ously over time – ranging from the Greek stories of gods and heroes to the Nazi myth of race. Given such clear versatility, there is no reason to assume that the contents of myths will crystallise and that the past contents of myths will remain as their contents for ever.

This is a crucial point. The reason why so many people today still maintain that myths have to deal with stories of gods and heroes is partly due to the fact that these are the myths with which we are most familiar. Stories of imaginary gods and heroes are the myths that even an enlightened approach, caught as it is in its own dialectic, is pre-pared to recognise as such. It comes as no surprise that most of the literature on myths deals with "primitive myths". The fact that so many myths were "found" among the "primitives" could work as further con-firmation of the self-presentation of scientific reason.

On the other hand, thinking of myth as the product of the "savage" or "primitive" mind has impeded us from seeing the myth by which

[14] Various authors have followed Vico on this point. See, for instance, Henry 2000 and Passerini 2003.

we – civilised, clothed human beings – live every day (Migdley 2003). And this is a problematic attitude that can open the way for the affirmation of myth in its most dangerous form – the myth without any possible mediation (Blumenberg 1985). In contrast, one should start from the assumption of a possible banality of myth.

To sum up, myths rely on figurative tools such as figures and images, but they do not necessarily do so at the service of any particular heroic content. To put it rather crudely, we do not need primitive blood rituals in order to have a myth. Everything can be an object of myth, just as everything can be an object of poetry. However, although myth – like poetry – evokes images and figures, poetry and myth do not coincide. Lyrics, for instance, are not myths – at least, not necessarily. In fact, and here we move to the third feature of myth, myths are a particular kind of poetry: they are narratives.

What is a narrative? At a very basic level, narratives are sequences of events, where the idea of sequence already implies that it is by being inserted in a narrative that events are given a certain meaning.[15] By sequences of events, however, I do not mean sequences of facts. Many authors have defined narratives as series of facts, where the term *fact* is understood as a description of what has happened. According to Labov, for instance, narrative "is one method of recapitulating past experience by matching a verbal sequence of clauses to the sequence of events which (it is inferred) actually occurred" (Labov 1972: 359–60).

This is still a widespread view of narratives[16] and it is rooted in the work of the Russian formalists of the beginning of the twentieth century – in particular, Propp and Tomashevski (Tomashevski 1965). A similar view has been used by French structuralists such as Barthes (1977). The basic idea, here, is that we can distinguish the narrative (*sjuñet, discours* or *recit*), that is the plot, as the organisation of *facts* from the *story* (*fabula, histoire*), that is the mere set of *brute facts*. According

---

[15] On the concept of narrative and, in particular, on the distinction between historical and mythical narratives, see also Chapter 10.

[16] For instance, in Cohan and Shires, we read "the distinguishing feature of narrative is a linear organisation of events" (Cohan and Shires 1988: 52–3). Or, in Toolan: "a minimalist definition of narrative might be: a perceived sequence of nonrandomly connected events" (Toolan 1988: 7).

to Tomashevski, "the plot is distinguished from story. Both include the same events, but in the plot events are arranged and connected according to the orderly sequence in which they were presented in the work ... in brief, the story is the 'action itself', ... [whereas the plot] is how the reader learns of the action" (Tomashevsky 1955: 67).

This approach presupposes the possibility of separating events – understood as facts, actions – from their organisation. However, it can certainly be argued that the distinction between the two is fundamentally problematic because there is no such thing as a "brute event". An event is such inasmuch as it *e-venit*, that is, it becomes perceivable against a background of non-becoming events. Therefore, an event is always already organised because, in as far as it *e-venit*, there must have been a choice: first, because it becomes, instead of remaining in the grey background of non-becoming events; and second, because it occurs in one way rather than in another. We all have experience of the different ways in which an event can be told: not just in what is not allowed to become, but also in the fact that it is made to be in one way and not in another. These operations imply a choice as well as the organisation of what is chosen.

Furthermore, what the event becomes for the narrator is not yet the event that it becomes for the receiver. Here, we face the limits of any approach that focuses only on the "content" of narratives.[17] A narrative is not a container into which the narrator puts meanings that are thereafter delivered into the mind of the receiver. Any narrative presupposes a context within which it becomes meaningful, that is, only within a context does it become a narrative. This context can be better described as a language-game made of acting and saying and, in particular, of "acts of telling" and "acts of interpreting"– where it is even difficult to distinguish between the two.

Most of the structuralist studies on narrative are devoted to the search for the structural elements of which a narrative is comprised, that is, for that surplus of meaning that makes an ordered plot emerge from a set of brute facts. To this end, many scholars have distinguished structures that are narratives from others that are not. For instance,

---

[17] On this point, see in particular White 1987, and the discussion of his work in Chapter 10.

according to Barthes, we must distinguish between cardinal functions (or nuclei) and catalysts (Barthes 1977: 93–4). Catalysts "merely fill in the narrative space" while cardinal functions fundamentally alter the status quo and they do so by providing an order to the events. Therefore, according to Barthes, while "catalysts are only consecutive units, cardinal functions are both consecutive and consequential" (Barthes 1977: 94).

However, in this search for the structural nuclei of the plot in a narrative, what gets lost is the role that the receiver plays and, particularly, the role that he or she plays in the language-games that give meaning to a narrative. A narrative is not a narrative if it is not narrated to someone, and this someone, the receiver, is never a passive receiver. As the phenomenology of the act of reading proposed by the so-called School of Konstanz has demonstrated, the analysis of the act of reading shows that the readers are fundamental to the construction of meaning of the events narrated (Iser 1976).[18] For instance, the reader will tendentiously provide logical connections that link one sentence to the other, when they are missing – and this happens even more often in a poetic text.

This is not to say that the elements that the narrator includes in the narrative are irrelevant for its meaning. In trying not to overemphasise the act of producing the narrative, the opposite mistake of overstressing the act of reading should not be made. It is by combining the two acts that a (meaningful) narrative is constructed. And the degrees and modality of this combination vary from text to text and from context to context. For instance, what characterises a piece of art is its higher degree of indeterminacy, which fosters a more active participation on the side of the receiver. This is what is at the basis of the asserted polysemy of the work of art (Gadamer 1988).

By proposing an interrelational and phenomenological approach to myth, I have emphasised and discussed three features of myth understood as work on myth: a myth operates with figurative means; it can deal with all sorts of contents; and, finally, it presents itself as a narrative. A further feature, however, still needs to be discussed. Indeed, not all narratives are myths. There is something in the "work on myth"

---

[18] On the relationship between the so-called theory of reception and Blumenberg's concept of the work on myth, see Leghissa 2002: 27.

(*Arbeit am Mythos*), namely, the process of telling-receiving and retelling of myth, that distinguishes it from other kinds of narrative (Blumenberg 1985). This is because a myth is a narrative that provides not just meaning, but also significance, and it does so by placing events in a more or less coherent plot. The work on myth is also the work on significance.

6

Naming the Unknown, Grounding Significance

Both Cassirer and Vico have approached myth from the point of view of scientific rationality as the *terminus ad quem*, and they have thus, at least partially, failed in their attempts to theorise myth in its autonomy. As Blumenberg pointed out in his *Work on Myth*, a more promising strategy is that of looking at myth from the point of view of what it follows, that is, of what it serves to overcome (Blumenberg 1985: 19ff. 1).

The basic performance of myth is to provide names. A myth is always "the myth *of*. . .". It is only by giving a thing a name that it can become "graspable" and therefore the object of a story. Providing names does not just render stories possible; naming the unknown is already a way of dominating the unknown. Denominating a thing is the first – if not the most interesting – answer to the question "what is this or that?" Moreover, by giving a name to the unknown, whole webs of other meanings are recalled.

In replying to Phaedrus' question "what is the soul?", Socrates says that he cannot say what a soul is in itself. This is the task, he admits, of a divine exposition in every sense. However, to say "what it resembles" is a perfectly human task (*Phaedr.* 246A). The soul, Socrates states, is a chariot. The image of the chariot is extremely powerful and generates a whole myth. A chariot has horses and a charioteer; this represents the *nous*, which guides the two horses: one black, made of opposites, and one white, which is good and beautiful. To lead the chariot is, therefore, inevitably very difficult. Each chariot aspires to follow its respective god in the *hyperuranion* in order to see the "land of truth", but because of its mixed composition, it is destined to fall and lose its wings. It is only through contemplating beauty that the charioteer can dominate the opposites and let the wings of the soul grow again (*Phaedrus* 256a).

Modernity, Blumenberg observes, is perhaps the epoch that has gone the furthest in providing names and, in a sense, it can be defined as the epoch that has found a name for everything. It is no coincidence, therefore, according to Blumenberg, that Francis Bacon connected the recovery of Paradise with the rediscovery of the original name of everything (Blumenberg 1985: 38). Bacon perceived the power of nomenclature clearly: it was manifest to him that it is only by naming and classifying the world that the bases for its mastery can be laid.

To name the unknown is not only to render familiar the unfamiliar. It is also a way of providing a means for orientation. Names are meanings and meanings are meanings in contexts of meanings; they recall other meanings and, in doing so, they provide a whole web that orients action. The sovereign can thus be defined as he or she who has the power to impose names. Hobbes observed that, however ingenious all other human inventions are, there can be no comparison with the invention of what he calls "speech". Speech, defined as "consisting of Names or Appellations and their connection", is the means by which human beings "register their thoughts, recall them when they are past, and also declare them one to another for mutual utility and conversation" (Hobbes 1985: 101). Defining things and their reciprocal connections is the sovereign's function par excellence. The first "author" of names, Hobbes also observed, was indeed God, the omnipotent God (Hobbes 1985: 100–1).

According to the narrative of Genesis, God dominates the world because he created it with his words (Genesis I: 1). At the beginning, earth was formless and empty, but God said "Let there be the light", and so on, and, by naming the things of the world, he created them. God also created human beings and he created them in his own image; as God created the world by naming it, it was through

the power of imposing names that the mastery of the world was given
to "man":

> and out of the ground the Lord God formed every beast of the field, and every
> foul of the air; and brought them unto Adam to see what he would name them:
> and whatsoever Adam called every living creature, that was the name thereof.
> (*Genesis* II: 19)

Names are not just the means by which webs of meanings are created and the world mastered, they are also reassuring in themselves
because they fill up an empty space. Ancient poetry was full of long
lists of names. Blumenberg observes that the reason why we now find
these long lists of names unpoetic is that we live in an epoch, that of
modernity, which aspires to give a name to everything. Our world is
therefore overwhelmed by names (Blumenberg 1985: 38).

All the same, the traces of this "filling-up" power of names can still
be found in the lists of names spread throughout ancient texts such as
those of Homer and Hesiod, and the Old and New Testaments. The
function of these lists was to reassure the reader about the familiarity
of the poet with what he was narrating: no empty space is left, because
the poet has a name for everything. Any biblical figure, for instance,
provided an occasion for an outburst of names, cast in the form of their
genealogies. These genealogies were not simply aimed at delineating
a continuity of a story. Sometimes the names that appeared were not
mentioned either before or after in the story. They played no other
role in the story – apart from just being there. This happens not just
for the genealogies of the great figures of the Old Testament – for
instance, Adam's (Genesis V: 1) or Abraham's genealogy (Genesis XI:
10). Christ's genealogies[1] in the New Testament are also full of names
that have *no sequitur* or prehistory: they simply are there – filling up a
space.

We need names to master the world, because we need names to master the emptiness. Emptiness generates fear – fear of something, but
also anguish (*Angst*),[2] that is fear without any object. As Blumenberg

---

[1] See, in particular, the genealogy of Christ provided in Matthew I: 1–16.
[2] In his essay on Blumenberg, Wallace observes that the term *Angst*, which is usually
translated as "anxiety", would be better rendered in English by the psychiatrists' paraphrase "intense fear or dread lacking an unambiguous cause or specific threat" (Wallace 1984: 95).

observes, a fright that has found the word again is a fright that is already over (Blumenberg 1985: 6–7). Magic manifestly exhibits the exorcising power of names. Anguish generated by the unknown can be dominated by pronouncing the right word. In a sense, magical words not only evoke hidden forces, they also exorcise them. By pronouncing names, the empty space of the unknown can be filled and – through this fullness – can be mastered.

Anguish (*Angst*) refers generally to the horizon of the empty possibilities that can present themselves. As Blumenberg points out by recovering a fundamental Freudian insight, anguish is never realistic, because it is never commensurate to the perception of a determined peril. Anguish has no object and is always pathological. Those who are prey to anguish are those who have lost the possibility of "putting something forward", of mitigating the absolute power of the unknown. Those who can name things, so Blumenberg argued, have the first powerful means by which to fight the "absolutism of reality" (Blumenberg 1985: 6).

Blumenberg defines this "absolutism of reality" as the condition in which human beings come close to losing control over the conditions of their existence, or, more importantly, when they believe that they lack any control over them (Blumenberg 1985: 3ff.). The concept of the absolutism of reality, he observes, is corroborated by theories of anthropogenesis. These depict the initial situation of humankind in terms of exit from the pluvial forest. The abandoning of the forest led to human beings' definitive acquisition of an erect position, which, in its turn, implied a widening of their horizon of perception. The erect being, who abandoned the advantages of a hidden way of life for those of the savannah, was obliged to face the challenges of a widened horizon of perception and visibility. It is this being that had to face the absolutism of reality.

Blumenberg was clearly influenced here by German philosophical anthropology, as elaborated by Max Scheler and Arnold Gehlen. According to them, human beings, in contrast to animals, are not adapted to a specific environment and are therefore open to the world (*weltoffen*). This has two basic consequences. First, according to Gehlen, human beings are subject to all sorts of stimulations and impressions from the outside world, and this places a great burden on them from which they must seek relief (*Entlastung*). The set of devices and apparatuses by which they can obtain relief is culture, which thus constitutes a sort of "second nature" (Gehlen 1988).

From these remarks, a second consequence is derived: to have a world is always the result of art – even if, to use Blumenberg's words, the world can never be a total work of art (*Gesamtkunstwerk*) (Blumenberg 1979: 7). The means through which all these actions, aimed at providing relief, take place is language. Myth, according to Blumenberg, together with magic, science and metaphysics, among others, is one of the possible means of obtaining such relief (*Entlastung*).

As Blumenberg noticed, there is a functional analogy between myth, science and metaphysics: by naming the unknown, they all contribute to its mastery (Blumenberg 1985: 34ff.). As we will see, this does not mean that there is no difference between them. It simply means that, again, as Blumenberg observed, myth defined a standard of performance that metaphysics and science could not fall short of satisfying.

Blumenberg also follows Gehlen in his reference to theories of anthropogenesis. From these, he derives the image of a primordial condition of humanity that he mixes with the old philosophical tradition of the state of nature (Blumenberg 1985: 3ff.). Blumenberg presents the "old state of nature" as a limit concept, but doubts can nonetheless be raised over the helpfulness of such a reference.

In fact, as Blumenberg seems to suggest in many places, whatever starting point one takes, the work of demolishing the absolutism of reality has always "already started" (1985: 7). We are always beyond the threshold of the absolutism of reality. There seems, therefore, to be no need to call on the state of nature, a category that might be misleading from a number of points of view. In particular, the idea of a state of nature cannot but evoke its normative corollary, that is, the precept to exit from such a primitive condition. In whatever way one presents this state of nature, something is always presupposed by the very fact that it is a *natural* state: that is, human beings must leave this condition and enter a civil(ised) one.

Blumenberg was probably influenced here by Gehlen's view of man as a deficient being (*Mangelwesen*). According to this view, human beings are not naturally assigned to a specific environment and are, therefore, incomplete beings in comparison with other animals. Due to their incomplete nature, they must undergo a process of disciplining. The deficient being (*Mangelwesen*) is also a being in need of discipline (*Zuchtwesen*) (Gehlen 1988).

The relief (*Entlastung*) from the excess of impulses to which human beings are subject because of their incompleteness is reached, according to Gehlen, in two basic ways. First, human beings distance themselves from the immediacy of drives and move on to the level of symbolic and intellectual action. Second, they seek relief through the mediation of institutions, given that these, by mediating the relationship of human beings with their needs, provide them with a stable horizon (Gehlen 1988).

Many authors have criticised this concept for its political implications and have seen in it the sign of Gehlen's connections with the authoritarianism of the Nazi regime. However, the idea of human beings as open to the world (*weltoffen*), which ultimately derives from Nietzsche, does not necessarily imply the disciplinary view that Gehlen draws from it. Gehlen opens his major work, *Man, His Nature and Place in the World* (1988), with the reference to Nietzsche's view of "man" as "the not yet determined animal" (*das noch nicht festgestellt Tier*). But the idea that human beings are not yet determined, not yet assigned to a specific environment, does not necessarily call for a view of human beings as beings that must be disciplined (*Zuchtwesen*).

In contrast, if one points to the fact that human beings are always not yet determined (*fest-gestellt*), that is, to the fact that they must re-elaborate the very conditions of their existence, then they appear as abundant beings (*Surpluswesen*) rather than as deficient beings (*Mangelwesen*). The idea of a need or lack (*Mangel*) immediately calls for a closure, and thus for discipline, but in this way it is only one aspect of the ambivalent relationship that human beings entertain with the conditions of their existence that comes to light.

The relationships between an always not yet determined animal and the conditions of his or her existence are ambivalent. The "not yet determined animal" does not completely control these circumstances, since, to put it in Heidegger's terms, he or she is always "thrown into the world" (Heidegger 2002a). At the same time, he or she does intervene over them in a way in which no other animals do. This is not the sign of a lack, but rather of abundance.

The work of myth is thus the work against an "absolutism of reality" understood in this way: at whatever stage we are, we have always already gone beyond this absolutism, because we have gone beyond pure chaos.[3] A synonym for "absolutism of reality" is indeed "chaos" (Angehrn 1996) – even though what gets lost in this term is the political register of the category of "absolutism of reality".[4] Whatever concept one decides to employ, it should be clear that the work against the "absolutism of reality" or "chaos" has always already started and that myth is the sign of its overcoming.

As Blumenberg observed, there is a functional analogy between myth, science and religion, inasmuch as they all are a means for the creation of meaning. What then, differentiates, the work of and on myth from other forms of the production of meaning (*Sinngebung*), such as science or religion?

In the first place, myth, in contrast to science, does not technically aim to explain something (*erklären*). As Malinowski observed in his essay, "Myth in Primitive Psychology", myths do not explain (or rather they do not explain in the sense in which science does), although they still make everything clear. Myth, in other words, is not an explanation that is put forward to satisfy a contemplative curiosity over the world. Instead, it derives its crucial features from the fact that it has a specific social function. As we read in a passage describing the role played by myths among the "primitive" peoples:

Myth as it exists in a savage community, that is, in its living primitive form, is not merely a story told but a reality lived . . . These stories live not by idle interest, not as fictitious or even as true narratives, but are to the natives a statement of a primeval, greater, and more relevant reality, by which the present life, fates, and activities of mankind are determined, the knowledge of which supplies man with the motive for ritual and moral actions, as well as with indications as to how to perform them. (Malinowski 1992: 100, 108)

While commenting on this passage, Kerényi observed that Malinowski understood that the function of myth is not to provide a scientific or "pseudo-scientific" explanation. However, according to

---

[3] Castoriadis makes a similar point in his work on the imaginary constitution of society. Instead of the concept of "absolutism of reality", he uses that of "chaos": whatever the stage of the institution of the society, the work of its imaginary significations against the absolutism of the chaos has already started (Castoriadis 1987).
[4] This political register of Blumenberg's concept of myth facilitates the task of linking philosophical theories of myth with the social sciences' treatment of political myth. All the same, even if Blumenberg's theory had political connotations, it is not specifically aimed at an understanding of political myth.

Kerényi, he lacked the proper word to describe this function; he rejected "explanation" (*Erklärung*), but the sense in which myth can make things "clear" (*klar*) remains obscure. However, the German language contains a word that adequately describes this: *begründen* (Kerényi 1963: 6).

The root of the concept of *begründen*, which can, perhaps, at best be translated as "to ground" or "to substantiate", is the term "*Grund*". *Grund* means both the abstract noun "reason" and the concrete noun "ground". Myths tell stories, they tell what the origins of things are, and, thus, at the same time, where they are going. They provide a "ground" but they do so by answering the question "whence?" rather than "why". In this way, they provide things with what in the German language corresponds to a *Grund*.

According to Kerényi, the difference between myth and science can be elucidated very well in Greek. Myth does not indicate *aitiai*, that is, causes. Or rather, it provides *aitiai* only to the extent that, as taught by Aristotle (Met. 1013a), the *aitiai* are *archai*, that is, beginnings or first principles. The happenings in a myth are not "causes" in the modern sense of necessary connections between events, but are rather grounds or primary states. And it is in this sense alone that they can be said to lay "the foundation" of things (Kerényi, 1963: 7).[5]

Myths are not just simple stories about origins. There are, indeed, stories of origins that are not myths. Together with Blumenberg, and perhaps against Kerényi,[6] we must recognise that the reason why myths succeed in their *begründen* is that they generate significance (*Bedeutsamkeit*). A myth is not just a story, but a story that works as a *Begründung* because it coagulates and reproduces significance (Blumenberg 1985). While all narratives provide facts with a meaning by simply inserting them in a plot, a myth is a narrative that has also succeeded in – so to speak – "making *significance*" of them.

Blumenberg defines the *Bedeutsamkeit* as a defence from indifference, mainly understood as indifference in space and time (Blumenberg 1985: 59ff.). Consequently, myth can be defined as that which

---

[5] On myth as a form of justification, see also Frank 1982. In the context of his discussion of German idealism, Frank also observes that the typically mythical justification is "*eine Begründung aus Zwecken*" (160).

[6] See in particular the passage where Kerényi states "it is no groundless generalization to say that mythology tells us of the origins or at least of what originally was" (Kerényi 1963: 7).

makes things closer to us. While something can have a meaning, but I can still be completely indifferent to it, something that is significant is something that I feel "close" to. This, at least, has one major consequence: science can be universal, whereas significance is always particular. That which is a myth, under certain conditions and for certain subjects, can be a simple story for others. Furthermore, that which is a myth for me "here" and "now" may, in the future, be relegated to the status of a simple story. What, then, lies behind this situatedness of significance?

As has been observed, Blumenberg derived the term *Bedeutsamkeit* (significance) from Dilthey.[7] The concept recalls the context of the discussion about the difference between human and natural sciences (respectively, in German, *Geistes-* and *Naturwissenschaften*). While positivist approaches, following the tradition of Hume, claimed the unity of scientific method on the basis of the dogma of the invariability of natural laws, Dilthey claimed the autonomy of the human sciences on the basis of their different objects: the mind (*Geist*), that is, what is specifically human, as opposed to nature (*Natur*).

However, the distinction between mind (*Geist*) and nature (*Natur*) seems to be very problematic in itself, in the sense that the mind can be seen as natural and that nature can be said to be mental. However, the connection of the term *Bedeutsamkeit* with the debate about the nature of the human sciences is illuminating. If human beings are not yet determined animals, they entertain a problematising relationship with the conditions of their existence. These conditions are "given" for most other animals, in the twofold sense that a fish dies out of water and that, as far as we know, it does not ask questions about this fact, whereas human beings question them: not only do humans change, at least to a certain extent, the conditions of their own existence, but they also question them. It is from all these questions that a need for significance is derived and the work on myth stems.

This does not mean that myth is the only way to provide significance and thus to fight the indifference of the world. It only means that, to put it in Geertz's words, the human being is an animal suspended in webs of significance (Geertz 1973: 5), and that myth is one of the

---

[7] On this point, see Jamme 1991: 116. Jamme does not, however, draw any conclusions from this fact.

ways in which this animal elaborates these webs and thus provides a "grounding" (*Grund*) for the conditions of his or her existence.

The plural is very important here. In the phrase "conditions of existence", the emphasis must be on the plurality of these conditions. Everything that is part of the experience of human beings is part of these conditions and can therefore be the object of this questioning. This point is crucial because not all myths aim to explain the whole sense of being, that is, the *condition* of the existence of human beings in the singular. Some of them do, but not all. To assume that they all do would preclude the possibility of seeing the work on myth in its variety, its richness, and also its banality.

On the one hand, myth differs from science because, instead of looking for the abstract relationships between causes and effects, it aims at "grounding" the world in which human beings live – a task that science, limited as it is to answering the question of "how?" cannot perform. To put it in Wittgenstein's terms, the problem of science is "how" the world exists, and not "why", and as a consequence he is right in saying that even when all possible scientific questions have been answered, the problems of life remain completely untouched (Wittgenstein 1961: 73).

On the other hand, myth does not coincide with religion or mysticism for this reason. Simplifying things, we can say that myth answers the question of "why?" by raising the issue of "whence"; as such, it can limit itself to telling a story about *some* of the conditions of existence, without necessarily aspiring to answer the question of the sense of life in general. Significance (*Bedeutsamkeit*) situates itself precisely between two extremes: meanings on the one hand (the *Sinnfrage*: "What is this?") and the sense of "Being" on the other (the *Seinsfrage*: "What is the sense of being?"). Significance is not (just) meaning, because there is meaning every time that there is language. But significance is not necessarily the question about the sense of the being either, because some myths do not aim to provide explanations of the ultimate meaning of being.

Thus, it is not necessary to question the whole sense of life in order to start the work on myth. Everything, even the most banal event, can be the object of a mythical narrative – just as everything can acquire significance. In other words, there is no need for any shedding of blood in order to have a myth. Indeed, the work on myth starts before we raise the issue of the meaning of death. Therefore, if we agree with Cassirer and Malinowski in saying that religion, notwithstanding its variety of manifestations, has always been and always will be "a question of life and death" (Cassirer 1973: 48), then we also have to conclude that religion is, in a way, an attempt to "bring myth to an end".

"Bringing myth to an end" is the expression used by Blumenberg to define the attempt at a closure exercised by any "final myths" (Blumenberg 1985: 263). As we have seen in our discussion of the sacred *logos*, by advancing a whole plot for interpretation of the sense of life and death, religious myths aspire to get rid of the need for significance. In contrast, the work on myth is driven by a need for significance that is continually fostered by the changing of the circumstances in which we live. In particular, while religion, by answering the question of the meaning of life and death, also radically aims to resolve the problem of the incongruence between "good" and "luck", the work on myth is fostered precisely by the impossibility of providing a definitive solution to the problem of this incongruence.

This is a crucial point. What Greek tragedy shared with Greek philosophy was the need to face the problem of the "fragility of goodness" that emerges from the uneven relationship between "good action" and "luck" (Nussbaum 1986). It is from this problematic relationship that the pathos of myth emerges. Religions aim to resolve this problem at its very roots, whereas the work on myth stems from the variety of possible configurations of the relationship between "good" and "luck". In contrast to philosophy, which mainly deals with this problem by rational argumentation, myth deals with it by telling stories.

If myth has to provide significance within the changing circumstances of fortune, it has to be open to a process of retelling. Hence, the "plurality of myth", something that different authors – from Aristotle to Blumenberg – have emphasised. Myth is pluralistic not only in the sense that its meaning is given by the interplay between the narrators and receivers of myth, but also in the sense that what can provide significance, and thus be a myth for someone, may not be a myth for another person. As a consequence, there is also no definitive answer to the question of the concrete means by which significance can be created. There are many ways by which significance understood in this way can be generated and they cannot be limited to any single form or type of content.

In particular, the work on myth can take place through conscious work on it, but it can also be located at an unconscious level. The concept of significance escapes most of the dichotomies created by an enlightened reason: "myth" versus "reason"; "passions" versus "reason"; "consciousness" versus "unconsciousness". Myths, indeed, can be learned by conscious learning, but can also be learned by unconscious exposure to them.

The exposure to certain mythical narratives can influence how we perceive ourselves and the conditions of our existence, and can thus also influence our orientations within them. In this sense, myths are stories that always bring a moral with them: they can be more or less dramatic, but nonetheless, by making significance of certain conditions of life, they always display a certain pathos. This must not, however, be understood in purely passive terms. Myths can be the product and the producer of the most inflamed passions, but passions can also turn out to be simple "upheavals of thought" (Nussbaum 2001).

Myths do not operate in a vacuum. Blumenberg's concept of work on myth (*Arbeit am Mythos*) suggests precisely this: each variant of a myth, as well as each different *mythologem*, works on the ruins of pre-existing edifices. The pre-existing material is then directed towards new exigencies and transformed in order to give significance to the new circumstances through a process that Blumenberg called "*Umbesetzung*", or "reoccupation" (Blumenberg 1971).[8] The ways in which this can happen are innumerable. The return of the identical, linear sequences, proximity in time, correspondence in places, circularity in space, and so on, can all be ways of reproducing and creating significance.

For example, the power of the *mythologem* of Homer's *Odyssey* rested in the circularity of Ulysses' voyage. Having left his Ithaca for the Trojan war, he has to overcome all sorts of human and divine obstacles on his way back. Going through the different vicissitudes of fortune, his travelling delineates a circular process. It is from this circularity that a cathartic effect was derived.

But myths are recounted, and as far as they are told-received, they are also possibly told again. The Ulysses that we find in the *Divine Comedy* is a Ulysses who paid the God of the Christians the high price of

---

[8] On Blumenberg's concept of *Umbesetzung*, see Leghissa 2002: 23.

his return to Ithaca. Indeed, the fraudulent Ulysses who has suggested the stratagem of the horse to overcome the Trojan resistance and violated the limit of Herculean columns imposed by God would never see his faithful Penelope again and would eventually die, swallowed up by the sea (*Inferno*, XVIII). With this episode, Dante aimed to show the dangers hidden in an absolutism of human *hybris*, and the way to do so was to break the circularity of the Homeric *Odyssey*.

In a letter to Carlo Linati, James Joyce wrote that the intention of his *Ulysses* was to render the myth *sub specie temporis nostri* (Joyce 1957: 21 September 1920). The odyssey of the banal itinerary covered in one day in Dublin at the beginning of the twentieth century by Leopold Bloom seemed to recover the circularity of Homer's *Odyssey*, but, in fact, breaks it, while paradoxically apparently recovering it. Leopold Bloom would then go home, but, in a monologue by Molly Bloom, we know that Penelope is thinking about being unfaithful to her husband. The "work on myth" (*Arbeit am Mythos*) continues and the reassuring circularity of the old myth breaks up when occupied by different circumstances.

Consequently, when Mircea Eliade, following Nietzsche, identified myth with the eternal return, he was pointing to only one of the possible means for the work on myth. To make recourse to the circularity of the eternal return is, indeed, a way of reproducing significance, but it is only one of the possible ways, and cannot therefore be identified with myth *tout court*. According to Eliade, the main function of myth as an eternal return would be to fix the exemplary model for every human deed, like rituals, in a way such as to provide an ahistorical and atemporal model. In his view, it would be to this model that we could make recourse each time we had to do something for which the *empeiria* did not provide a guide (Eliade 1954).

However, not all myths are sites for a hierophany understood in this way. Not all myths are based on the eternal return of the identical, and not all myths are sacred myths. For instance, the myth of the foundation of Rome was a truly historical myth, in the sense that it referred to a peculiar and singular event in the profane world of history. There was some dispute, however, as to the date: Cato placed the founding of the city in 755 BC whereas Varro's more careful calculation placed it 753 BC. But the point remains that the city was founded not in the sacred world of primordial time, which is destined to return, but in the profane world of everyday life.[9]

Identifying myth with the eternal return of the identical is perhaps the consequence of having approached myth as the product of a primitive mentality. Myths have often been identified with magic and religious beliefs and practices, and thus have also often been assimilated with rituals under the general category of "primitive consciousness" (Cassirer 1977). The parallel myth-ritual has been pushed so far that the so-called ritualistic school defined myths as spoken correlatives of acted rites.[10]

The problem with this view is not just that it neglects the fact that, as has been observed, not all myths have a ritual origin or are associated with a significant corpus of rituals (Tudor 1972: 29). By conflating myth and ritual into a common category of mythical or primitive thinking, the danger is that the specificity of myth is completely overlooked. Myths are indeed the sign of a work on myth that is fostered by the need to provide significance in constantly changing circumstances, and it must therefore be open to the possibility of retelling. Rituals, in contrast, are literally what is "well done" or "done according to the rules" – from the Latin *rite*. Therefore, in order to be effective for the cohesion of a social group, myth and ritual must operate in opposite directions: rituals must be kept unchanged, while myths must continually change. When this is not possible, narratives simply cease to work as myths.

Rituals represent a stability and continuity that is acted out and re-enacted in a visible way. They imply a visible continuity. By dint of repetition they deny the passage of time, the nature of change, and the extent of indeterminacy in social relations (Moore 1975: 167). In contrast, the work on myth, in order to be effective, that is, in order to generate myths, and not simple narratives, must also be the work of significance within conditions that are given *hic et nunc*. In other words, myths are always situational and must therefore always be retold from the point of view of the *present*. This is, in the final analysis, what moves the whole work on myth (*Arbeit am Mythos*).

[9] For this critique of Eliade, see Tudor 1972: 62.
[10] We will come back to this point when discussing the relationships between political myth and rituals in Chapter 8 and 9.

The emphasis on the difference between myth and ritual is more the result of a phenomenological approach to myth than the application of functionalism. In particular, to adopt a functionalist approach at this stage would mean deciding upon the role of myth within politics from the very beginning. If one assumes with Malinowski, for instance, that myth supports and maintains the social state of affairs (Malinowski 1992), then there is no need to develop a philosophy of political myth. On the contrary, it is only after having established what a myth is that the issue of its relationship with politics can be properly dealt with.

The approach to myth sketched in this chapter can perhaps be better understood as "interpretative". Indeed, even if it does not presuppose a functional relationship between myth and the social-historical element, this approach moves from a theory of meaning that presupposes some kind of relationship between the two. Wittgenstein did not write the book on anthropology that he alluded to in his *Remarks on Frazer's Golden Bough*. The interpretative anthropology proposed by Geertz can perhaps be considered as an attempt to write such a book (Geertz 1973; 1983; 2000). Following Geertz's anthropology, we can say that myths – insofar as they have a meaning – presuppose a context and therefore a semiotic system within which only they can make sense and significance.

However, Geertz did not focus on the specificity of myth. As a consequence he did not elaborate on the distinction between meaning and significance. In contrast, the view of myth defended here is based on the assumption that not only do we need meanings to orient us in the world, but we also need significance to render the world less indifferent to us. The task of the next chapters is to investigate the consequence that this will have when it comes to political life and political circumstances.

III

POLITICAL MYTH

So far, we have seen that to approach myth from the point of view of its claim to truth, as is the case with most contemporary theories of political myth, means to bring myth to a terrain that is not its own. In particular, the genealogy sketched in Part I has shown that this entails an approach to myth from the point of view of an absolute truth, to which only a unique God or an enlightened reason can aspire. In order to avoid the traps of the dialectic of the sacred *logos* and of the Enlightenment, which condemn myth as untrue and unreal, Part II proposed the adoption of an interrelational and phenomenological approach to myth. Myth, as we have seen, is best understood as a process involving a multiplicity of subjects, a process of continual work that responds to a perpetually changing need for significance. Human beings need names to orient themselves in the world, but they also need significance in order to live in a world less indifferent to them.

At first sight, one may think that such a human need would tend to wither away under conditions of modernity. The process of modernisation has deeply transformed European societies, as well as the relationship that human beings have with one another, and with society as a whole. One could therefore assume that the affirmation of a rational orientation of action, a highly developed social differentiation and an increased secularisation have brought about a condition in which there is no longer any need for mythological narratives: in the modern epoch, it is the rational Copernican man who, against any absolutism of the tradition, is the subject of the process of legitimation.

History has disavowed this self-presentation of modernity. Myth has always reccurred in Western civilisation — and the more powerful the attack against it, the more disruptive the forms in which it has reappeared. While the eighteenth century Enlightenment's critique of myth did not deny the legitimacy of the need from which myth stemmed, nineteenth century positivism, by denying as meaningless any enquiry that is not subsumable to the principle of verification, denied legitimacy to this very need. As a consequence, it favoured the return of myth without mediation, that is, myth as has been used by totalitarian regimes (Blumenberg 1985).

Modernity has not diminished the need from which myth stems. Rather, it can be argued that it has actually enhanced this need. To put it in Weberian terms, the old peasant may well die "fulfilled by life", having completed the circle of biological life, but the civilised human being, who is inserted in a never-ending process, one that transcends him or her and about which he or she is able to understand only a very limited part (Weber 2004: 13), is destined to feel a greater need for significance. The process of disenchantment (*Entzauberung*) implies an increased intellectualisation, which, on the one hand, reflects the human awareness of being able to master the world, but, on the other, given the high level of specialisation of knowledge, also means an increased distance from the possibility of understanding the conditions under which we live. To use another Weberian example, while the savages know how the instruments they use in their everyday life work, we are surrounded by many objects and means that we depend on and whose mechanisms are completely unknown to us (Weber 2004: 13ff.); hence the possibility of an increased distance from the world and, consequently, also an increased need for significance.

It comes as no surprise then that it is precisely in the conditions of modernity that the role played by political myth becomes conspicuous. The complexity of modern societies, the rapid change that they have undergone by transcending the individual's space of experience, has rendered more acute the need for a symbolic mediation of political experience. Complex and vast political phenomena that transcend the individual's horizon of experience need to be imagined even more in order to be experienced. The concept of political myth points to the fact that this imaginary mediation can also take the form of a narrative that coagulates and reproduces significance, that is, the form of a myth.

Myth, however, must not be understood as a regression into superstition. By criticising Bayle's approach, considered as paradigmatic of the Enlightenment's attitude towards myth, and by analysing the role played by the myth of the state of nature, in Chapter 7 I argue that myth can play an important part in the critique of political reason. There is therefore no a priori reason to condemn myth.

This does not mean that political myths are always a means for critique or for progress. On the contrary, the subsequent discussion of the classical theories of political myth, in Chapter 8, shows that political myths can be a means for critique and progress (Sorel) as well as for the most annihilating forms of domination (Cassirer). This, in the end, will depend on the specific circumstances in which the myth operates. A philosophy of political myth can only say, with Spinoza, that, if all societies rely in one way or another on political imagination, what they differ in is the degree to which this imaginary dimension can be subjected to critical discussion.

However, what was missing in the classical theories of political myth was a specific focus on political myth as a process rather than as an object. By applying Blumenberg's concept of myth as work on myth, in Chapter 9 I argue that a political myth is best defined as the work on a common narrative by which the members of a social group (or society), so to speak, make significance of their experience and deeds. In this sense, political myths are a normal component of modern political life, together with ideology and utopias, with which they sometimes overlap but from which, however, they must be kept distinct.

7

Myth and the Critique of Political Reason

The aim of Bayle's *Various Thoughts on the Occasion of a Comet* (2000) was to undermine the influence of superstition in politics. To this end, by criticising the view of comets as presages of misfortune, he made his notorious claim that a decent society of atheists is possible: sound political life does not require religious beliefs and it might even be harmed by them. This claim, revolutionary for his epoch, was advanced with every precaution possible, and the book was first published anonymously.

According to Bayle, when events are reduced to their natural causes, they no longer warn us of anything, and this deprives the people of an infinite number of "vain imaginings", the diviners of a considerable part of their employment, and the statesmen of the possibility of taking advantage of these events (Bayle 2000: 141). Statesmen have fomented these beliefs in all times because, as Bayle clearly states, "nothing is as powerful as superstition for keeping the populace in check. However unruly and inconstant they may be, if their minds are once struck by a vain image of religion, they will obey the diviners better than their chiefs" (Bayle 2000: 99).

The strategy adopted to undermine the role of superstition in politics is thus twofold. First, Bayle argues that the beliefs in presages are ill-founded because, if we analyse the phenomenon of comets with an "altogether pure reason", we see that there is nothing in them that links them with the advent of fortunes and misfortunes: the link between their happening and any sort of calamity is purely imaginary and stems from people's natural inclination to treat the slightest thing as a presage (Bayle 2000: 97–8, 141). Second, Bayle points to the danger of these beliefs for a sound political life. Here, he advances the claim that a decent society of atheists is possible. In the part devoted to arguing "that atheism is not a greater evil than idolatry" (144–240), Bayle, with his usual technique of disguising himself, gradually leads the reader to the conclusion that atheism is superior to both idolatry and biblical worship. To this end, Bayle argues that religious beliefs do not constitute a brake on human behaviour, because human beings act according to their passions and not their opinions, so that "both [atheists and Christians] could never constitute a society if a brake stronger than that of religion, namely human laws, did not repress their perversity" (159). Furthermore, he suggests, religious beliefs might even undermine the possibility of a decent political life; both idolatry and biblical worship, in his view, have led human beings to commit atrocities that they would never have committed had they not been filled with religious zeal. Referring to the civil strife that followed the conversion of Henry IV, Bayle goes as far as to affirm: that had the Court of France been atheistic, it would never have maintained such conduct (193ff.).

Bayle argues that it is human law, and thus coercion, that makes society possible, because human beings are prey to their passions (171), and then also points to all the atrocities that have been committed in the name of religion (193ff, 242ff.). Hence, he can conclude that "a society of atheists would perform civil and moral actions as much as other societies do, provided that it punishes crimes severely and that it attaches honour and infamy to certain things" (212). In his view, neither the possibility of a society nor that of morality is undermined by atheism: it is human law that holds society together, and morality rests upon the idea of decency, which does not depend on a belief in God, because decency is rooted in human nature. An atheist, Bayle observes, is certainly capable of returning a deposit when he sees that his good faith will earn him the praise of a whole city and that his infidelity could one day subject him to reproach (223).

Bayle's criticism of superstition is paradigmatic of the Enlightenment's attitude towards the role of religious beliefs in politics: a decent political life does not require religious beliefs and might even be harmed by them. According to some critics, Bayle's criticism shows how high the stakes are in deriding the Enlightenment and its political achievements. We see in Bayle's words something of what the world was before the rise of modern political philosophy, that is, we see that: "absent the appeal to reason, the world teems with miracles and malevolent spirits". Thus – so this view concludes – those who celebrate the collapse of reason on the grounds that it will give rise to a more thorough toleration of all "difference" or "otherness" should be aware that this will, in all likelihood, give rise to religious superstitions (Bartlett 2000: xxiv).

Despite all the evidence to the contrary, let us admit for the moment that modern political philosophy has actually succeeded in liberating politics from "miracles and malevolent spirits". The problem still remains, as Bayle himself points out in many places, that this appeal to "an altogether pure reason" (Bayle 2000: 18) deprives human beings of an infinite number of "vain imaginings". These images, as Bayle recognises, stem from the natural inclination of human beings to form images and to see in certain events signs for something else. Myths, those particular narratives that answer a need for significance, are also among the products of this natural inclination.

Now, if the religious beliefs that Bayle criticises do come from this imaginary faculty, for it is not possible to believe in religious dogmas without imagining them, certainly not all the images that this faculty produces are religious. In particular, not all the images that, in Bayle's terms, may appear "vain" to an "altogether pure reason" are necessarily superstition, that is, heteronymously given beliefs.

The problem is that the Enlightenment, in its attempt to ground political life on the autonomy of the individual and the critique of tradition, has unified all that is not grounded in pure reason under the heading of "superstition" and, in so doing, has assimilated all the "vain images" to religious superstition. But there is no such dichotomy as "pure reason" versus "religious superstition". There is much more inbetween. Myth certainly escapes this dichotomy, since it cannot be reduced to "pure reason". On the other hand, this does not mean that myths are superstitious beliefs. Indeed, there are myths that are religious myths, but not all myths are religious.

To put it bluntly, religion is always a matter of life and death (Cassirer 1973: 48), while a myth is not necessarily so. The need for significance (*Bedeutsamkeit*) from which myth stems is not merely need for meaning (*Sinnfrage*), but it is also not necessarily the question about the ultimate meaning of life and death (*Seinsfrage*). While religion, by providing an answer to the ultimate question, tends towards a closure of meaning, that is, to reinterpreting all that happens (*e-venit*) within its categories, a myth is not necessarily so, precisely because it does not necessarily aim at a closure. Myths, as narratives aimed to answer a need for significance, must be open to the possibility of changing in accordance with the changing circumstances and the new needs that these circumstances generate.

Thus, even if modern reason has undermined the role of religious beliefs as the horizon of sense in the experience of the world in general, and of politics in particular, it has not undermined the role of myth. Even if modern political philosophy has detached politics from its transcendental anchorage in the great chain of being, this does not imply that it has also denied any possible recourse to mythical narratives. In fact, as we shall see, it does not need to do so.

It seems as if the reason that is at work in modern political discourses can hardly be described as an "altogether pure reason" from this point of view. The aim of this chapter is to show that even modern contractualism, which, it has been claimed, represents the apex of the struggle of political theory against myth (Cassirer 1973: 13), has had recourse to mythical narratives. These narratives, however, do not represent a premodern residual. As we will see, they can also play an important part in the critique.

Social contract theorists are usually credited with having provided a purely rational foundation of political power. In contrast to mainstream medieval political theory, the necessity of a common power is not derived here from the *Sacred History*, but from the *will* of individual human beings. In the post-Galilean clockwork universe, the existence of a polity is no longer a ring in the great chain of being, but simply a human artefact.

The great revolution behind the idea of a "social contract" is that the existence of a political power can now only appear as justified on the basis of the will of individual human beings. According to some scholars, this revolution has also brought with it a dismissal of myth. For instance, according to Cassirer, by dissipating the mystery surrounding the origins of the polity and linking them back to the will of individuals, social contract theorists have also succeeded in getting rid of myth (Cassirer 1973: 13).

Hence, according to the self-presentation of an enlightened reason, one would indeed expect to find no traces of myth in social contract theories, but only the working of a pure reason. Hobbes, for instance, after having laid the foundations of the rights of the sovereign power and of the subjects in the commonwealth, claims to have derived them from the "Principles of Nature onely [*sic*]; such as Experience has found true, or Consent (concerning the use of words) has made so" (Hobbes 1985: 409). It is only when moving on to handle the nature of a *Christian* commonwealth that Hobbes admits the need to refer to the supernatural revelations of the will of God, and then to the tales told by the prophets.

Thus, when analysing the first two parts of *Leviathan*, we would indeed expect to see only our natural reason at work – where reason, according to Hobbes, is the faculty that does nothing else but conceive a total sum from the addition of the parts; or conceive a remainder from the subtraction of one sum from another. When it comes to words, reason is therefore the faculty of conceiving of the consequences of the names of all the parts to the name of the whole or from the names of the whole and one part, to the name of the other part (Hobbes 1985: 110). However, if we analyse the overall reasoning concerning the justification of sovereign power, we do not see such a pure reason at work.

In fact, a great narrative triggers the mechanism of political obligation, that is, the necessity of being in awe of sovereign power – the narrative of the state of nature. According to Hobbes, human beings are driven to institute a sovereign power in order to escape the state in which human beings naturally are, which is a state of perpetual (potential) war. In such a condition every human being is a potential *lupus* for the other (*homo homini lupus*), so that any single human being is equally exposed to the possibility of death (Hobbes 1985: 183ff.). Once the state of nature is depicted in such a way, the next step in the argument consists of showing how natural reason prescribes each man to exit from that state (Hobbes 1985: 189ff.). While in this second moment it is only a pure reason that is at work, that is, a Hobbesian reason that merely calculates the consequences of living in such a state and then prescribes exit from it, the reason that creates the narrative of the state of nature is not a pure reason. As we will see, there are many signs that suggest that this narrative has also worked as a myth.

The recourse to a mythical narrative within philosophical theory should not come as a surprise. Recent theories, in particular, have emphasised that philosophers in their rational theorising have also had recourse to images, metaphors, narratives, and even myths. Among the mythological narratives that have played a major role among political philosophers, there has been the idea of a "state of nature" (Midgley 2003). A detailed analysis of the use of the narrative of the state of nature in contemporary political theory has, for instance, suggested that this narrative, which is indeed presented as a device of "pure reason", is, in fact, not so "pure": it would be better to say that it works to a great extent like a myth (La Caze 2002: 94–118).[1]

This is not to say that interpretations of the Hobbesian state of nature as a mental experiment, or even as a rational device, are misplaced.[2] It simply means that they only comprehend one aspect of the function that this narrative can play. To put it plainly, only a reason caught in the dialectic of the Enlightenment can assume a dichotomy of myth versus reason so that when reason is at work there is no space for myth. Indeed, there is, in principle, no reason to assume that within a philosophical system that presents itself as based on rational inferences there can be no space for myth.

Hobbes, together with most other social contract theorists, explicitly claims that his state of nature must be understood as a rational device, an "inference made from the theory of passions" (Hobbes 1985: 183ff.). All the same, if we look at myth as a process and we move on to analyse the way in which the image of the state of nature works, it seems that not only does this image take the form of narrative, but also that this narrative comes from and, at the same time, generates a series of figures, images and symbols that answer to what we have called a need for significance. In other words, it seems as if this narrative works as a myth.

In order to see whether the state of nature is a myth or not, we must not take the myth as an object and look at its content. Even if

---

[1] La Caze focuses her attention precisely on the "analytic imaginary", that is, on the repertoire of images, metaphors and myths recurring in the writings of contemporary analytic philosophers. In particular, she suggests that Rawls' narrative of the "veil of ignorance" and the "original position" work as a myth (La Caze 2002: 94).

[2] See for instance the classical work by Kavka (1986), who interprets Hobbes' view in terms of rational choice theory.

Hobbes had conceived of the state of nature as a historical event, as
Locke was to do, it could still be argued that it worked as a myth.[3]
Indeed, it is at the whole work on the myth, that is, at the way in which
this narrative was told and received, that we must look. This, first and
foremost, implies that even if the state of nature only works as a rational
device for a contemporary reader, it was not necessarily so for Hobbes'
contemporaries. Significance, as we have seen, is always positional.

After describing the state of nature, Hobbes continues by saying
that for those who do not trust his view of the state of nature because
it might appear strange to them that nature should dissociate, and
render men apt to invade, and destroy one another, it can be shown
that experience itself confirms this inference (Hobbes 1985: 183ff.).
When confronted with the possible objection that there was never a
time or condition of war such as he is depicting, Hobbes replies that
even if there has never been such a condition, there are people that live
now in such a "brutish manner": these are the "savages" of America.

Why did Hobbes need to make reference to the "savages" of America
if he only wanted to build a rational device? Hobbes does not just refer
to the peoples of America. He qualifies their way of life with precise
terms:

in such condition, there is no place for Industry; . . . no Culture of the Earth,
no Navigation, nor use of commodities that may be imported by Sea; no com-
modious Building; no Instruments of moving, and removing such things as
require much force; no Knowledge of the face of the Earth; no account of
Time; no Arts; no Letters, no Society; and which is worst of all, continuall
feare, and danger of violent death; And the life of man, solitary, poore, nasty,
brutish, and short (Hobbes 1985: 186).

The words Hobbes used to describe the "savages" of America recall
a whole work on the narrative of an original state of humankind that
had begun much earlier and that received a new powerful emotional
appeal with the discovery of the "New World". In particular, the construction of the image of the "savage" through a series of negations
was almost a topos of the time. By the time of Hobbes' writings, this
was a cliché in the literature – mostly made up of travel reports, novels

---

[3] As we will see, most modern political myths stem from historical narratives, that is,
from narratives that present themselves as historical events. Examples are the myth of
the French Revolution and the myth of the Italian Resistance.

and philosophical treatises. In the second half of the seventeenth century the stereotype of the "savage" became fixed in a definition that was repeated in dictionaries such as that of the French Academy published in Paris in 1694.[4]

The origins of the topos of the *homines sylvestri* go back to the large number of reports from the exploration of the "New World" that started circulating at the beginning of the sixteenth century and, by Hobbes' time, were already a widespread literary genre. In particular, it is to the native populations of North America that the topos refers since the inhabitants of regions such as Central America and Peru, who did not live naked and had constructed stone buildings, were considered to be more civilised populations. The natives of North America, in contrast, continually at war with each other, appeared to be the real "savages", the bottom of the civilisational scale.

As Landucci points out, it is around the figure of the savage that the results of the first experience of a radical diversity crystallised; the shock of their discovery was so deep that some authors of the time saw in it the source of all speculation in moral and political philosophy (Landucci 1972: 20). Indeed, in whatever way the savages' ways of life were evaluated, positively or negatively, it still remains that the characterisation was made in terms of their radical difference.

Both when it is seen as the first expression of the discontent of civilised Europeans (Freud 1989), and when it is seen as the complex of the superiority of the European colonisers (Gliozzi 1977), the image of the savage is recognised as a very powerful source of significance. The discovery of America was indeed an enormous shock that needed to be digested by Europeans and the figure of the "savage" brought together the emotional replies of the European. As Pagden has pointed out, the different variants of the figure of the savage can be read as attempts to reposition the "oneiric horizon"[5] of an original state of humankind in different spaces and times: the dream was expanded to a vision of a world in which a different kind of life was lived, and in which taboos were eliminated or exchanged for others (Pagden 2000: xviii)

---

[4] For what follows, see Landucci 1972, and Pagden 1982; 2000.
[5] Pagden recovers here Le Goff's concept of "oneiric horizon". See, in particular, Le Goff 2000.

Thus, it is not by chance that Hobbes' passage, which makes a long list of the arts that locate human beings *supra conditionem caeterorum animalium* (above the conditions of other animals) and the Europeans above the savage, is almost a topos in his writings. The figure of the savage is a very powerful image that mobilised extremely rich resources of significance, as is suggested by the literature of the time. Despite the fact that some authors have contested the importance of the figure of the savage in Hobbes' theory by saying that his men in the state of nature are not primitive men,[6] the savage does play a crucial role for Hobbes, who continuously exhibits him, from the *Elements* to *De Cive* and *Leviathan*, as *exemplum* of his state of nature. However, what is of most importance in reconstructing the work on this myth is that this figure played a fundamental role for Hobbes's audience, for whom the reference to the state of nature was not only "a purely rational device", but also recalled the whole work on this myth.

The narrative dimension of the state of nature can take different forms. While for authors such as Rousseau this condition was completely lost, for Hobbes and his contemporaries the state of nature was also a condition into which human beings could always return, if they did not stand in awe of a common power. In particular, the descriptions of the continual state of intertribal wars, which impressed all travellers, echoed the shock of the recent European civil wars for Hobbes and his contemporaries.[7] Hence, the natural condition of the savages was characterised in a completely negative way. The state of nature was depicted as a "brutish manner of living" because it lacked all that Hobbes held as praiseworthy in the world in which he lived, a world he perceived as being in danger in the religious civil wars: peace, first and foremost, and then industry, culture, navigation, comfortable buildings, knowledge and an account of time (Hobbes 1985: 186–7). In other words, the savages were what the Europeans were not, or, rather, what they no longer were because they have left the state of nature (Landucci 1972; Padgen 1982; 2000).

As a result, the state of nature has a crucial function in grounding – in the sense of the German *begründen* – the present state of things

---

[6] See, in particular, the classical interpretations by Warrender and Macpherson (Warrender 1957: 143; Macpherson 1964: 18–29).

[7] This state of war appeared as reasonless to the first explorers. We now know that they were most probably wars for the division of hunting territories (Landucci 1972).

for the "civilised Europeans". This grounding, however, is not only achieved by a pure reason calculating abstract consequences, but also by inserting the advent of civil society into a narrative that coagulates significance: chaos at the beginning, and then order.

The fact that the narrative of the state of nature also worked as a myth is not a premodern residual. The fact that a political theory can also be the site of the work on myth does not mean that it has failed in its attempt to ground politics on the autonomy of individuals. Myth, indeed, does not necessarily imply heteronomy and can also be a means for critique.

The best way to show the manner in which the myth of the state of nature can, and indeed has been, a means for questioning is, perhaps, to reconstruct the changes it has undergone. In particular, it is in Rousseau's utilisation of myth that this is most evident. As we have seen, the opposition of chaos and cosmos is perhaps one of the most typical narrative schemes for recreating significance. Rousseau substantially modifies this twofold scheme by adding a third dimension to the *mythologem* of the state of nature/civil society, in the form of a different point of departure. In this way, he introduces a further element of the critique towards modernity: by recalling the work on the myth of a happy original state of nature he gives expression to a widespread discontent of civilisation.

Despite the fact that it is very difficult to reconstruct the different phases of the exit from the state of nature described in his *Discourse on the Origin and Foundations of Inequality Among Men*, it appears legitimate to state that, in his thinking, the narrative scheme of the state of nature is a threefold one: no longer, as in Hobbes, a linear passage from chaos to cosmos, but a passage from the *cosmos* of the primeval state of nature to *chaos* following the exit from that state and towards the possible reconstitution of a *cosmos* through the institution of a social contract.

Human beings, according to Rousseau, are not naturally driven to a war of everybody against everybody: philosophers such as Hobbes, who depicted them in this way, thought they were describing savages but, in fact, were depicting civilised human beings (Rousseau 1997a, 151). What authors such as Hobbes depicted are human beings who are dependent on each other because they have many needs, and are therefore prey to violent passions. But these are not savages, who, according to Rousseau, have such limited needs and moderate passions that they are completely independent of each other, and are, therefore,

genuinely free. Rousseau's savages live a solitary life, and have very basic
needs that they can easily satisfy with the help of nature; as a consequence, they have calm passions and very sporadic contacts with each
other (1997a: 142). Far from being in a condition of war of everybody
against everybody, this state of nature is a condition of peace from
which human beings can exit only as a consequence of an unhappy
series of fortuitous circumstances such as the institution of private
property (1997a: 139, 164).[8]

In this way, Rousseau sharply questions the idea of a linear progress
from chaos to order. On the other hand, it can be held that, by neglecting the mythical nature of this narrative, he still has one foot in the
presuppositions of the Enlightenment, which assumes that, where reason is at work, there can be no space for myth. Indeed, at different
points, Rousseau claims that the state of nature must be understood as
a rational device. He clearly states that "the enquiries that may be pursued regarding this subject ought not to be taken for historical truths,
but only for hypothetical and conditional reasoning, better suited to
elucidate the nature of things than to show their genuine origin, and
comparable to those our physicists daily make regarding the formation
of the world" (1997a: 132). Now, if the reference to "only hypothetical
and conditional reasoning" leaves space for interpreting this construction as a myth, with this reference to the discourses of the physicians
he seems to deny the mythical side of the idea of a state of nature.

All the same, it can be argued that what he does is precisely to
contribute to the work on the myth of the state of nature. By adding a
new moment to the narrative scheme of chaos and cosmos, Rousseau
gives a new interpretation to the narrative of the state of nature and
thus a new grounding (*begründen*) to the civil society (*société civile*) that
emerges with the exit from this state. By doing so, Rousseau is not only,
as he claims, raising a chain of hypothetical and rational reasoning in
his readers, he is also raising a whole series of images, figures and
narratives that respond to a need for significance.

Thus, it is not by chance that the referent changes, too. Instead
of referring to the savages of North America, Rousseau's referent is

---

[8] In the first part of the second *Discourse* Rousseau talks of the exit from the state of
nature as a "singular and fortuitous concatenations of circumstances, . . . which could
very well never have occurred" (Rousseau 1997a: 139).

the people of the Caribbean, who, in his view, of all existing people, had deviated least from the state of nature (Rousseau 1997a: 156). Rousseau refers continuously to this *exemplum*, in one instance to say that, despite their nakedness, they do not fear other animals because they have developed all their faculties, so that they have never been eaten by ferocious beasts; in another instance, that they live in perfect calm and that their passions are so calm that, despite the hot climate in which they live, they are less subject to violent passions and jealousy; and in another, that, as a consequence of their very limited basic needs, they have not developed reason, so that they sell their cotton bed in the morning and come back and cry to have it back in the evening, because they could not even foresee that they might need it again.

By referring to the "savages", reinterpreted in this way, Rousseau could fundamentally reinterpret the self-narrative of modernity. In this view, modernity does not represent a linear progress from chaos to order but, first of all, an exit from a state of freedom and peace in order to enter one of dependence and disorder. This narrative thus recalls an entire series of images and symbols that give expression to the discontent of civilisation – at least for the readers of the time. In particular, the image of the happy savage depicted in his writings could not but evoke the oneiric horizon of a paradise lost and, as a consequence, the whole work on myth that has taken place around this narrative. To sum up, he refers to a myth and he does so in order to contribute to a critique of modernity.

Rousseau's attitude towards modernity is, however, more ambivalent.[9] In his view, once the exit from such a primeval state of nature has taken place,[10] one way to recover the same freedom that human beings enjoyed there is by means of political freedom. According to

[9] One of the points where this ambivalence is most evident is Rousseau's view of civil religion. After having constructed all his theory on the principle of individual freedom, Rousseau ends his *Social Contract* by saying that it is impossible to be a good citizen without a civil religion, whose dogmas include the belief in the existence of God (Rousseau 1997b: 150–1).

[10] By primeval state of nature, I mean the condition in which human beings are at their very beginning, which is described in the first part of the second *Discourse*, in order to distinguish it from the condition in which they find themselves after the introduction of private property, which is described in the second part of the *Discourse*: the error made by Hobbes and others who followed him was to take this condition, which is already a degenerated one, to be the original state of nature (Rousseau 1997a).

his *Social Contract*, through the institution of such a contract, human beings each give themselves to everybody and then to nobody, recovering thus a new form of freedom. In this way, they are only subjected to the general will and therefore cease to depend on the will of other single individuals (Rousseau 1997b: 49ff.). This, in the *Social Contract*, is said to be the only moral freedom, because it is the only freedom that renders human beings masters of themselves. According to Rousseau, "the impulsion of mere appetite is slavery, and obedience to the law one has prescribed to oneself is freedom" (1997b: 54).

Notwithstanding his critique towards modernity, Rousseau seems to argue that only through subjection to the law as an expression of the general will can human beings, properly speaking, be autonomous, that is, free. And, as we have seen in Chapter 3, this identification of freedom with subjection to the law is indeed paradigmatic of the Enlightenment.[11]

This alternative between the autonomy of a general law and the heteronomy (and thus the serfdom), which Rousseau formulated at the political level, was proposed again by Kant in both the moral and the political dimension. It is well known that Rousseau deeply influenced Kant's moral and political thinking.[12] In particular, Kant followed Rousseau in interpreting freedom as autonomy, that is, as giving the law to oneself. In *Perpetual Peace*, for instance, after criticising as an "empty tautology" the view of political freedom as a warrant to do whatever one wishes unless this means doing injustice to others (*arbitrium*), he states that "external and rightful freedom should be defined as a warrant to obey no external laws except those to which I have been able to give my own consent" (Kant 1991d: 99).

This identification of autonomy with the autonomy of a pure reason that follows a universal law is paradigmatic of the project of Enlightenment. On the other hand, as I want to show, not even Kant's political theory is completely "pure" from mythical elements.

[11] Here I am referring only to the theory exposed in the *Social Contract*. As many interpreters have noticed, together with the political way described by the *Social Contract*, there is for Rousseau also another road to recover freedom. This is the private way, which is described in other works such as the *Nouvelle Héloïse* and *Émile*. See, for instance, Taylor 1989: 294–7, 356–70, or Pulcini 2001: 90–126.
[12] As many commentators have shown, Kant's political thinking is dependent on his moral thinking, because it depends on the categorical imperative. On this point, see Kersting 1992, and Bottici 2003 and 2004.

Kant's view explicitly posits the issue of autonomy as the basic principle of any rightful state.[13] In his *Metaphysics of Morals*, he presents his system of right as derived from a priori principles of reason. The concept of right, defined as "the sum of the conditions under which the choice of one can be united with the choice of another in accordance with a universal law of freedom" (Kant 1991b: 56), is derived via progressive qualifications from the concept of obligation, or the categorical imperative which, in turn, is elaborated in the *Critique of Practical Reason* (1998). In his view, an autonomous reason is a reason that takes its principles from itself. There are no other ways to autonomy. This view, as we have seen, can only bring with it a condemnation of myth.

But, in fact, if we move on to analyse the way in which the necessity of the institution of a lawful condition is established, once more we do not see a "pure reason" at work. Kant, like the other natural law theorists, refers to the category of social contract and the correlated image of the state of nature. In Kant's political writings, too, there is a narrative of the exit from the state of nature and the creation of a politically lawful condition. And it can be shown that this narrative works to a certain extent as a myth.

Kant insists on neglecting the mythical side of his state of nature even more than do Hobbes and Rousseau. He explicitly states that the state of nature must not be understood as a historical fact, since a fact drawn from experience could never, in his view, generate a right: the social contract is said to be an "an *a priori* idea of reason" (Kant 1991c: 79).[14] For instance, in *Metaphysics of Morals*, he affirms that

It is therefore not some fact that makes coercion through public law necessary. On the contrary, however well disposed and law-abiding man might be, it still lies a priori in the rational idea of such a condition (one that is not rightful) that before a public lawful condition is established, individual men, peoples, and states can never be secure against violence from one another, since each has its own right to do what seems right and good to it and not to be dependent upon another's opinion about this. (Kant 1991b: 123–4)

But how could reason state that each human being has the right to do whatever seems right and good to him or her? What tells us that

---

[13] See, in particular, his definition of the concept of right in the *Metaphysics of Morals* as derived from that of freedom (Kant 1991b: 48ff.).

[14] On this point, see Bottici 2003; 2004.

this is not pure reason, but a reason that refers to the narrative of the state of nature? From the way in which he describes this condition, it is clear that Kant refers to this narrative with the awareness that what this narrative evokes in his audience is not a "pure" chain of rational reasoning.

As is well known, Kant depicts this condition not as a Hobbesian condition of war of all against all, but as a condition in which right is only provisory (Kant 1991b: 77ff.). This remains an unlawful condition because right cannot be secured: human beings must, therefore, leave this condition because a "civil society", that is, a society that can guarantee the mine and thine through public laws, cannot exist in such a natural state (Kant 1991b: 67). The term *civil* is here counterpoised to the condition of the state of nature, which is the condition in which the *savages* live. Thus, in Kant, too, there is not only the narrative scheme of the passage from a natural condition to a civil society, but also the reference to the contraposition of the "civilised men" and the "savages" that we have seen playing a fundamental role in both Hobbes and Rousseau. And the way in which he uses it suggests that for both Kant and his readers this narrative not only evoked rational reasoning, but also constituted a powerful font of significance that grounded – in the sense of *begründen* – the identity of the "civilised Europeans".[15]

In *Perpetual Peace*, Kant describes the condition of the savages as that of a "lawless freedom", or "freedom of folly", as counterpoised to the "freedom of reason", for "they [the savages] would prefer rather to engage in incessant strife than submit to a legal constraint which they might impose upon themselves" (Kant 1991d: 102–3). Kant is well aware of the power that the figure of the savage evoked and has no doubt that his reader will have a similar reaction. As he openly puts it, "we regard [savages' behaviour] as barbarism, coarseness, and brutish debasement of humanity" (Kant 1991d: 103). In other words, it is by evoking the passionate contempt of his reader for the "savages" that Kant hoped to persuade his audience of the necessity of a social contract between states.

---

[15] On the dichotomy of "savage" versus "civil", see, in particular, Landucci 1972 and Padgen 1982; 2000.

Thus, even Kant, the advocate of the autonomy of pure reason, when elaborating his system of morals, leaves space for the work on the myth of the state of nature. However, by identifying the critique with the pureness of reason and autonomy with the law, he seems to deny any legitimacy to myth as part of the critique. On the other hand, it can be argued that, it is the very identification of autonomy with pure reason that is fundamentally problematic.

As we have seen, not all myths are religious myths. Quite on the contrary, what characterises myth is precisely its plurality, that is, the plurality that stems from the work on myth, from the fact that, having to ground a world subject to change, myth has to be open to a process of continual retelling. In this work on myth, which questions its own products, one can see a possible means for critique. The previous analysis of the way in which the *mythologem* of the state of nature changed and worked as a means for critique is an example of the possibility of combining myth and the quest for autonomy.

Autonomy must not be identified with following the moral law given by reason. Kant arrives at this view of autonomy through the series of corresponding dichotomies that emerge throughout the *Critique of Practical Reason*: particular maxims versus universal law, material principle versus formal principle of action, inclinations versus reason, pleasure versus duty, heteronomy versus autonomy (Kant 1993). Kant encompasses not only religious morals, but also, for instance, all the moralities of pleasure in the heteronomy. In his view, a person who follows his or her own inclinations acts in a heteronymous way. It is only by subjecting oneself to the categorical imperative of the law that a person can be autonomous. The problem here is the identification of inclinations with something that is necessarily heteronymous. In what sense, we may ask, are inclinations the discourse of an "other" as much as the words prescribed by an omnipotent God can be said to be the discourse of the other?

We cannot here explore the details of a discussion of Kant's view of autonomy and the shortcomings of the dualistic view of human beings that it presupposes. It is, however, sufficient to point to the limited character of such a view. The possibility of autonomy does not necessarily mean pureness of reason. Autonomy literally means giving oneself one's own laws, that is, self-rule. The mistake of the Enlightenment is precisely to have identified all that is not grounded on an altogether pure reason with heteronomy and superstition. However, returning to Bayle, it can be sustained that a "mythical" society of atheists is not only possible but also desirable.

This does not mean that myth is always a means for critique. While discussing classical theories of political myth, the next chapter will also further discuss this point. A political myth is not always a form of regression, as Cassirer argued, nor a form of progress, as Sorel seems to suggest. Rather, as Spinoza points out, political myths can be a means for both, depending on the circumstances in which they, operate and, in particular, on the degree to which they are subjected to critical discussion.

8

Classical Theories of Political Myth

If modern political theory has, to a great extent, neglected the role that myth plays in politics, there has been a moment in European history when this role became tragically conspicuous. The massive use made by totalitarianism of political symbols and myths, and the achievements reached by this, not only manifestly exhibited the power of myth, but also posed a major intellectual problem for those intellectuals who had believed in the Enlightenment's promise of a liberation of politics from myth.

The first book in Western political philosophy that, from the very title, promised to deal with a modern political myth was published in 1946: it was Cassirer's posthumous *The Myth of the State*. The man Ernst Cassirer, a German of Jewish origin, who had left his homeland just after the advent of Nazism, could not but perceive the morally tragic challenge posed by the "appearance of a new power: the power of mythical thought" (Cassirer 1973: 3). The philosopher Cassirer, who had spent most of his intellectual life developing a theory of the symbolic forms in which myth was presented as a primitive form of consciousness, also appeared to feel the intellectual challenge, as did other theorists educated in the school of the Enlightenment.[1]

---

[1] Cassirer is, in the first place, one of the major representatives of the so-called neo-Kantian Marburg School, which identifies a series of intellectual trends that drew inspiration from Kant's thinking in the late-nineteenth and early-twentieth centuries. Beyond his major work, *The Philosophy of Symbolic Forms* (1977), Cassirer is also the author of a monograph on Kant's life and theory (1981) and of an essay called the *Philosophy of Enlightenment* (1951).

The *Myth of the State* begins:

> In the last thirty years we have not only passed through a severe crisis of
> our political and social life but have also been confronted with quite new
> theoretical problems.... If we look at the present state of our cultural life we
> feel at once that there is a deep chasm between two different fields. When
> it comes to political action man seems to follow rules quite different from
> those recognised in all his mere theoretical activities.... Scientific knowledge
> and technical mastery of nature daily win new and unprecedented victories.
> But in man's practical and social life the defeat of rational thought seems
> to be complete and irrevocable. In this domain modern man is supposed to
> forget everything he has learned in the development of his intellectual life.
> He is admonished to go back to the first rudimentary stages of human culture.
> (Cassirer 1973: 3–4)

In Cassirer's view, myth is not just a simple way of thinking or
speaking: myth, in his view, is a whole form of life (*Lebensform*). As such,
Cassirer's myth encompasses all that anthropologists have described
using such different names as magic, religious practice and belief, worship and ritual (Krois 1979: 199). In this ensemble there is no space
for a distinction between myth, religion and ritual: "myth" became
the general name for all these beliefs and practices; and it is in them
that Cassirer identifies the form of life (*Lebensform*) that holds together
primitive societies.

In Cassirer's view, the difference between modern and traditional
societies is precisely the difference between a community (*Gemein-
schaft*) held together by mythical beliefs and practices and a society
(*Gesellschaft*) that is a product of the will. The latter corresponds to
what he also calls a community of will (*Willensgemeinschaft*), while the
former is a community of fate (*Schicksalsgemeinschaft*) (Krois 1979).

If myth is what characterises traditional forms of political communities (what Cassirer calls *Gemeinschaften* and *Schicksalsgemeinschaften*),
then the problem is to explain how the appeal to the myth of the Aryan
race could have been so successful in a modern polity. Drawing from
Doutté's anthropological analysis of magical and religious practices,
Cassirer affirms that a political myth is a "collective desire personified" (Cassirer 1973: 280). But if myth is a collective desire, how can
the emergence of such a desire be explained in the case of modern
polities?

The Myth of the State, which presents itself as an analysis of the role that myth plays in the state, is, in fact, the reconstruction of Western attempts to get rid of myth. The text starts with a section where myth is defined as the form of life that characterises traditional societies and then moves on to analyse "the struggle against myth in the history of political philosophy", a section that occupies two-thirds of the work. The "myth of the state" appears only at the end of the text, in a section that, significantly, recalls Rosenberg's *The Myth of the Twentieth Century*, one of the main ideological texts of Nazism (Rosenberg 1941). It is only here that Cassirer faces the problem of the presence of myth in modern polities.

Cassirer's answer is twofold. First, political myths are desperate means. The return of myth, he asserts, is only explainable as the last resort for facing a situation of deep crisis when rational means are not available. According to him, "in desperate situations, man will always have recourse to desperate means – and our present-day political myths have been such desperate means" (Cassirer 1973: 279). He describes this even more clearly when he writes that, with the advent of modernity:

the mythical organisation of society seems to be superseded by a rational organisation. In quiet and peaceful times, in periods of relative stability and security, this rational organisation is easily maintained. It seems to be safe against all attacks. But in politics the equipoise is never completely established. . . . In all critical moments of man's social life, the rational forces that resist the rise of the old mythical conceptions are no longer sure of themselves. In these moments the time for myth has come again. For myth has not been really vanquished and subjugated. It is always there, lurking in the dark and waiting for its hour and opportunity. This hour comes as soon as the other binding forces of man's social life, for one reason or another, lose their strength and are no longer able to combat the demonic mythical power. (Cassirer 1973: 280)

However, Cassirer himself realises that this is still not an answer. To say that myth has returned because rational means were unavailable is not an explanation of why this happened. Cassirer is led to look elsewhere and precisely at the power of what he calls the "new techniques of power".

While according to Cassirer, political myth is collective desire personified, here we find myth made according to plan. The new political

myths do not grow up freely; they are not the wild fruits of an exu-
berant imagination. They are artificial things fabricated by very skilful
and cunning artisans. Here, one can argue, Cassirer seems to be facing
a counterexample to his own previous theory of myth as a primitive
form of consciousness. But instead of reconsidering his theory, he
attributes this anomaly to the development of new techniques: "It has
been reserved for the twentieth century", he argues, "our own great
technical age to develop a new technique of myth" (Cassirer 1973:
282).

Cassirer's general theory of mythical consciousness seems to be
inadequate to explain the presence of political myth in modern politics, and *The Myth of the State* is indeed more a book on the Western
attempts to get rid of myth than a book on political myth in general.
Having classified myth as a primitive form of consciousness that *has*
to be superseded by modern rationality, he can only explain the presence of myth in terms of regression. Certainly his analysis of the "new"
techniques of power that were put in place by Nazism is of great help
in order to understand the success of this particular political myth,
that of the Aryan race, but it does not say much about the human
need from which political myths stem in general. Three of these new
techniques are analysed at length: the magical use of words, the use
of rituals, and the recourse to prophecy. However, his analysis remains
entrapped in an enlightened approach to myth.

First, according to Cassirer, in order to understand the fabrication
of such a personified collective desire as that of the Aryan race, one has
to refer to a change in the function of the language used by Nazism.
Cassirer's philosophy of language allows for two possible uses of words:
the semantic and the magical. The semantic, which is the main one,
consists of using a word in order to describe an objective state of affairs,
whereas the magical consists of using words in order to produce certain
effects. Even if the semantic function is never missing, because without
it there could be no human speech, the magic word has an overwhelming influence in primitive societies. The magician or sorcerer does not
describe a state of affairs, but aims to produce certain effects, and by
them to change the course of nature and history (Cassirer 1973: 283).

Politicians, Cassirer continues, unite within themselves two figures
that have appeared separate until now – the *homo faber* is now also
homo magus (Cassirer 1973: 283). However, Cassirer does not explain

how such a change is possible; he simply notes that ordinary words are infused with further meanings and that new-fangled words are charged with feelings and violent passions (Cassirer 1973: 283).

But the skilful use of words, he observes, is insufficient, because, if the word is to have its effect, it has to be supplemented by the introduction of new rites (Cassirer 1973: 284). Again, it is primitive societies that provide the example of a form of life which is punctuated by thousands of rituals and social practices. In Cassirer's view, the progress of anthropological research has falsified Rousseau's image of the savage: far from being the free and unfettered creature described by Rousseau, the savage is hemmed in on every side by the customs of his people and is bound by the chains of innumerable rites grounded in tradition. The effect of all these rites is the obliteration of the responsibility of the subject. In primitive societies there is no individual responsibility, only a collective one. Similarly, he held, totalitarianism, by deleting the distinction between the private and the public sphere, succeeded in inundating the life of the individual with a multitude of rigorous and inexorable rituals (Cassirer 1973: 284).

Methods of repression and compulsion have always been in use in political life, but, Cassirer notes, modern myths did not begin by demanding or prohibiting certain actions: "they undertook to change the men in order to be able to regulate and control their deeds" (Cassirer 1973: 286). The modern techniques of power, which overwhelm the individual with an ensemble of rituals, suppress the sense of individual responsibility and, in this way, destroy freedom.[2] Freedom, Cassirer argues following Kant, is not something that is given by nature but is instead a task, an ethical imperative: to be autonomous. By melting the individual into the collective responsibility, the very sense of freedom is destroyed but, at the same time, human beings are relieved from a heavy burden, that of personal responsibility (Cassirer 1973: 288). The destruction of the freedom of the subject and his or her autonomy is the sign that we are leaving modernity: the advent of the new techniques of power represents a fall into a primitive form of life.

Though Cassirer's analysis gradually becomes more detailed, it still does not fully explain how such a deep change was possible if, as he argues, it represented such a revolution. Why, in other words, did

---

[2] On the relationship between myth and freedom in Cassirer, see Henry 1986.

modern individuals accept the exchange of their freedom for a return to a "primitive" form of life?

Cassirer identifies the new politicians with the magicians of primitive societies. The new sorcerers not only use words in a magical way, they also promise the medicine to cure all evils. This leads Cassirer to the third feature of the new techniques of myth: the sorcerer, the *homo magus* is, at the same time, the *homo divinans*. He not only provides the cure for everything, he can also reveal the will of gods and foretell the future. Again, a parallel between primitive and modern societies is introduced:

To be sure, we no longer have the primitive kind of sortilege, the divination by lot; we no longer observe the flight of birds nor do we inspect the entrails of slain animals. We have developed a much more refined and elaborate method of divination – a method that claims to be scientific and philosophical. But if our methods have changed, the thing itself has by no means vanished. Our modern politicians know very well that the great masses are much more easily moved by the force of imagination than by the sheer physical force. And they have made ample use of this knowledge. The politician becomes a sort of public fortune-teller. Prophecy is an essential element in the new technique of rulership. The most improbable or even impossible promises are made; the millennium is predicted over and over again. (Cassirer 1973: 289)

Reading this passage one cannot but think of our contemporary political techniques: at first sight it seems it is still the case that "the most improbable and impossible promises are made" and "the millennium is predicted over and over again". We will come back to this point later on, but for now it is important to stress that there are reasons to suspect that Cassirer's statement that "prophecy is an essential element in the new technique of rulership" still holds true. This suggests that the Nazi's recourse to prophecy is not an anomaly in modernity: far from being a prerogative of totalitarianism, it seems to be part of the techniques of power of very different political regimes.

Cassirer continues by analysing the way in which philosophical conceptions such as that elaborated by Spengler in his *The Decline of the West* could have fomented in their readers a prophetic sense of fatalism that prepared the way for the new prophets. What is interesting to note here is that when Cassirer moves on to specifically analysing the way in which the new myths work, all the dichotomies that he had built before break down. For instance, Spengler's catastrophic prophecy cannot be grasped through a dichotomy such as "semantic" versus "magic" uses of the word. Cassirer himself could not but admit that Spengler's words, even if they were not directly aimed at dominating people's deeds and minds, worked both as semantic and magic devices: they served to describe a presumed state of affairs (the decline of the West), and to produce effects in their readers (to stimulate their reaction). The great success of Spengler's book, must lie in its title more than in its content; the title *The Decline of the West* was an "electric spark" that set the imagination of Spengler's readers aflame (Cassirer 1973: 289).

But to take another view, in the light of Wittgenstein's philosophy, it appears legitimate to ask whether the distinction between a semantic and a magical use of the word is possible at all. As Wittgenstein's critique of the possibility of explaining meanings on the basis of merely ostensive definitions has shown, meaning cannot exist without a whole made of language and actions, that is, language-games. The meaning of a word lies in its use, and its use is always aimed at describing something by producing certain effects and vice versa. To put it in Cassirer's terminology, there cannot be a semantic meaning without a magical use of words.

The point is that, as we have seen in Chapter 5, Cassirer's general philosophy is still within the Enlightenment's presupposition of a philosophy of the subject. In his view, the two main forms of experience of meaning are of the mythical consciousness and of the scientific consciousness, and the distinction between the two is drawn on the basis of the possibility of distinguishing between the subject and the object of the representations. According to Cassirer's *Philosophy of Symbolic Forms*, scientific representations are based on a clear distinction between the subject and the object of knowledge, while in the mythical consciousness the subject is overwhelmed by its object; and this explains why, in his view, myth can have a magical impact (Cassier 1977: vol. II).

Against those who believe that Cassirer's general philosophy is not a philosophy of the subject, because he points to the social character of the mythical consciousness (Krois 1979: 203), it can be argued that Cassirer still remains within the presuppositions of a philosophy of the subject. He conceived of myth *tout court*, and not just the totalitarian model of myth, in such a way precisely because he counterposed it to the scientific representations: he does not conceive of the subject of mythical representation in a "solipsistic" way, precisely because he counterpoised it to the "solipsistic" subject of scientific enquiry. Consequently, in this he remains within the Enlightenment.

From the point of view of a theory of political myth, the problem seems to be that, by analysing myth as a form of consciousness or as an entire form of life, the differences between such phenomena as myths, religious beliefs and practices, as well as rituals of all sorts, all get lost. But myth, religion and ritual are very different things. First, myth is not religion, and, though it can be argued that human beings are overwhelmed by a religious representation that claims to be the ultimate truth, the same does not hold for myth.[3] In particular, mythical constructions are not impenetrable to rational arguments: Cassirer's own critique of "modern myths" demonstrates precisely the opposite.

Second, the two categories of myth and ritual must be kept separated. In fact, even if the work on myth is in a sense a language-game made of language and action, the concept of ritual brings in a new dimension that is not covered by the concept of myth. As we have seen, ritual is not *any* action. Only a particular class of action can be classified as ritual. Ritual, from the Latin word *rite*, is literally "what is well done", or "what is done according to the rules". Even if political myths and political rituals are quite often associated, the two work in different ways within a society: political rituals must be kept unchanged to be effective, whereas political myth, insofar as it provides significance within perpetually changing circumstances, must remain open to the possibility of being renegotiated according to new experiences and needs. To put it plainly, a political myth expresses itself through variants, the political ritual through fixed rules.

Hence it can be argued that it is precisely because Cassirer remained linked to the Enlightenment dichotomy of "mythical consciousness" versus "scientific consciousness" that his analysis of the myth of Aryan

---

[3] A similar point is made by Tudor when he observes that it is not true, as Cassirer argues, that, in myth, all reality and events are projected into the fundamental opposition of the "sacred" and the "profane" since there are many myths in which the sacred plays no role whatsoever (Tudor 1972: 35). The reason why Cassirer argued this is that he saw in the modern totalitarian myth-maker "the priest of a new, entirely irrational and mysterious religion" (Cassirer 1973: 282). But myths, despite all the enthusiasm that they can inspire, are not a form of religion.

race, even if it provides important insights as to the functioning of a totalitarian myth, is ultimately unable to explain the presence of myth in modern politics. Only by following the Enlightenment identification of myth with all that pure reason is not, with a whole form of life encompassing religion as well as magic, could he have assumed that, since modernity has undermined the role of religion, it should also have disposed of myth. However, as other scholars have pointed out, political myths are not always a form of regression and the role that they play in modern politics should not be seen as an anomaly.

At the beginning of the twentieth century and thus well before *The Myth of the State*, another book was published in which an alternative theory of political myth was developed – Sorel's *Reflections on Violence* (1975).[1] Its major argument about political myth is that myth is not religion, and it is precisely for this reason that it can and should play a role in modern politics. Indeed, while Cassirer saw in myth a form of "regression", Sorel presents political myth as a form of "progress".

Sorel, in contrast to Cassirer, was not a professional philosopher. In all his writings, he is continually taking a polemical distance from the intellectuals. The *Reflections on Violence*, a collection of articles written in the context of the discussion on syndicalism, clearly has an activist intent: to develop a severe critique of the parliamentary socialists and their neglect of the primary role played by proletarian violence in history. Therefore, his theory of political myth stems from a practical engagement with one of the typically modern phenomena: the proletarian struggle.

In Sorel's view, proletarian violence, and not the sophisticated moves of parliamentary socialists, is the real engine of history. And the myth of the general strike is the highest point of proletarian violence, a complex of images that immediately evoke all the different manifestations of the war engaged by socialism against capitalism.

Sorel's reasoning is quite straightforward:

In the course of these studies, one thing has always been present in my mind, which seemed to me so evident that I did not think it worth while to lay much stress on it – that men who are participating in a great social movement always

---

[1] According to some interpreters Sorel's *Reflections on Violence* remains "the most interesting attempt to elaborate the notion of political myth" (Tudor 1972: 12).

picture their coming action as a battle in which their cause is certain to triumph. These constructions, knowledge of which is so important for historians, I propose to call myths; the syndacalist "general strike" and Marx's catastrophic revolution are such myths. (Sorel 1975: 22)

According to Sorel, the action engaged in by human beings in big social movements cannot be explained without powerful images such as myths: the more dramatic the action, the more powerful these images. Much as the Christian martyrs were moved by the catastrophic representation of the Apocalypse, so the passage from capitalism to socialism must take the form of a catastrophe in order to be effective as a *pouvoir moteur* (Sorel 1975: 164).

Why should we use the concept of myth to describe these images? First, it can be argued that Sorel meant to distance himself from all kinds of positivistic explanations. There are facts, according to Sorel, that cannot be explained by the sophistry of an intellectualist (1975: 23ff.). For instance, the readiness to sacrifice their own lives shown by the Napoleonic soldiers or by the Greeks and Romans cannot be explained on the basis of purely rational explanation. In order to explain such facts, according to Sorel, we must have recourse to Bergson's analysis of the way in which human beings create an artificial world that is placed in the future and that is formed by movements that depend entirely on us (1975: 30). Precisely for this reason, these complexes of images can be defined as myths. This also enables us to distinguish them both from utopia and religion.

The general strike is a myth and not a utopia because it is not a theoretical model. The general strike is a "determination of the will". A myth is not the construction of the single mind of a theorist who, after having observed and discussed facts, establishes a model for comparing existing societies and measuring the good and bad that they contain (Sorel 1975: 32). A myth cannot be divided into its parts and judged according to their correspondence to reality or their feasibility: a myth, in Sorel's terms, is a whole made of images that can express a specific determination of the will only when they are together.

What interested the revolutionary syndicalist Sorel was indeed to understand in what conditions a socialist revolution was possible. In this respect, it is crucial for him to distinguish myth from utopia. So he states that, despite the fact that socialism has been a utopia for a long time, it has now reached a completely different stage. Socialism, in his view, is no longer a utopia because it has become a preparation of the proletarian masses that wanted to suppress the state and property (1975: 34).

Thus, if, on the one hand, the general strike is no longer a utopia because it is now a determination of the will, it must also, on the other, be distinguished from religious beliefs. Sorel explicitly wrote that people living in this world of myths are secure from refutation, and this led many to assert that socialism is a kind of religion. For a long time, people have been struck by the fact that religious convictions are unaffected by criticism and from that they have concluded that everything that is below science must be religion (Sorel 1975: 35).[5] But not all that which is not science is religion.

Sorel, in contrast to Cassirer, emphasises this point, and this enables him to recognise the role of myth in modern politics. Thus, while Cassirer, by moving from the presupposition of Enlightenment, interprets political myth as a form of regression, Sorel, who distinguishes myth from religion, is able to recognise the presence of myth in modern societies and to show the circumstances in which its presence can be a form of progress. If modernity has undermined the role of religion as a horizon of sense in the experience of the world, it has not undermined the role of myth. On the contrary, it is precisely in typically modern phenomena such as the big social movements that the role played by mythical constructions became evident. It is only because people taking part in big social movements can represent their action as an event within a narrative that assures the triumph of their cause that they engage in such actions as the proletarian struggle. As Sorel wrote:

These results could not be produced in any very certain manner by the use of ordinary language; use must be made of a body of images which, by *intuition alone*, and before considered analyses are made, is capable of evoking as an undivided whole the mass of sentiments which correspond to the different manifestations of the war undertaken by socialism against modern society. (1975: 130)

---

[5] Curiously, the English translator rendered the French "*au-dessous de la science*" with "beyond science", whereas the fact that Sorel posits myth and religion *under* the level of science is very significant.

Thus, it is not important to know whether the single details that form a myth will actually be part of the future history. It might even be the case that nothing that they contain will ever happen; this will not undermine their *pouvoir moteur*. In our everyday life, we continuously experience the huge gap between what actually happens and our preconceived notion of what happens, but this does not prevent us from continuing to make resolutions. To conclude, myth, according to Sorel, must not be judged as an astrological almanac that foretells the future, but as a means of acting on the present (1975: 135).

But if it is true that myths cannot be falsified, it is also true that they can be discussed. Sorel is ambiguous on this point, although, on many occasions, he seems to conceive of myth as an absolute dimension beyond the possibility of discussion. For instance, he goes as far as to write that "the idea of the general strike is so admirably adapted to the working-class mind that there is a possibility of its dominating the latter in the most absolute manner... thus the power of the dispute would be reduced to nothing (1975: 139).[6]

In fact, this statement contrasts with what Sorel does, which is to critically discuss a myth. In particular, in the fourth article of the *Reflections on Violence*, an article devoted to the defence of the general strike against the criticism of many parliamentary socialists, Sorel discusses the myth of the general strike from the point of view of its rationality. Sorel defends this myth by showing how it corresponds to Marx's doctrine. In Sorel's view, the general strike is well adapted to convey all the most important views and values of this doctrine in an immediate image: the division of the society into two classes, the idea of class struggle, and the revolution against the present state of things. This is a crucial point that can be grasped only by looking, at the same time, at what Sorel actually says about the myth of the general strike and at what Sorel actually does with the myth. If one looks at both dimensions, it becomes impossible to argue that, for Sorel, myth is only a matter of faith that eludes any possibility of critical discussion (Tudor 1972: 15): indeed, it is exactly critical discussion in which Sorel engages in his work.

---

[6] In other places, Sorel defines myth as an integral experience (*une expérience intégrale*) that cannot be permeated by rational arguments (Sorel 1975: 142).

The reason why Sorel, in contrast to what he does, seems to hold that myths are not subject to rational discussion is that he remained linked to what we can call a "dualistic view of the self". He interprets Bergson's psychology according to a theory of the two selves. As we read in the Introduction to the *Reflections*, in Sorel's view there are two different selves: on the one hand, the free creative self and, on the other, the rational, external and spatial one. It is to the latter self that the stable affirmations of science are due, whereas myth is the product of the other self (1975: 29). The two selves, therefore, appear as inevitably separated.

However, Sorel does not go much further than this very brief reference to Bergson's psychology. He was not as interested in the psychological implications of his theory of myth as he was in its practical ones. His major point was to show that proletarian violence is the real engine of history, and, to this end, he points to the *pouvoir moteur* of the general strike. In doing this, though, he formulates a theory of political myth in which he recognises that there cannot be a mobilisation of political action without a powerful set of images that assure those who are engaged in this action about the triumph of their cause. Sorel does not investigate the psychological implications of such a view deeply: for the point he wanted to make in the *Reflections*, some scattered references to Bergson were enough. And this is the reason why the psychological theory of the two selves, to which he refers, remains inadequate to support his own analysis of political myth.

Sorel's conception of political myth cannot be grasped through a dualistic approach, nor can what he actually does when dealing with the myth of the general strike. Gramsci points to this when he criticises Croce's interpretation of Sorel. Croce himself thought of myth as the product of a sphere of the human mind – the sphere of passions – which is impenetrable to rationality, and, for this reason, he held that Sorel, by rationally discussing the myth of the general strike, dissolved it (Gramsci 1975: vol. II, 1308; trans. mine). To this view, Gramsci replies that only such an intellectualist and idealistic approach as that of Croce could have assumed this. In Gramsci's view, the myth of the general strike is neither a mere piece of paper (*una cosa di carta*) that could be dissipated by some doctrinarian pages, nor the expression of a set of passions that are impenetrable by rational discussion (Gramsci 1975: vol. II, 1308; trans. mine).

Why, one could argue following this line of reasoning, should we assume that reason does not have its own passions and that, vice-versa, passions cannot be reasonable? Why should passions disappear when rational considerations appear? Any dichotomy of "passions" versus "reason" reveals its serious limitations. What Sorel does while discussing the myth of the general strike is no different from what we all do when reflecting upon a future course of action: we consider its correspondence to our own views, values and passions, without it being possible to separate out all these components. Far from dissolving myth, Sorel reinforces it by discussing its correspondence to Marxism. In other words, he shows the morals of the story, and thereby reinforces the determination to act on its basis.

A more detailed theoretical framework for a theory of political myth can be found in Spinoza's thinking. While most early modern political philosophy neglected or marginalized the role of political myth, a fully developed theory of political imagination can be found in Spinoza's *Tractatus Theologico-Politicus* (1951b). Pierre-François Moreau recently asserted that, to see another such detailed analysis of the symbolic conditions of the existence of a polity, and emphasis on the logic of adhesion and identity, we would have to wait until the twentieth century, for Hannah Arendt and Jürgen Habermas (Moreau 1994: 495).

Maybe we did not have to wait until Arendt, since sociology, for instance, from its very beginning has largely dealt with such phenomena;[7] but Moreau rightly points to the fact that Spinoza constitutes an anomaly within modern political theory. Not only, in contrast to other modern philosophers, does he analyse the symbolic conditions for the conservation of political power; he also combines this analysis with a radical theory of democracy.[8] It is therefore striking that Spinoza's contribution to an understanding of political myth has been so largely neglected.[9]

In the fifth chapter of the *Tractatus*, Spinoza clearly states that all kinds of state laws must be instituted in such a way that human beings

---

[7] One just has to think of the founding fathers of sociology, Durkheim and Weber. See, for instance, Weber 1969.
[8] According to Balibar, for instance, Spinoza's *Tractatus* is a true democratic manifest (Balibar 1985: 35–62).
[9] For instance, neither Tudor nor Flood mentions Spinoza among the theorists of political myth (Tudor 1972; Flood 1996).

are bound not by fear (*metu*) but by hope of something that they desire in a particular way (*spe alicuius boni, quod maxime cupiunt*).[10] Spinoza's theory of political imagination can be considered as a reflection on the problem of how such a hope can be socially created.

To this end, Spinoza analyses the role that prophecy played in the creation and conservation of the ancient nation of Israel. The approach that Spinoza adopts in this analysis is not theological, but theological-political, or, to put it in more contemporary terms, "sociological". Spinoza is not interested in defending the truth of the Jews' prophecy, but in analysing the role that it played within society. From this point of view, Spinoza inaugurates the modern study of religion (Preus 1989: 72).[11] From the very outset, he describes the method that he employs in the interpretation of the Scriptures on the basis of two premises. The first can be described as a shift from an approach to the *truth* of the text to one that focuses on its *meaning*, and the second as the recognition of the *contingency* of meaning, that is, of the fact that meaning is contingent because the text is contingent (Lang 1989: 328).

First, Spinoza explicitly states that, in the interpretation of the Bible – and by implication of any text – we are, in the first place, at work not on the truth of passages, but only on their meanings (Spinoza 1951b: chs. VII, XII). Two extremes must thus be avoided when interpreting the Scriptures: that of the "dogmatists", the rationalists or philosophical allegorists who, in order to save the truth of the text, attribute to the prophets what they never even dreamed of; and that of the sceptics, the literalist interpreters who force us to accept all the possible prejudices of the ancient *vulgi* as divine utterances (Spinoza 1951b: 190–9).[12] Both these extremes, according to Spinoza, are

---

[10] See Spinoza 1951b: 74. There are many places in the *Tractatus* in which Spinoza makes a similar point. Here the critique seems to be directed towards Hobbes.

[11] On this point see, for instance, Preus 1989: 72; and Lang 1989: 296. Lang argues that the theory of interpretation of the *Tractatus* is an anticipation of the modernist turn towards a politics of interpretation. According to Lang, Spinoza not only argues that interpretation presupposes or implies a political framework, but even that interpretation is itself a politics. For our purposes it is not necessary to go as far as this.

[12] The similarities between Spinoza's criticism of the literalists and dogmatists as interpreters and Vico's criticism of the "two conceits" have been noted: that of nations that claim that their own myths are literally true, and that of scholars who maintain that

concerned more with the *truth* of the text than with its *meaning*, and they fail thus to understand the contingent character of the meaning. God, though, does not have a style, as Spinoza often repeats, and therefore all differences and incongruities of the Scriptures cannot but be attributed to the contingency of the context in which the texts were written. But since meaning cannot be separated from use, and thus from its context, then it must be contingent in itself.

Meaning, in Spinoza's view, is contingent because it is determined by the *use* of a word. This view leads Spinoza to go as far as to say that the Scriptures can be said to be "sacred" only insofar as they are designed to promote piety, and continue to be sacred only as long as they are "religiously used". As we read, in a passage that could have been written by Wittgenstein:

Words gain their meaning solely from their usage, and if they are arranged according to their accepted signification so as to move those who read them to devotion, they will become sacred, and the book so written will be sacred also. But if their usage afterwards dies out so that words have no meaning, or the book becomes utterly neglected, whether from unworthy motives, or because it is no longer needed, then the words and the book will lose both their use and their sanctity. (1951b: 167)

Spinoza's analysis of the role of prophecy for the ancient Hebrews is thus the occasion for a more general reflection on the social nature of meaning. Spinoza, who was excluded from the Jewish community in Amsterdam, was in the main able to work free from the ordinary constraints that determined both popular and scholarly perspectives on religion in Europe at that time. He did not have to bear the apologetic burden to save the religious meaning of the text that he studied or of the people that produced the text (Preus 1989: 72). This put him in a position where he could adopt a genuinely *critical* approach towards the texts so that many authors have seen in his analysis the origins of modern critical theory (Norris 1991, Hippler 2000).

Biblical prophecy, according to Spinoza, does not derive, as Maimonides held, from a particular kind of knowledge. Prophecies are not the result of a divine revelation since no divine revelation, as

what they know is as old as the world, that is, that the rationality with which they now apprehend the world was shared from the very beginning (Preus 1989). On Vico's two conceits, see Chapter 5.

traditionally understood, exists: God does not have a particular style and he adapts himself to the particular circumstances of the linguistic and historical context in which prophets live. The obscure, enigmatic and figurative character of prophecies derives not from God, but from the vivid *imagination* of the prophets. As a consequence, in order to prophesy, one must not have a more perfect mind, but a more vivid imagination (Spinoza 1951b: 13ff.).

On the other hand, as has been recently pointed out, imagination, in Spinoza's view, is not "imaginary", that is, false (Hippler 2000: 97). Imagination, according to his *Ethics*, is simply a set of ideas produced on the basis of present or past bodily impressions. In its turn, an idea is a "concept of the mind" (Spinoza 1985: 447) and the mind is nothing other than an expression of the body – the body that is felt and thought (1985: 457). As is well known, the mind and the body are, in Spinoza's view, simply two attributes of God, that is, the ways in which God, the unique substance, is given to us. Furthermore, according to Spinoza, the structures of the two attributes are parallel: "the order and connection of ideas is, at the same time, the order and connection of things" (1985: 451).[13]

However, the parallelism between body and mind, or extension and thinking, does not mean that all ideas are adequate. On the contrary, what characterises imagination is precisely its inadequacy, because, in Spinoza's theory of knowledge, imagination is only the first level of knowledge. Nevertheless, even if these ideas are not yet adequate, since it is only through intellectual knowledge that adequate ideas can be obtained, they are not necessarily false, because a mind has false ideas only insofar as it considers these bodily perceptions to be adequate ideas when they are not (1985: 468–71). In his view, if imagination cannot be considered as adequate knowledge, it nonetheless plays an extremely important role in the sphere of praxis.

As Spinoza points out, prophetic imagination concerns the practice of life and virtue and the authority of the prophets is based on this moral role (Spinoza 1951b: 27ff.). As he clearly states, the certitude

---

[13] As is well known, the polemical objective of this conception is Descartes' radical dualism of the *res cogitans* and *res extensa*. It would be interesting to investigate further the link between Spinoza's radical monism and his conception of political imagination: prima facie there seems to be a strict link between his ontology and his denial of the purely "imaginary" character of imagination.

stemming from biblical prophecy is a moral one: "the certitude afforded to the prophet by sign was not mathematical (i.e. it did not necessarity follow from the perception of the thing perceived or seen) but only moral" (Spinoza 1951b: 29). On many occasions, Spinoza repeats that the intent of the Scriptures is mainly a moral one and the certitude of the prophets derives from the fact that their mind was totally given to what was right and wrong (Spinoza 1951b: 27ff.).

It has been argued that, since, for Spinoza, the categories of good and right do not exist outside of a political community, one can conclude that prophecy is valid because the prophet belongs to a community whose laws and rules the prophet fully embodies (Hippler 2000: 99). Thus, the social function of prophecy is to recall these norms in the memories of the members of society. But if the prophets can only be prophets in the community whose norms they embody and if the aim of prophecy is precisely to strengthen the community's adhesion to those same values, then the prophets and the community are products of each other, that is, they have a purely circular relationship (Hippler 2000: 100).

Rosenthal has advanced a similar interpretation of this point, which also seems to suggest a way out of this circularity (Rosenthal 1997). For Rosenthal, Spinoza chose the example of the Hebrews because the analysis of the role of prophetic language enabled him to make a general point about the way in which an appeal to an imaginative narrative example contributes to the justification of a particular set of institutions: when the prophets called the Hebrews "the chosen people", they were performing a function essential to any society: they were using imagination to transcend individual interests and to create a common standard of judgements and of behaviour (Rosenthal 1997).

The concept that makes this passage possible is that of the exemplar of human nature, which is developed in the fourth part of *Ethics* (Rosenthal 1997: 247). Here, Spinoza defines "good" and "bad" from the point of view of utility: "By good, I shall understand what we certainly know to be useful to us", and "by evil, I shall understand what we certainly know prevents us from being masters of some good" (Spinoza 1985: 546). Clearly the problem arises of how to determine this utility because what is useful for one person at any given time and place may not be useful to another. So if the value terms "good" and "bad" are to mean something more than the mere subjective utility of an individual, then it is necessary to find a basis for transcending the particular judgement of the individual; this is the purpose of the concept of the "*exemplar* of human nature".

Thus, after the definitions of good and bad, Spinoza points the reader back to the preface of the fourth part of the *Ethics*, in which he says:

I shall understand by "good" what we know certainly is a means by which we may approach nearer and nearer to the model (*exemplar*) of human nature that we set before ourselves. By evil, what we certainly know prevents us from becoming like that model. (Spinoza 1985: 545)

Spinoza then goes on to explain that exemplars, thus defined, serve as a bridge from subjective to objective judgement because they are formed not on the basis of an individual judgement, but on the basis of a *universal idea* (1985: 545ff.).

What is a "universal idea" according to Spinoza? As Rosenthal points out, according to Spinoza so-called universal ideas are not "adequate ideas", that is, the clear and distinct foundations of reason, but are rather inadequate, incomplete, and confused images of the world. Spinoza distinguishes between "common notions", which are the foundations of our reasoning on the one hand, and notions that derive from other causes and are therefore ill-founded on the other (Spinoza 1985: 475). Despite their names, "these notions are not formed by all [human beings] in the same way, but vary from one to another, in accordance with what the body has more often been affected by, and what the mind imagines or recollects more easily" (1985: 477). Thus, universal ideas can also be characterised as the notions we are accustomed to feign (Spinoza 1985: 544) and should, therefore, be called "beings of imagination" rather than "beings of reason" (Spinoza 1985: 446).

Spinoza's notion of the exemplars of human nature cannot but recall Vico's concept of "imaginative universals". In both cases, we have certain constructs of the imagination that, far from being simply individual creatures, aspire to be universal in their nature. In both cases we have universal beings of imagination. It is precisely due to this "universality" that they can serve to mediate between individual and universal judgements. In turn, this concept of imaginative universals cannot but recall Aristotle's concept of myth as developed in the so-called *Poetics*.

As we have seen, *mythoi*, according to Aristotle, are superior to history precisely because history tells things as they happened, whereas *mythoi* tell them as they could have happened, and, for this reason, contain a more universal truth.[14] This, in Aristotle's view, is the universality of the knowledge of different human characters, or, to put it in Spinoza's terms, the knowledge of the different "*exemplars* of human nature".

While Vico, by historicising his analysis of the role of imaginative universals and attributing this role to the childhood of humankind, limits his theory of imaginative universals to a certain historical phase of humankind,[15] Spinoza, like Aristotle, considered the power of imagination to create order as a normal feature of human beings at any time and in any society. This is the reason why Spinoza's analysis of the role played by imagination in prophecy can become the basis for a more general theory. The example of Jewish prophecy is the basis for constructing a whole theory of political myth – a theory that allows us both to reconstruct the role that myth plays in politics as well as to set the limits for the legitimacy of its use. As we will see, instead of labelling political myths as a form of "regression" or "progress", Spinoza's elaborate theory provided the means for analysing the legitimate conditions of their use.

The fact that Spinoza understood his analysis of the history of the ancient Hebrews as a basis for a more general theory is made patent in the structure of the *Tractatus*. Indeed, the text, after having dealt with all aspects of the constitution of the nation of Israel, ends with a chapter on the "Principles that can be drawn from the Hebrews' history" followed by another two chapters that are dedicated to show, on the basis of this example, that freedom of thought and speech does not harm the state, but is actually fundamental to its survival (Spinoza 1951b: chs. XIX, XX). From the very preface to the text, Spinoza clearly states that the aim of the *Tractatus* is precisely to argue for the freedom of thinking and speech. His main argument is indeed that, if all societies are, in a sense, imaginary, where they differ is the degree to

---

[14] See Chapter 3.
[15] For an analysis of Vico's view of myth, see Chapter 2. On the possible influence of Spinoza on Vico as well as on the difference between the two, see Preus 1989.

which this imagination is subject to critical scrutiny. As a consequence, despite the fact that most people live at the level of imagination, the state should still guarantee the possibility to those who can to elevate themselves to higher levels of knowledge and exercise a *critical* function (1951b: chs. XIX, XX). What Spinoza actually does in his critique of the Sacred Scriptures is precisely this.

In his critique, Spinoza wanted to make a general point about the role of political imagination, but the reason why he chose the Jews is also linked to the particular circumstances in which he wrote. It has been shown that the seventeenth century Dutch saw themselves in the light of three important sets of narratives or myths: their heroic struggle against the Spanish, the story of the Batvians depicted in the writings of Tacitus (and other Roman historians) and drawn upon by Grotius (among others) and, finally, the story of the ancient Israelites (Rosenthal 1997: 267). It is in reference to the latter founding myth that Spinoza chose the Jews. Spinoza's contemporary Dutch Calvinists had spread the belief that their nation was chosen to endure and triumph over their labours in order to maintain a certain political order. Spinoza's use of the ancient Israelites is meant to be the basis for analysing and setting the limits to the legitimate use of such political myths.

Let us develop this point by going back to the analysis of Jewish prophecy. According to Spinoza's reconstruction, after the exodus from Egypt, the people of Israel had fallen again into a pure state of nature, because having left the laws of Egypt to which they had been hitherto subjected, they had not yet been able to build other laws. In this context, Moses had called the Jews the "chosen people" and had used the idea of the covenant with God as a means of morally encouraging his people to subject themselves to a lawful condition. This use of prophecy made by Moses was, according to Spinoza, legitimate because the Jews were, by that time, a lawless band of people cast out into the desert, and Moses, in order to give them a law, had to place their particular experience into a framework of a divine plane in which they played a special role.

The people listened to the prophecy because it provided them with a consistent set of expectations about the results of their action. The recourse to prophecy was thus necessary because, in this situation, the

Israelites were not able to otherwise perceive the necessity of a polity.
As Spinoza observes:

If any one wishes to persuade his fellows for or against anything which is
not self evident, he must deduce his contention from their admission, and
convince them either by experience or by ratiocination. . . . But the deduction
of the conclusion from a general *a priori* truth, usually requires a long chain of
arguments, and, moreover, very great caution, acuteness, and self-restraint –
qualities which are not often found; therefore, people prefer to be taught by
experience rather than deduce their conclusion from a few *axioms*. Whence it
follows that if anyone wishes to teach a doctrine to a whole nation (not to speak
of the whole human race), and to be understood by all men in every particular,
he will seek to support his teaching with experience and will endeavour to
suit his reasoning and the definition of his doctrines as far as possible to the
understanding of the common people, who form the majority of mankind.
(Spinoza 1951b: 76–7)

Thus, given that only the learned can elevate themselves to intellectual knowledge, whoever wants to communicate to a whole nation
has to have recourse to imagination. This does not mean that these
histories are necessarily false. On the contrary, the reference to imagination as a way to "teach by experience" leaves the issue of the truth of
these images open. Spinoza also explicitly admits the possibility that
the content of such stories is true. The point is that only the person who
can attain the level of intellectual knowledge will also have a concept
of these images as clear and distinct (1951b: 78ff.). The Scriptures,
whose true moral content, according to Spinoza, can be summarised
in very few principles, were written for an entire people and therefore had to communicate through stories that appealed to people's
imagination. However, these very few principles could also be grasped
with the faculty of reason (*lumine naturali*); this, in Spinoza's view, is,
however, reserved for the learned few.

As Spinoza explicitly argues, the intent of the histories of the Bible
is precisely to inspire devotion and obedience (1951b: 77ff.).[16] As a
consequence, the populace (*vulgus*) must not know all the stories of the

---

[16] It should be noted that Spinoza, in order to assert that the Scriptures teach certain
principles through the narrations of stories, uses the expression "*atque heac Scriptura
sola experientia comprobat, nempe his quas narrat, historis*", meaning these things are
proved by the Scriptures only through experience, namely through the stories that
they tell.

Bible, but only the stories that can move their mind to obedience and devotion in the strongest way (*quae maxime eorum animos ad obedientiam et devotionem movere possunt*). In the case of the Jews cast out in the desert, among these stories were the prophetic stories of their chosenness.

Biblical prophecy therefore played a double role for the Jews in the particular situation in which they found themselves. First, like all the other stories from the Bible, they transmitted a moral message. Second, the story of their chosenness, by addressing their particular needs, contributed to grounding – again in the sense of *begründen* – the specificity of their polity: theocracy. The biblical prophecy, by recalling the covenant with God to the Jews, made respecting the law appear as necessary.

In this sense, it does not differ from the other political myths to which Spinoza refers. Among them, he quotes, for instance, the myth of the foundation of Rome: all kings, Spinoza observes, that have usurped power have always tried to make the people believe that they had divine origins, because only if the people thought these rulers were gods could the people support their governments (1951b: 217). To sum up, prophecy is only one of the possible ways in which "to arrange laws so that people are kept in bounds by the hope of some greatly-desired good, rather than by fear, for then everyone will do his duty willingly" (1951b: 74).

To this end, Moses introduced the ceremonial laws. After having analysed Moses' use of prophecy, Spinoza observes:

Lastly in order that the people which could not govern itself be entirely dependent on its ruler, he left nothing to the free choice of individuals (who had hitherto been slaves); the people could do nothing but remember the law and follow the ordinances laid down at the good pleasure of their rulers; they were not allowed to plough, to sow, to reap, nor even to eat.... This, then, was the object of ceremonial law: that men should do nothing of their own free will, but should always act under external authority, and should continually confess by their actions and thoughts that they were not their own masters, but were entirely under control of others. (Spinoza 1951b: 75)

For Spinoza, as for Cassirer, specific rituals accompany political myths. The function of rituals is to continually remind the people of their duty to obey the laws. This role is not, however, a prerogative of the Jews' ceremonies. A few paragraphs later, Spinoza analyses the

similar role played by Christian ceremonies. In his view, they do not
possess any sanctity in themselves, but were ordained for the preservation of the society (1951b: 76).

The specific social function of Christian ceremonies was to remind
people to obey the law. In the case of the Jews, people used to slavery and who were thrown into a state of nature, the ceremonial laws
prescribed took a particularly detailed and alienated form. Furthermore, Spinoza observed, all these rituals serve not only to remind the
people of their obedience to the law, but also to separate the Jews
from other peoples (1951b: 56). Among these rituals, circumcision,
a way of writing the covenant with God on the body, played a crucial
role so that, Spinoza observes, circumcision alone would be sufficient
to explain how the Jews survived as a nation through the centuries,
notwithstanding the destruction of their state.

Writing this obedience on their own bodies through circumcision
is the strongest means for political discipline. The parallelism between
the order of ideas and that of things takes the form of a sign on the body
here. The importance of the exterior or bodily sign is also confirmed
by a reference to the Chinese who, according to Spinoza, by means of a
distinctive mark on their heads, which they most scrupulously observe,
kept themselves apart from everyone else so that they preserved their
unity even when they had no empire (1951b: 56).

The reference to the history of the Jews, however, also serves to draw
the limits of the legitimate recourse to political myths and rituals. As for
political rituals, we have seen that, according to Spinoza, the extremely
strict ceremonial prescriptions that Moses gave to his people are only
justified on the basis of the contingent situation in which the people of
Israel found themselves: a people cast in the desert after many years of
slavery. The institution of ceremonies served to remind them of their
obedience to God's laws in every single act of their lives, for a people
that, having just come out of slavery, could not think for themselves.
But in no way must these ceremonies be considered as possessing any
sanctity in themselves (1951b: 76). Instead, we can assume that, in a
polity formed by people not used to slavery, political rituals – however
necessary – must not take such a meticulous and alienating form.

The contours for a legitimate use of political myth are drawn in a
similar vein. Again, the history of the Jews works as an exemplar. After
the death of Moses, Spinoza says, the Jews' theocracy degenerated

into superstition and this finally led to its collapse. In his view, this is due to the fact that, while Moses used prophecy as a means of morally inciting his people, but never confused the laws of the Jewish theocracy with the eternal laws of nature, the priests that followed him interpreted the "laws of right conduct" as "laws of nature". Thus whereas Moses always showed that he was aware of the epistemological limits of prophetic foundation because he separated the powers of political authority from those of the priestly caste, the priests abused their authority and claimed the right to interpret and enforce the laws directly (Rosenthal 1997: 259).

In fact, as we have seen, the role of prophecy is that of an exemplar, of a universal idea that serves to mediate between subjective and objective judgements. Its aim is to teach knowledge about the right conduct, not to assert the truth about nature itself. According to Spinoza, when the beings of imagination are taken as true laws of nature, they turn into superstition. The epistemological and practical status of an exemplar is that of a human construct that serves to compare things and their relative values and to promote emulation, but, despite the fact that they claim to represent the ideal or model of all things of a certain kind, they might, in fact, represent only one particular image or a series of images blurred together. There is no guarantee that they constitute an adequate knowledge.

Therefore, to take them as the bearers of an absolute truth such as that expressed in the knowledge of the laws of nature is to fall into the trap of superstition. Political myths must be recognised in their plurality, a plurality, in Spinoza's terms, which is derived from the fact that the universality of the exemplars of human nature is the universality of what we are accustomed to feign. If we fail to recognise this, and take political myths as laws of nature, then we transform them into superstition.

In Spinoza's analysis of the history of the Jews we find the basis for a whole theory of political myth, which enables us to both understand the role that myth plays in politics and to normatively set the limits for myth's legitimate use. In his view, even if imagination is not an adequate kind of knowledge, such as that which can be reached by the intellect, it is, however, not necessarily false: it turns into falsehood, or superstition, only when it is taken beyond its limits. These, as we have seen, consist in teaching the right conduct.

Political myths, we can conclude, should not be taken as expressing an absolute truth, because there is always the possibility that they contain an inadequate form of knowledge. For this reason, the state should enable those who can to elevate themselves to the level of intellectual knowledge. In other words, they should be given the possibility to exercise a critical scrutiny. Political myths are not necessarily a form of regression (Cassirer) or a form of progress (Sorel): they can be both because there is no a priori guarantee that the knowledge they contain is adequate. However, if all societies are in a sense imaginary, because they will have to resort to imagination in one way or another, what they differ in is the degree to which this imaginative dimension can be subjected to critical discussion.

Despite the fact that all the three theories analysed here are derived from the analysis of specific examples, Spinoza's reflections provide the basis for a more comprehensive theory of political imagination, which contains both analytical and normative insights. As we have seen, though, according to Spinoza, imagination, as a set of bodily determined ideas, is necessarily passive. In his view, it is only at the level of intellectual knowledge that autonomy, and thus real morality, can be attained. However, it is possible to question such a completely passive view of imagination, as we saw in Chapter 3, and will discuss again in Chapter 10. As Castoriadis has pointed out, together with a repetitive, bodily and socially determined imagination, there is also a radical or primary imagination that explains the possibility, even within a disciplinary society, of a radical political imaginary and thus of a critique (Castoriadis 1987).

In spite of this limit, Spinoza's reflections provide very stimulating insights as to the nature and limits of political myth. The next step consists in drawing some conclusions from this discussion, by spelling out what a political myth is, and how it differs from other related imaginary constructions. In doing so, we will return to the theory of myth presented in Part II. However rich, none of the classical theories of political myth analysed here treat myth as a process rather than as an object, as following Blumenberg, I will now try to do.

9

Political Myth, Ideology and Utopia

Following the preceding discussion of the classical theories of political myth, we can now attempt to draw some conclusions as to what a political myth is and how it works. In the first place, all the authors we have been analysing stress the narrative dimension of myth. Cassirer holds that it is a narrative that, by connecting past, present and future events, posits itself as prophetic: the "myth of the twentieth century" is the myth of a superior race, the Aryan one, which, precisely on the basis of the narrative of its glorious origins, is deemed to rule the world. Sorel also points to the narrative dimension of political myth: it is thanks to this dimension that the people involved in major social movements can represent their upcoming action as part of a sequence of events that assures the triumph of their cause. Finally, Spinoza, too, who deals with political myth by using the Jewish prophecy as an exemplar, stresses the narrative dimension that is implicit in the idea of "chosenness", in the story of the Covenant between God and the Jews that is the foundation of Jewish theocracy. In this case, we have a narrative dimension that encompasses the past, the present and the future: the biblical prophecy looks at the past, since the aim of this prophecy is to recall the terms of the Covenant with God, and, on this basis, it is able to predict the salvation of all the peoples on Earth through the "elected people" of Israel.[1]

[1] See, for instance, Jeremiah 31: 31.

While all these authors point to the narrative dimension, they also stress that there is something more at stake in a political myth. For instance, they all make reference to "prophecy", however differently it may be understood, as foreseeing the future (Cassirer), as a prediction of catastrophe (Sorel) or as a reminder of a past Covenant (Spinoza). In other words, they all stress that the narrative that constitutes a political myth also grounds – in the sense of *begründen* – the conditions in which the human beings who believe in these myths find themselves. Following Blumenberg, we have called this dimension significance. Myth, to sum up, is a narrative that answers a need for significance.

The reference to the idea of "prophecy" should not, however, be misleading. If it is true that political myths are, in a sense, prophecies, it must also be added that they are, most of the time, secular prophecies. Myth, as we have seen, does not coincide with religion. What is significant is not simply that which possesses a meaning, nor is it necessarily that which explains the meaning of life in general: something that is significant is something that situates itself between the two extremes of a simple meaning and the meaning of life and death.

This also clarifies the particularistic nature of myth, and thus the reason why all these authors have dealt with singular political myths. What makes a political myth out of a simple narrative is the fact that the work on this narrative can, in a certain context and for certain subjects, come together and produce significance. Significance is always particularistic in the sense that what is significant for me here and now is not necessarily so in another context. At the same time, the sphere of significance always refers to some possibility that what is significant for me here and now can also be recognised as significant by somebody else who shares the same conditions.

Spinoza points to this when he states that prophecy conveys exemplars of human nature. As we have seen, though these are "universal ideas", they are not necessarily adequate ideas, since the universality at stake here is that of "what we are accustomed to feign". In other words, it is not an absolute universal, but a relative one, and precisely a universal relative to the conditions in which these beings of the imagination are created.

This leads us to a crucial point. Political myths are always told from the standpoint of the present (Tudor 1972), and it is precisely for this reason that political myths are best defined in terms of a continual process of "work on myth": it is in light of the continual change in their present conditions that human beings are impelled to go back to their political narratives, revise them in light of their new needs and exigencies through their reception, or, when this is not possible, dismiss them.

To sum up, a political myth can be defined as the work on a common narrative by which the members of a social group (or society) make significance[2] of their political experiences and deeds. Consequently, what makes a political myth out of a simple narrative is not its content or its claim to truth, as Lincoln and Flood have argued (Lincoln 1989; Flood 1996), but the fact that this narrative creates significance, that it is shared by a group and that it affects the specifically political conditions in which this group operates.

Therefore, the work on political myth unfolds in a dimension, that of the articulation and creation of significance, that escapes any sharp contraposition between cognitive, practical and aesthetical spheres. A political myth can, at the same time, have a cognitive, practical and an aesthetical dimension, without it being possible to distinguish clearly between them.

As Flood has also pointed out, political myths provide fundamental cognitive schemata for mapping the social world: it is by reducing the complexity of social life to the relative simplicity of its narrative plot, that a comprehension of the multifaceted character of experience is possible (Flood 1996). This, in its turn, points to the practical dimension of myth, as has been underlined by Sorel: the people involved in social action need to represent their upcoming action in the form of a narrative or sequence of events that assures the triumph of their cause. As we have seen, a narrative of events does not simply imply a temporal sequence of what comes into being, but also a configurational dimension, or a plot, which construes a significant whole out of scattered events. This leads to the aesthetical dimension of myth or, as Tudor has put it, to the fact that political myths are narratives of events cast in a dramatic form (Tudor 1972). It is in the articulation

[2] To "make significance" does not simply mean to "make sense", but must be understood in the sense shown in Chapter 6.

of a drama that the pathos of political myth emerges (Lincoln 1989). This, however, cannot be separated from other dimensions: thinking too, not only acting, can have its pathos.

Going back to our previous examples, one can conclude that the myths of the Aryan race, the general strike and the Jewish prophecy are all political myths because they are all *shared narratives* that answer a need for *significance*, and they are all *political* because the significance that is at stake here is that of political conditions and actions.

This does not mean that a myth can only be political if its content is political. According to Tudor, what renders a myth specifically political is precisely its subject matter. As we read in his *Political Myth*, just as natural myths deal with natural phenomena and religious myths deal with gods and their worship, so political myth deals with politics (Tudor 1972: 17). As a consequence, a political myth is, according to this view, "one which tells the story of a political society" (Tudor 1972: 138).

However, within this view the problem emerges of how to determine the contours of a specifically political subject. For example, the Christian myth of the apocalypse to which Tudor himself devotes great attention was not political per se. There is nothing specifically political in the claim that the world is transitory, that it was created by God, and, in the fullness of time, will be destroyed. And, in fact, such an idea has not generated political myth at all times and epochs. It is only when it has been inserted in particular contexts that it has generated powerful political myths – the accurate analysis by Tudor of the myth of the millennium being a case in point.

Thus, what renders a myth specifically *political* is not an already political content of the story that it tells, but the fact that the story that it tells comes to "make significance" of the specifically *political* conditions for a certain social group or society. Here, by political conditions, I mean provisionally the conditions concerning the struggle for the distribution of power and resources which can, as a last resort, have recourse to physical force.[3]

---

3 This is a standard definition of politics, whose origins go as far back as Weber, at least (see, for instance, Weber 1978: vol. I, 54–5, vol. II, 901). As will emerge, particularly in Part IV, it is precisely by analysing the work on political myth that one is, however, led to rethink this definition of politics. Indeed, it seems as if an always greater part of political power is exercised through means other than the threat to recourse to physical coercion.

As a consequence, in order to catch the specifically political connotation of a myth one must look at the whole "work on myth". As more recent theories of political myth such as that elaborated by Flood have pointed out, in dealing with political myth it is not only at the production of myth that we must look, but also, and foremost, at its reception (Flood 1996: 7). It is the way in which a story works within a given context, the way in which it is received, that is whether a story can or cannot provide significance and then affect the political conditions that determines whether it is a political myth or not.[4]

Political myths are not, to use Gramsci's expression, pieces of paper (*cose di carta*). If we want to perceive the work on a political myth, it is not under the dust in our libraries that we have to look. This work cannot be perceived by simply looking at the stories that are deposited in books and archives. The work on myth is a process that can take place in very different settings: speeches, icons, arts, both visual and otherwise, rituals and almost all other kinds of social practices.

Indeed, the possible sites for the work on political myth can hardly be counted.[5] We can only point here to the pervasiveness of the work on myth. All activities and practices can become vehicles of political myths inasmuch as they can embody a narrative dimension that satisfies the need for significance. Any kind of social activity can host the work on the particular kinds of narratives that Blumenberg called *mythologems* in order to stress the fact that it is implicit in the concept of myth that there can be variants.

As a consequence, political myths are not usually learned once and for all. Most of the time, they are apprehended through an at least partially unconscious cumulative exposure. This also elucidates the "condensational power" of political myths, that is, their capacity to condense things into a few images or "icons" (Flood 1996). By means of a synecdoche, any object or gesture – a painting, an image, a song, a

---

[4] Tudor also seems to get close to arguing this when he states that "a myth is always told from the standpoint of the present" and this carries the implications that, as the circumstances in which human beings find themselves change, so they reconstruct their myth (Tudor 1972: 21, 125), but he does not include this feature in his final definition of political myth. This, perhaps, is because he conceived his *Political Myth* more as an introduction to the different approaches to political myth rather than as a systematic attempt to construct a theory of political myth.

[5] Some suggestions on the possible sites for the working of myth in contemporary societies can be found in Chapter 12.

film, an advertisement, a gesture – can recall the whole work on myth that lies behind it.

This pervasiveness of myths, on the one hand explains the difficulty of scientifically analysing them and, therefore, the related discrediting that is pending on this topic. On the other hand, it has led many authors to conflate myth with other forms of human expression and social practice. As we have seen, Cassirer considered myth as a whole form of life encompassing most different phenomena, such as totemism, religion, and ritual. However, a distinction must be drawn between what is a political myth and what can be the sites for the work on a political myth.

First and foremost, as we have seen, one must analytically distinguish between political myths and rituals. In everyday life, they are often associated since it is also through rituals that the work on political myths can take place. This does not just hold true for the so-called primitive societies or forms of life – to which the ritualistic theory of myth devoted most of its attention (Tudor 1972 28ff.). For instance, an important body of rituals, such as national festivals, commemorations of the crucial events of national history, and so on, accompanies most national foundational myths. Most national days, from the American Fourth of July to the French Fourteenth of July, are examples of political rituals that are connected with political myths, in these cases the myth of American Independence and the myth of the French Revolution.[6]

But, as Tudor observes by criticising the ritualistic theories of myth, not all political myths are accompanied by any significant body of rituals (for example the myth of the Norman yoke), while some political rituals, such as inauguration ceremonies, are not directly connected with any myth (Tudor 1972: 30). The point to be stressed here is that, as we saw earlier on, myth and rituals can work within the social historical context through two different modalities. The "ritual" expresses itself through fixed rules and is effective only as far as these rules remain unchanged. In contrast, a myth, and, in particular, a political myth, expresses itself through variants; if a political myth is always told from the standpoint of the present and it is in the present political

---

[6] On the link between national day celebrations and political myth, see, for instance, Thorsen 2000.

conditions that it must provide significance, then it follows that it can be effective only insofar as it is possible to go back to it and transform it according to the changing circumstances and needs. In the last analysis, political rituals must remain unchanged in order to promote social cohesion, whereas political myths, having to ground (*begründen*) always-changing circumstances, must be open to change in order to promote the same purpose.

For example, in Italy the ritual celebration of the Twenty-Fifth of April has remained fundamentally unchanged, while the corresponding myth of the Italian Resistance against Nazism has changed considerably in the last fifty years (Pavone 1995; Paggi 1999; and Stråth 2000). The work around the narrative of the Resistance has coagulated and given significance to very different actors in very different contexts. As Pavone observes, the problem in dealing with the Resistance as a historian is that the Resistance as a historical problem is quite often intermingled with the work around the Resistance as a "civic problem" in general, but also as a myth in particular (Pavone 1995: 185).[7] The narrative of the Resistance has not only worked as a narrative that legitimates the new Italian Republic – as is signalled by the widespread formula "republic born out of the Resistance" (*Repubblica nata dalla Resistenza*) – but has also worked as a narrative that, by operating at the crossroads between memory of the past and expectations for the future as embodied in certain human exemplars, provided significance to different generations and in very different contexts.[8]

Political myths must always be up to date, otherwise they cease to be political myths and become something else. And they are not simply abstract models with which to compare existing political conditions. They can also be abstract models, but they are never just this. They are always at the same time a determination to act – they are narratives that prompt people to action precisely because they answer a need for

[7] On the difference between mythical and historical narratives, see Chapter 10.

[8] As Pavone observes, the study of the myth of the Resistance cannot but start from the study of the innumerable tales, novels, films, documentaries, monuments, etc., which, in the last fifty years, have been the privileged sites for the working on the myth of the Resistance (Pavone 1995). This does not mean that there is one single myth of the Resistance and even less that the narrative of the Resistance always works as a myth: as Paggi points out, in order to establish whether this narrative is working as a myth or not, one has to start from specific regional and local contexts (Paggi 1999).

significance. Political myths therefore cannot be falsified: the fact that what they contain has not or will not be realised does not diminish their power. As Sorel pointed out, political myths must not be judged as astrological almanacs, but as a means for acting in the present.

This does not mean that they are impermeable to critical discussion. The fact that they cannot be falsified by what actually happens does not mean that they cannot be rationally discussed. What Sorel, Spinoza and Cassirer do in their theories is precisely to discuss them critically. The point is that the way in which the discussion must be carried out is not in relation to their real or unreal content, but to their appropriateness as a means for acting in the present – the moral of the story that they tell, that is, the values that they purport, on the one hand, and their capacity to create significance in these particular conditions, on the other.

This, of course, holds for the pure ideal-typical political myths. In fact, as we shall see, the political myths with which we are most familiar are often intermingled with other kinds of discourses. This is the consequence of the pervasiveness of political myth. The myth of the Aryan race is, for instance, constructed on the basis of scientific findings, which clearly bring to the fore other kinds of considerations that call for a different method of judgement: the biological finding upon which it rests and its mythical side must be judged with different tools, even if in reality the two kinds of discourse are intermingled.

Even if there is no dichotomy of myth versus science similar to the one from which we departed in this work, there still remains a difference between the two that cannot but bring in different kinds of considerations. As Spinoza pointed out, when the two orders of considerations are not kept separate, they risk falling into superstition, as happened when the moral message encompassed in the Jewish prophecy of Israel's election was taken as a law of nature. This is what Spinoza feared may have happened if his contemporaries, the Dutch Calvinists, had interpreted the myth of their "chosenness" in such terms.

Similarly, in many national myths, we have a melange of mythical and other elements. Clearly these bring different sorts of consideration to light and call for different tools of evaluation.[9] The Italian Resistance and the French Revolution are neither pure myths nor

---

[9] On the relationship between myth and historical narratives, see Chapter 10.

pure historical events. They can work as both, but we must, accordingly, analyse them with the most appropriate tools. As we shall see in Chapter 10, even if pure historians do not exist, what historians do, and what we expect them to do when they present their historical narratives, is to refer to a method that asks them to base their narratives on documents and testimonies, that is, on other (in principle revisable) narratives. The ideal-typical myth-maker – let us submit for the moment that there is a pure one – does not refer to other evidences because the capacity to address the present conditions is a sufficient condition. The myth-maker wants to incite people to action, not to reconstruct the past accurately. If he or she looks at the past, it is done with the immediate intent of inciting people to action.

Even if some historical narratives, such as the French Revolution or the Italian Resistance, work and have been working in certain contexts as political myths, there are plenty of historical narratives that are not political myths. Furthermore, there are also political myths, such as that of the general strike, that – as Sorel points out – are all constructed in a future dimension; and this is sufficient, at the ideal-typical level, for keeping historical and mythical narratives separate.

Not even all the founding narratives are political myth. What decides which narratives can become political myths is a narrative's capacity to answer a need for significance, and not all the founding narratives are able to do this in certain conditions and contexts. It is not a matter of objective interests at stake: the question is not which narrative can be better used in order to uphold certain material interests. Not all the possible narratives that suit those interests could have aspired to the role of political myths. This explains why a political myth cannot simply be fabricated around a table. Instead, political myths must insert themselves within certain conditions, and are mostly intermingled with other kinds of discourses, although they must not be conflated with them.

One of the reasons why political myth was given so little attention in theoretical debate is that it has often been deployed together with other and more familiar kinds of discourse. Political myths tend to be obscured by them. And the reason why this happens is easy to understand. We almost never see a pure myth-maker at work: the mythical account will inevitably deal with matters also touched upon by writers, philosophers, historians and scientists, and it is most often only to them that the critical discussion applies itself. One of the concepts with which political myth is most often conflated is ideology.[10] As we will see, however, notwithstanding the important interconnections between the two, political myth and ideology must be kept analytically separated and used to address only partially overlapping social phenomena.

A classical example of the attempt to deal with political myth under the heading of ideology is Raymond Aron's *The Opium of the Intellectuals* (2001). Written in the 1950s as an analysis of the reasons for the uncritical attitude of the French communists towards the politics of the Soviet Union, the book had a clear polemical intent. This is patent from its very title, in which Aron turns Marx's criticism of religious alienation upon French Marxists themselves, in order to point out that Marxism, far from leading to liberation from alienation, had itself turned into a form of religious alienation.

In his view, this loss of critical attitude is evident in the communists' tendency to impose the same eschatological scheme everywhere and thereby overlook the complexity of reality and the radical diversity of historical circumstances. This, in Aron's view, is particularly evident in the working of three of the political myths that he analyses: the myth of the left, the myth of the revolution, and the myth of the proletariat. All these myths, according to Aron, correspond to the same eschatological scheme of Christianity: an agent of salvation elected as vehicle for the redemption of humanity on the basis of its sufferings (Aron 2001: 66ff.).

In this view, there are three characteristics of political myths understood as ideologies: 1) they are systems of ideas that reveal a universal truth, and are therefore totalising; 2) they mobilise passions; and 3) they are utopian insofar as they neglect the complexity of reality and of the specific historical circumstances. On this basis, Aron was also predicting the advent of "the end of ideologies": in the aftermath of World War II, after the defeat of fascism and the affirmation of democracy, the longing for ideology was, in his view, superseded by a careful pragmatism more inclined to look at the specificity of different contexts.[11]

[10] As we have seen, Flood 1996 is a typical example.
[11] Among the supporters of the "end of ideologies" thesis, see Bell 1960 and Shils 1958.

There is, however, a double problem with this treatment of political myth. First, from the point of view of a theory of political myth, it is subject to the same kind of criticism that can be raised against any attempt to unify myth and religion under common headings such as Cassirer's "mythical consciousness" or "the opium of intellectuals". I will not repeat previous considerations, but simply observe that if political myths are characterised as narratives that provide significance and that, by locating human action within a coherent narrative, prompt people to act, this is not a sufficient condition for conflating them with religion. If it is true, as Sorel, and, more recently, Tudor have observed, that Marxism, when inserted in certain contexts, has also worked as a political myth, this is not a sufficient condition for conflating myth with religion, on the one hand, or with ideology, on the other (Tudor 1996: 126).

Second, it can be argued that this view is constructed in such a way that it is destined to fall victim to its own arguments: the criticism of ideologies as the opium of the masses that was used by Aron against Marx, who first formulated it, can well be used against Aron himself. This becomes evident at the end of the book when Aron is confronted with the objection that democracy and nationalism are also ideologies since they have also been able to instil an ardour that was no less passionate than the one instilled by the myth of a classless society (Aron 2001: 266–7). Aron's reply to this possible objection consists of vindicating the uniqueness of communism as an ideology precisely on the basis of its prophetic structure.

Let us now look more closely at what, according to Aron, this means, that is, at what precisely characterises ideology understood as prophecy. For Aron, communism, like all kinds of prophecies, is constructed around three elements: 1) condemnation of the status quo, 2) the depiction of what should be; and 3) the individuation of a subject capable of transforming the present into a future condition (Aron 2001: 265ff.). But in this sense, the "end of ideologies" thesis is itself an ideology. Clearly, it entails a condemnation of the age of ideologies, as well as the prophetic assertion of its immanent end and the individuation of a subject, the disengaged social theorist, who can, if not lead this transition, at least prepare its way.

The problem is that, once one enters into the polemical use of the concept of ideology, it becomes impossible to extricate oneself from it – it triggers a vicious circle. The dichotomy of "ideological" versus "real" upon which this use ultimately rests can always be turned against those who employ it. Aron remains a victim of his own polemical usage of the concept of ideology. However, as many authors have pointed out, together with this polemical use of the term ideology, there is another, more neutral, one.[12] As has been stressed from different sides, notwithstanding the multifaceted varieties of the possible uses of the term ideology – Eagleton counts at least fifteen of them (Eagleton 1991) – they can all be subsumed into two types.

The first kind in use is more restricted and might be defined as the negative, or at least as polemical: ideology, in this view, fundamentally refers to some kind of false consciousness or masquerade through a fictitious disguising of the true reality of facts. The hallmark of this use, as we have seen in Aron's theory, is the contrast between what is "ideological" and what is "real". This term was first employed by Napoleon, who used it to criticise the abstract idealism of *les idéologues* in contrast with the "reality" of facts (Dierse 1976).

As is well known, the term was most influentially used in this sense by Marx and Engels, who contributed profoundly to the physiognomy of the polemical use of the concept.[13] Initially, Marx and Engels used the term in their criticism of German ideology, that is, the fundamentally illusory attempts of the "Young Hegelians" to modify the society they lived in through the sheer criticism of ideas (Marx and Engels 1976).

The entire body of German philosophical criticism, so they wrote, from Strauss to Stirner is confined to criticism of religious conceptions. . . . Their advance consisted in subsuming the allegedly dominant metaphysical, political, juridical moral and other conceptions under the category of religious or theological conception . . . The Young Hegelian ideologists, in spite of their allegedly "world-shattering" statement, are the staunchest conservatives. The most recent of them have found the correct expression for their activity when they declare they are only fighting against "phrases". They forget, however, that they themselves are opposing only other phrases to these phrases and that they

---

[12] See, for instance, Dubois 2001, Freeden 2001, Stoppino 1989, and Thompson 2001.
[13] According to Mannheim, the anticipation of this concept of ideology goes as far back as Francis Bacon's critique of the *idola* or prejudices (Mannheim 1960: 55). Nevertheless, it was not until the time of the French Revolution that the term ideology began to be used in the common sense of the term.

are in no way combating the *real* existing world when they are combating solely
the *phrases* of this world . . . It has not occurred to anyone of these philosophers
to inquire into the connection of the German philosophy with German *reality*,
the relation of their criticism to their own material *surroundings*. (Marx, Engels
1976: 29–30; emphasis mine)

The polemic is conducted against a topos in German literature, whose
origins go as far back as the epoch of the French Revolution, according
to which Germany, economically and politically backward in comparison with France, could only undertake in *thought*, that is, through
philosophical criticism, the same revolution that France had put into
action. The criticism of this "ideological view" is conducted through a
continual contrast between the level of ideas and that of reality. In this
sense, the early usage of the term by Marx and Engels is closely related
to Napoleon's criticism of *les idéologues*.

With his *Contribution to the Critique of Hegel's Philosophy of Law*, Marx
had already attempted to vindicate the need for a "material basis
of the revolution" against the view advanced by the "German ideologists" (Marx 1975). Against the illusions of these ideologists, who
could only think of revolutions "in a glass of water", Marx had, from
1843, been emphasising that the weapons of criticism cannot replace
the criticism of weapons (1975). Two years later with Engels, in *The
German Ideology* (1976), the dichotomy of "ideological" versus "real"
takes the form of a contrast between "idealism" and what is now called
the "materialistic conception of history". Its method is very efficiently
synthesised:

the premises from which we begin are not *arbitrary* ones, not dogmas, but *real*
premises from which abstraction can only be made in the *imagination*. They
are the *real* individuals, their activity and the *material conditions* under which
they live, both those which they find already existing and those produced by
their activity. These premises can thus be verified in a purely empirical way.
(Marx and Engels 1976: 32)

With historical materialism, particularly in its successive elabora-
tions where the reference to the material conditions of existence was
to take the form of a detailed analysis of the economic modes and relations of production, the term "ideology" tends to widen so as to cover
the whole complex of social historical phenomena – not only religious
and philosophical ones, but also political and juridical ones – in other

words all that is super-structural in respect to the economic structure, the real material conditions for the reproduction of life.

As has been observed from various approaches, Marx and Engels' analysis of ideology is a permanent acquisition: it contributed to rooting the evanescent world of ideas in the solid ground of the social structure, to showing the necessity of ideological constructions. If the Marxist view of ideology is no longer hegemonic in academic debate, this is, to a great extent, due to the fact that it became a piece of standard intellectual equipment (Geertz 1964).

On the other hand, the questions raised by a theory of political myth do not coincide with those faced by Marx and Engels. What is of interest here is not to raise the issue of why ideological constructions are necessary, or to what kind of mode of production they correspond, but rather why human beings, among the different human constructions of meaning, also need to make recourse to narratives that respond to the need for significance. Conflating myth and ideology, therefore, can only be impoverishing.

In particular, from the point of view of a theory of political myth, the problem is that, by contrasting both political myth and ideology with the "real material conditions of existence", not only does it become difficult to draw any distinction between myth and ideology, but, moreover, there is the risk of falling once more into the Enlightenment's dichotomy of "myth" versus "reality". Marx's analysis of the uses made by the French revolutionaries of the myth of the Roman Republic is a good example of this risk.

In the preface to the second edition of *The Eighteenth Brumaire of Louis Bonaparte*, Marx stated that his intention was "to demonstrate how the class struggle in France created circumstances and relationships that made it possible for a grotesque mediocrity to play a hero's part" (Marx 1969: 395). He began his essay by observing that human beings do not make their history under circumstances chosen by themselves, but under circumstances that they found as already given and transmitted from the past. Among these circumstances is the tradition of the dead generations "that weighs like a nightmare on the brain of the living" (1969: 398). In his view, even when human beings seem to be engaged in creating something entirely new:

precisely in such epochs of revolutionary crises they anxiously conjure up the spirits of the past to their service, and borrow from them names, battle slogans and costumes in order to present the new scene of world history in this time-honoured disguise and this borrowed language. Thus Luther donned the mask of the Apostle Paul, the Revolution of the 1789 to 1814 draped itself alternatively as the Roman Republic and the Roman Empire, and the Revolution of 1848 knew nothing better to do than to parody, in turn 1789 and the revolutionary tradition of 1793 to 1795. (1969: 399)

Marx is referring to one narrative, that of the Roman Republic, which is likely to have worked, to a great extent, as political myth for the French revolutionaries. However, Marx is interested here in the phenomenon of ideology and thus states that the French revolutionaries needed to perform the task of their time in Roman costumes and with Roman phrases, because, unheroic as bourgeois society is, it had need of heroism and sacrifice to come into being. As he wrote: "in the classical austere traditions of the Roman Republic, its gladiators found the ideals and the art forms, the *self-deceptions* that they needed in order to conceal from themselves the bourgeois limitations of the content of their struggles and to keep their passions at the height of the great historical tragedy" (1969: 399; emphasis mine). Similarly, Marx further observes, at another stage of development, a century earlier, Cromwell and the English people had made their bourgeois revolution by borrowing "speech, passions and illusions" from the Old Testament: "only when the real aim had been achieved, when the bourgeois transformation of English society had been accomplished, did Locke supplant Habakkuk" (1969: 399). Ideology, thus, is a self-deception, but a self-deception that is necessary.

Moving from this analysis, the only aspect that can be said to unite political myths and ideology is their being a form of self-deception, which, however necessary, is meant to present particular interests in the form of universally recognised principles. Indeed, when analysing the events of the Eighteenth Brumaire, Marx constructs his account through a long chain of conceptual oppositions that reflect the fundamental opposition between imagination and reality: "Roman *phrases*"[14] versus their "*real* task", "the antediluvian Colossi and the resurrected Romans (from Brutus and Gracchi to the senators and Caesar)" versus

[14] Marx used the same contraposition between "phrases" and "reality" in order to criticise the attempt of the German ideologists to make a revolution by simply criticising ideas. As we have seen, for Marx and Engels, these were merely "revolutions in a glass of water".

"the sober *reality* of bourgeois society and its *true* interpreters such as
its Says, Constants, Guizots and its *real* military leaders", "the heroic
self-deceptions" versus "the bourgeois *limitations* of their struggle", "the
magnification of their tasks in *imagination*" versus "the finding of a
solution in *reality*" (Marx 1969: 399–401; emphasis mine).

However, the problem raised by a theory of political myth is the
question of why people needed to represent their action precisely in
this way and not whether this served to conceal the real interests at
stake. In other words, why did the French revolutionaries need to
perform the task of their epoch in Roman customs, and not Greek or
Turkish? Why could only the narrative of the Roman Republic provide
significance to them in those particular circumstances? Marx's theory
does not aim to deal with these questions. Indeed, he does not say much
about the difference between the imaginary constructions, which are
cast in a narrative form and respond to a need for significance (that is,
what we have called "political myths"), and those that do not present
these features.

All the same, one could assume that, by elaborating a different view
of ideology, the concept of political myth may still be treated together
with that of ideology. For instance, as has been noted, in Marx there are
signs of a passage from a polemical, and thus particular, view of ideology to what has been called a "total view of ideology". Karl Mannheim,
who explicitly proposed the adoption of a neutral concept of ideology, has strongly emphasised this point.[15] In his view, although the
particular conception of ideology, by presenting ideas as the more or
less conscious disguise of the real nature of a situation, makes specific
assumptions as to the mystifying relationship between the two, what he
calls the "total conception of ideology" simply presupposes that there
is a correspondence between a given social situation and a given perspective or point of view (Mannheim 1960: 51). In this second sense,
we refer to the ideology of an age or a concrete social historical group,
for example, a class, when we are concerned with the characteristics
and composition of the total structure of the mind of this epoch or of
this group (1960: 49–50).

According to Mannheim, while the first conception of ideology that
focuses on the errors of the individuals is the field of psychology, the

---

[15] See Dubois 2001, Freeden 2001, Stoppino 1989, and Thompson 2001.

second one is the field of what he calls a "sociology of knowledge". This should be a discipline concerned with ideology in the sense of interwoven systems of thought and modes of experience that are conditioned by the social circumstances shared by groups of individuals. Marx, by tracing ideology back to its social roots, took an important step from the particular to the total concept of ideology, but, by remaining attached to the idea of ideology as false consciousness, he still had one foot in this particular view of ideology (Mannheim 1960: 57).

It is crucial to assume a neutral concept of ideology, as first inaugurated by Mannheim, in order to discuss ideology's relationship with political myth. This does not mean that, by using a neutral definition, one aims to transcend the historically situated character of any sociology of knowledge: the intellectual is always within ideology, and is never a free-floating being transcending the inevitable perspectiveness of any enquiry.[16] To assume a neutral meaning simply means not to make any strong ontological assumption over the nature of the relationship between ideology and the social historical framework. Following Mannheim's insights, this simply means that we assume that there is a strict relationship between the two, without, however, entering into any substantive characterisation of their relationship. Indeed, it is to such a definition of ideology that contemporary theorists of political myth have been referring (see Tudor 1972, and, more recently, Lincoln 1989, and Flood 1996).

According to Christopher Flood, for instance, political myth situates itself precisely between ideology thus conceived and what he calls the sacred myth, that is, myth as it is used within religious systems. In addition, the two definitions of ideology to which he refers are examples of the neutral meaning: ideology, he states picking up one of the most common definitions in contemporary social science, is a "belief system that explains and justifies a preferred political order for society, either existing or proposed, and offers a strategy (processes, institutional

---

[16] According to Freeden, Mannheim would, on the contrary, have attempted to overcome the relativism through his own sociology of knowledge, since he would have granted to the free-floating intellectuals the capacity to incorporate the perspective of different groups into a holistic relationism and, thereby, to attain a critical approximation of truth (Freeden 2001). Irrespective of the correctness of this interpretation, the important point to stress here is that this is not what we mean by a "neutral" type of use of the concept of ideology.

arrangements, programs) for its attainment" (Flood 1996: 13). Otherwise stated, in his view, ideology is a "set of ideas by which men posit, explain and justify ends and means of organised social action, and specifically political action, irrespective of whether such action aims to preserve, amend, uproot or rebuild a given social order" (Flood 1996: 13).

The advantages of this perspective are clear. From the point of view of a theory of political myth, first, it does not carry with it any assumption about the reality or unreality of both ideology and political myth, and, second, it enables us to address one important common feature of political myth and ideology. Such definitions do not make any assumption about the nature of these beliefs: they do not limit ideology to false/true or conscious/unconscious beliefs and ideas. In other words, they do not analyse ideology from the psychological point of view, that is, from the point of view of the single individual, and they therefore make no assumptions as to the degree to which these motivations must be present in the consciousness of single acting individuals. Indeed, in order to analyse the impact of a political myth or, more generally, of an ideology, one cannot limit oneself to the level of individual psychology (let us admit for the moment that this is possible), since it may well be the case that not all the elements that constitute a political myth or an ideology are present in all their parts *hic et nunc* in the single mind of an individual.

As Geertz noted, only the first answer to the question "Why do individuals need ideology?" can be psychological (Geertz 1964). A huge amount of literature that draws inspiration from Freud's discoveries tells us that ideologies are collections of invested symbols that are needed in order to overcome the chronic misintegration of society – be it in the form of the scapegoat theory, according to which ideology is a symbolic construction that drains off emotional tension through the creation of a symbolic enemy, or any other way of overcoming the strain created by the very condition of living in a society. In any case, it is always at the psychological level that the determinant of the production of ideology is located. Again, the acquisitions in this field are enormous and permanent. But what interests us, to go back to the Marxian example, is not an analysis of the emotional disequilibrium that led to the investing of Roman customs with such ideological power. The crucial question for us is why they needed to perform their task using the customs of others in the first place, and, in the second, why they needed to use Roman rather than other customs.

As Geertz himself, among others, has pointed out, ideologies are mapping devices whose cognitive impact is secondary in comparison to their practical function: ideology serves to provide a map of the social reality that orients both at the cognitive as well as at the practical level (Geertz 1964). The reason why such symbolic templates are necessary is that human behaviour, in contrast with that of lower animals, is not for the most part determined by innate, physiologically determined patterns of behaviour: birds learn how to fly without wind tunnels and, whatever reaction they may have in the face of death, this is to a great extent physiologically preformed. In contrast, the extreme generality and variability of human capacities of response mean that the patterns of their behaviour are predominantly guided by cultural rather than innate templates (Geertz 1964: 63). As we have seen, the tool-making and lying animal is "an incomplete – or more accurately, self-completing animal":[17] the agent of his own realisation, he creates the specific capacity that defines him out of his general capacity for the construction of symbolic models. In particular it is through the construction of ideologies, schematic images of political order and actions, that he makes himself a political animal (Geertz 1964: 63).

An important qualification must, however, be added to this definition of ideology. Both Geertz's concept of ideology as "cultural system" and Flood's first definition refer to the concept of "system". This implies a further dimension that is not covered in Flood's second definition of ideology as a simple set of ideas – the systematic character of the set of ideas constituting ideology. In order to analyse the relationship between political myth and ideology we must abandon this element.

Indeed, only certain types of ideology, such as those to which the thesis of "the end of ideology" refers, have a systematic character. In comparison to them, contemporary forms of ideology evoke the image of an *archipelago* in contrast with that of a continent (Boudon 1999). As Boudon reminds us, we have ideologies about what should be done about unemployment, educational opportunities, crime or drug

---

[17] See also the discussion of Gehlen's recovery of Nietzsche's definition of the human being as a not yet determined animal in Chapter 3.

addiction and about a myriad subjects. But these theories are weakly
related to one another, so that the concept of system can hardly be
applied here. We have ceased to believe that they could be derived
from an all-encompassing theory. We have all kinds of local ideologies;
we no longer believe in general ideologies (Boudon 1999). In other
words, ideology is today much more pervasive than a "system of
beliefs".

Thus, we can conclude that an ideology is a set of ideas by which
human beings posit, understand and justify ends and means of a more
or less organised social action.[18] The intersection with the concept of
political myth is indeed clear: a political myth also entails a set of ideas
by which human beings posit and represent the ends and means of
social action. Both political myth and ideology are mapping devices
that orient in the social and political world.

However, not all such sets of ideas constitute a political myth. In
order to constitute a political myth, two further conditions must also
be met. First, this set of ideas must take the form of a narrative, that is,
of a series of events cast in a dramatic form. And not all ideologies have
a narrative form. Second, precisely on the basis of this narrative form,
it must be able to ground (*begründen*) or to coagulate and reproduce
significance. To put it plainly, political myths are narratives that put a
drama on stage. And it is from the impression of being part of such
drama that the typically strong pathos of a political myth derives.[19] I can
theoretically share an ideology which leaves me completely indifferent
on the emotional level, but no political myth can ever be shared and at
the same time remain emotionally indifferent. In this case, it is simply
not a political myth for me. And this, I think, is ultimately the reason
why the concept of political myth and that of ideology should be kept
separated.

---

[18] In respect of the original formulation of this definition (Flood 1996: 13), where
reference is made to ideology as a means of "positing, explaining and justifying",
I have omitted the second verb, since in the most general sense of the term "to
explain" this is already implicit in the verb "to justify", whereas in the strongest sense,
that of a "scientific explanation", this would not enable me to encompass political
myth within it. Similarly, I have modified the reference to "organized social and
specifically political action". The action that is promoted by a political myth, as well
as by ideology, can in fact be more or less organised.

[19] Many contemporary theorists of political myth insist on this point: see Tudor 1972
and Flood 1996.

The same holds for the relationship between political myths and modern utopias. Many authors have dealt with myth under the heading of utopia, in the sense of a general state of the mind that is incongruous with the reality within which it occurs. A utopia is, *latu sensu*, the description of an unrealisable state of things.[20] According to Mannheim, for instance, both myths and utopias are indeed the products of wishful thinking:

When imagination finds no satisfaction in existing reality, it seeks refuge in wishfully constructed places and periods. Myths, fairy tales, other-wordly promises of religion, humanistic fantasies, travel romances, have always been continually changing expression of that which was lacking in actual life. (Mannheim 1960: 184)

In this view, the utopian mentality works in opposition to the status quo and aims at its disintegration, whereas ideology, even when it does not precisely correspond to the status quo, nevertheless tends towards its preservation because it is congruous with it. In other words, utopias are revolutionary because they tend to burst the boundaries of the existing order (Mannheim 1960: in particular 173–84). As Ricoeur more recently also argued, ideology always aims at the integration and thus conservation of society, while utopia aims at its subversion (Ricoeur 1986: 417–31).

Apart from the general problems connected with the definition of the category of "reality" which, as Mannheim himself in many places recognises, is a definition that is always historically situated (Mannheim 1960: 91, 174), the problem, from our point of view, is the impossibility of defining political myth in relation to its congruence/incongruence with social reality thus conceived. Indeed, not all political myths are revolutionary, inasmuch as not all ideologies, at least as we have defined them, are conservative. Moving from such a characterisation of the "utopian mentality", it is impossible to grasp the difference between political myth, utopia and ideology.

However, if by "utopia" we understand *strictu sensu* the literary genre that was inaugurated by Thomas More's *Utopia*, then similarities and differences between this genre and political myth come to light. The

---

[20] On utopia, particularly from the point of view of the social utopias, see Maffey 1989 and Cazes 2001.

literary genre that goes from More to the negative utopia of Orwell's
1984 through authors such as Campanella, Fontenelle and Fourier,
is precisely characterised by the narrative form in which it casts the
description of the *ou-topos* – "the place that is nowhere", according to
the fortunate expression coined by More. Typically, the description of
the perfect or ideal society takes the form of a narrative by a traveller
of his discovery of this *ou-topos* (no-place) – or perhaps *eu-topos* (good
place)[21] – which is classically an island or at least a territory isolated
from other societies.

But it is not just the narrative form that unites political myth and
utopias. As has been observed, modern utopias were forms of radical
secularised theodicy. Utopias address the problem of the existence of
evil, but, in contrast to Christian theodicy, they begin from the assumption that any form of evil is resolvable in this world through a radical
reorganisation of social life (Moneti 1992: 406). Therefore, independent of the relationship with reality, we can say that what characterises
utopias in this sense is their regulative function, where by "regulative",
I mean, following Kant, the capacity of ideas to serve as guiding ideals
independent of their being more or less constitutive of the world of
phenomena.[22]

Both political myths and utopias have a regulative function. Despite
the fact that political myths can also be articulated in the dimension of
the past, as is the case with most of the foundation myths, their function
is always to address the present conditions and orient us within them.
The same holds for utopias: both positive and negative utopias, independent of their being more or less realistic, are always programs for
the reform of the present.

In other words, both political myths and utopias can be the sites
for the work of the radical imagination. Imagination, as Castoriadis

[21] As Maffey reminds us, the problem of the meaning of the neologism coined by More
was a big problem for the interpreters of More from the very first years of the work's
publication: *U-topia* can mean *Eu-topia* (the good place) or the *Ou-topia* (the no-
place). Indeed, Thomas More himself seems to allow both interpretations (Maffey
1989: 1215).
[22] In this sense authors from the Frankfurt School recovered, against Marx and Engels'
critique of utopian socialism, the positive function of utopia: as Marcuse observed, in
an age where the end of utopia is a real possibility because there seems to be no limit
to technical mastery even over the laws of nature, it is necessary to go from science
to utopia – and not the other way round as Marx and Engels held (Marcuse 1980).

points out, creates *ex nihilo* – not *in nihilo* or *cum nihilo*, as romantic theories of imagination tend to assume (Castoriadis 1997). This means that, together with the repetitive and passively conceived imagination, as was depicted by Spinoza, there is also a creative or radical imagination: it is from this creative side of the imagination that the critical impact, exercised by both utopias and political myth, stems. However, political myths are not necessarily the site for the work of the critical imagination: as the example of the myth of the Aryan race shows, they can also be the opposite. Yet, despite the fact that political myths, in contrast to utopias, do not always exercise such a critical function, there is always the possibility for them to do it, and in this possibility lies their regulative function.

Another difference between political myth and utopia is that, while utopias are radical secularised theodicy in the sense that they aim to extirpate evil through the construction of a perfect society, political myths do not necessarily aim at a radical solution once and for all for all the problems. Utopias are theoretical constructions that have a regulative function because they are the means for measuring the general good and bad contained in any society, whereas political myths are regulative because, as Sorel pointed out, they are direct determinations to act here and now. It is their capacity to put a drama on the stage that provides them with a regulative function. In other words, utopias are "no-places", whereas political myths are invitations to act here and now: *hic Rhodus, hic saltus.* (Hegel 1991: 21)

Precisely because political myths respond to a need for significance here and now and because, in contrast to utopias, they do not necessarily aim at a definitive answer to the problem of theodicy, they must be open to the possibility of being retold according to the changing circumstances. Utopias can be eternal. A political myth can be old, even ancient, but never eternal. In other words, political myths also address the problem of the theodicy, that is, the problem of the congruence between good and luck, but they do not necessarily aim to resolve it once for all. Instead, we could say that it is precisely the impossibility of providing a definitive answer to this dilemma that fosters the need for significance and thus the continual retelling of myth.

When the work on myth aims to provide a definitive answer, it generates closed myths, that is, myths that tend towards the elimination of contingency. These, however, are only a particular kind of myth, such as religious and naturalised myths. Both of these are myths that deny their historical nature, either by invoking their sacredness or their naturalness. Political myth, on the contrary, lives out of history. Thus, while a narrative can be utopian by nature because it violates its alleged laws,[23] nothing could ever be mythical by nature because it is always history that nourishes the work on myth.

This chapter, with the theory of political myth that I put forward, represents the culminating point of the philosophy of political myth that I have tried to delineate in this work. Such conceptual framework has shown both how myths in general and political myths in particular should be understood and why we need them. To sum up, political myths, understood as work on a common narrative by which a social group provides significance to its political conditions and needs, ultimately stem from a universal human need, the need to live in a world less indifferent to us. The discussion of the relationship between myth, ideology and utopia helps further position this concept of myth within the spectrum of related concepts. The following chapters further develop this task by analysing the relationship between myths and two other concepts that are often associated with them in current debates: history and identity.

---

[23] When Marcuse announced the end of utopia, he did so by pointing to the possibility that modern technology had rendered the idea of a supposed "limit by nature" obsolete (Marcuse 1980). Undoubtedly, the so-called laws of nature are also historical, but they are historical in a different sense: they are historically determined, but they do not live out of history as political myth does.

IV

MYTH AND POLITICAL IDENTITY

Political myths are narratives that coagulate and reproduce significance. They consist of the work on a common narrative by which the members of a social group or society represent and posit their experience and deeds. As such, they are an important part of what, following Castoriadis, can be called the social imaginary (Castoriadis 1987). Once political myths are defined in this way, the problem becomes one of analysing their relationship with other kinds of narratives that are also constitutive of the social imaginary.

In particular, both myths and historical writings are positional, in that they are told from the standpoint of the present. In other words, if the historian can also be defined as a "turned-back prophet" (Schlegel and Schlegel 1992: Frag. 80), in what ways does he or she differ from an ideal-typical myth-maker? Or, to put it in another way, in what ways do political myths and historical writings respectively contribute to present identities, or in what ways are the result of them?

These are the questions addressed in the following chapters. In particular, in Chapter 10 I discuss the relationship between historical and mythical writings, the extent to which they can possibly overlap, and also the reasons why they must be kept analytically distinct. By discussing various positions of the contemporary debate, I argue that only when historical narratives come to respond to a need for significance do they work as political myths. In other words, both historical and mythical writings contribute to the shaping of what, following Castoriadis, we will call "social imaginary", but they do so in different ways.

This, in its turn, leads us to explore the ways in which political myth relates to cultural, social and political identities. By criticising Schmitt's view of political myth as a symptom of an already constituted identity, in Chapter 11 I argue that the work on political myth is not just the result, but also the producer of common political identities. Furthermore, in contrast to Schmitt's usage of the term, I argue for a differentiation between the different forms of identity – personal, social, cultural, political, and so on – which aim to avoid normatively problematic outcomes, such as those generated by any homogenising view of identity.

This does not mean, however, that we should disregard the possible overlapping between different forms of identity. In particular, by confronting the issue of political identity from the standpoint of political myth, it becomes evident that there is no clear-cut separation between political and cultural identity. If not all cultural myths are political, there is always the possibility that the work on a cultural myth, which has nothing political *in se*, can come to affect specifically political conditions, and thus to contribute to the shaping of a political identity.

Finally, in Chapter 12 I advance some hypotheses on the possible sites for the work of political myths today. This is, properly speaking, the task of a sociology of political myth, for the construction of which this chapter provides only some preliminary suggestions. Indeed, there are reasons to suspect that, under the contemporary conditions, the work of political myth, disseminated in archipelagos of icons covertly recalling each other, becomes not only potentially global, but also less and less locatable. Thus, the hypothesis is suggested that political myths today operate through the interplay of the banal and the extraordinary, where, by "banal", I mean, etymologically, that which has become a commonplace by virtue of its continual use within a community. This, in its turn, would render the work on political myths much more insidious than it ever was, because this work now increasingly eludes the possibility of a critical discussion.

10

Myth, Historical Narrative and the Social Imaginary

According to one view, history consists of a collection of events, the faithful reproduction of which is the task of the historian. The historian reconstructs events as they actually happened and reproduces them in a narrative, the truth of which resides in the correspondence between the story told and the story actually lived by the people. According to this view, the literary aspect of historical narrative is limited to a few stylistic embellishments – as opposed to the kind of inventiveness presumed to be inherent in mythical and fictitional narratives.[1] The criterion for distinguishing between mythical and historical narratives would thus consist of the reality of the latter as counterpoised to the unreal or fictitious character of the former.

Recent theories, though, have sharply questioned this view.[2] A variety of approaches, ranging from those of French structuralism and poststructuralism, to historians drawing inspiration from the Annales group, to those of literary theorists and philosophers, such as Barthes, Foucault and Kristeva, tend to dissolve the distinction between "real" and "fictitious" narratives, by arguing that there is no ontological difference between the two. Notwithstanding the huge differences between

[1] As White observes, the passage in which the Prussian historian Leopold von Ranke characterised the historical method in terms of its opposition to the principles of representation found in novels and, subsequently, resolved to write history in such a way as to relate only what had actually happened in the past has become canonical in the historiographical profession's credo of orthodoxy (White 1973: 163).
[2] For a reconstruction of the debate, see White 1987; K. Jenkins 1997; and Stråth 2000.

such approaches, they all emphasise that a narrative is not a form
that can be added to the content without altering it: narrative, in this
perspective, is a form already full of content. Thus, mythical and historical narratives cannot be counterpoised as fictitious and real stories;
rather, they tend to converge. As some have argued by pushing this
argument to its extreme formulation, history would then be nothing
but the myth of Western societies (Friedman 1992; Young 1990).

Thus, whereas Fernand Braudel, for instance, has attacked narrative
history as intrinsically "dramatising" reality, Roland Barthes has challenged the very distinction between "historical" and "fictional" narratives, while, more recently, other authors of postmodern inspiration
have dissolved the opposition of "myth" and "history" by concluding
that both are the products of a politics of identity. In all these cases,
the idea of an intrinsic opposition between historical and mythical narratives has been reversed into its opposite, namely the thesis of their
essential coincidence.

Notwithstanding some common assumptions regarding these disparate theoretical positions, such as the common emphasis on the
language-mediated character of the human experience, they all clearly
bring very different issues to the fore. According to Braudel, what is
wrong with narrative history is that it claims to describe things as they
really happen, but it consists in fact of a heavily interpreted account of
them. In particular, what he criticises in this approach is the fact that,
for narrative historians, the lives of human beings necessarily assume
the form of a drama, dominated by the actions of often exceptional
individuals who emerge as the very protagonists of history, that is, as
the masters of their own fate as well as of ours (Braudel 1980: 11).

Narratives, according to the view taken by the historians who follow
the Annales approach, are intrinsically "novelising" and even dramatising reality. In contrast to this kind of historiography, they propose
a "scientific" reconstruction of reality. This, they argue, can only be
accomplished by looking at deeper and long-term historical processes,
rather than personalised and dramatised events.

It is worth nothing that this position was born more as a justification for the promotion of a historiography devoted to the analysis of
"long-term" impersonal processes in demography, economics and eth-
nology than as an incentive for analysing the nature of "narratives": the

rejection of narrative history by this historiography is due to a distaste for its conventional subject matter, past politics, as much as to the conviction that narratives are inherently "novelising" and therefore anti-scientific (White 1987: 32). Thus, the suspicion that it is not so much the intrinsic dramatic nature of narrative that is at stake here, but the distaste for a genre of literature that focuses on human agents as masters of their own destiny becomes legitimate.

Furthermore, the view of narrative as intrinsically dramatising is at odds with the whole literary experience of the last century. As modernist literature clearly shows, it is in fact possible to narrativise without novelising and dramatising. Indeed, at least from Pirandello onwards, it has been a common experience to view theatre that does not entail dramatisation. Thus, the point of the discussion should rather be an investigation of what a narrative properly consists of and to what extent writing history without narrative is possible. In other words, do we have narrative only when we talk about "dramatised" and "novelised" political events, or are narratives much more pervasive than this view suggests?

According to Roland Barthes, for instance, narratives are much more pervasive than dramas, since they are almost ubiquitous. Barthes holds that narrative, with its pervasiveness and its ability to be expressed with the most widely differing materials and languages, is "international, trans-historical, transcultural: it is simply there, like life itself.... Under this almost infinite diversity of forms, narrative is present in every age, in every place, in every society; it begins with the very history of mankind and there nowhere is nor has been a people without narrative" (Barthes 1977: 78).

However, this does not mean that every narrative is a myth according to Barthes.[3] In *The Discourse of History*, Barthes seems to hold that history can be represented in different ways, some of which are not mythological insofar as they do overtly call attention to their own process of production and indicate the constructed rather than given nature of their object. When, at the beginning of this essay, Barthes states it is his intention to show that historical discourse does not differ

---

[3] On Barthes' conception of narrative, see also Chapter 5, whereas on his conception of myth, see Chapter 12.

from imaginary narration, it is most probably the claim to an objective account of history that he is criticising. As he asks,

the narration of past events, commonly subject in our culture, since the Greeks, to the sanction of historical "science", placed under the imperious warrant of the "real", justified by principles of "rational" exposition – does this narration differ, in fact, by some specific feature, by an indubitable pertinence, from imaginary narration as we find in the epic, the novel, the drama? (Barthes 1986: 127)

The question is clearly rhetorical. Barthes is persuaded that by simply looking at its very structure, one can see that this kind of historical discourse is, in its essence, a form of ideological elaboration: historical narratives are the result of an "imaginary elaboration", of a performative speech-act through which the utterer of the discourse "fills out" the place of the subject of the utterance. It is this performative speech-act that is responsible for what Barthes calls the "reality effect", that is, a new meaning that is extensive to all historical discourse and ultimately defines its pertinence and its reality itself. Thus, Barthes concludes, "historical discourse does not follow the real, it merely signifies it, constantly repeating '*this happened*', without this assertion being anything but the signified wrong side of all historical narration" (Barthes 1986: 139).

According to Barthes, then, it is quite understandable why, at the privileged moment in the nineteenth century when history attempted to constitute itself as a genre, historiography should have come to institute narration as a privileged signifier of what is real: narrative history refuses to assume the real as signified and thus, paradoxically, the narrative structure, which is the hallmark of myth, becomes for these historians the very sign and proof of reality (Barthes 1986: 140). Barthes thus contrasts this narrative history with what he considers a "veritable transformation" of contemporary historiography, which, by shifting the emphasis onto structures rather than events, has, in his view, liberated history from narrative (Barthes 1986: 140).

Clearly, for Barthes, a narrative always implies a form of "distortion". He made this point explicitly in his "Introduction to the Structural Analysis of Narrative":

The function of narrative is not to "represent", it is to constitute a spectacle still very enigmatic for us, but in any case not of a mimetic order. The "reality" of a sequence lies not in the "natural" succession of actions composing it, but in the logic there exposed, risked and satisfied... Narrative does not show, does not imitate; the passion which may excite us in reading a novel is not that of a "vision" (in actual fact, we do not "see" anything). Rather it is that of a meaning, that of a higher order of relation which also has its emotions, its hopes, its dangers, its triumphs. (Barthes 1977: 124)

In his *Mythologies*, Barthes argued that myths are a form of ideological distortion of reality, and, in particular, one that presents that which is a product of contingency as natural, and therefore, eternal (Barthes 1972). Narrative history is also intrinsically distorting in this sense because it presents as "facts" that which is instead the constructed spectacle of a narrative. However, even if one accepts Barthes' definition of myth as distortion, the problem within this perspective remains that, not only myth, but all kinds of narratives, both mythical and historical, insofar as narrative is distorting per se, are to be characterised as "distorting" and thus "ideological" (in Barthes' use of the term). How then can we distinguish between more or less mythological historical narratives? In other words, is there no historical narrative without distortion? What is the "reality" that they distort?

As we have seen in his approach to narrative, Barthes moves from the assumption, drawn from the Russian formalists, that one can distinguish between two levels in a narrative: that of the *story* or argument of the narrative, and that of the *discourse* or organisation of the argument, this latter only comprising tenses, aspects and modes of the narrative (Barthes 1977: 87).[1] However, as we have seen, there is no "natural" succession of events that only comes to be organised later. If Nietzsche is right in saying that there are no facts as such but that we must always begin by introducing a meaning in order to have a fact (Barthes 1977: 138), then there is no basis for distinguishing between a "natural" succession of events and their "organisation" (Barthes 1977: 124). Indeed, as far as we perceive of a succession of events, they are always somehow already "organised" and thus invested with a meaning. To put it plainly, whatever earlier stage of the perception of a sequence of events we take, the work of organisation has always already started.

Contemporary theorists have pushed this kind of argument further. Robert Young, for instance, seems to hold that, if writing history always

---

[1] For a discussion of Barthes' treatment of narrative, see Chapter 5.

implies a process of organisation of the events in a narrative plot, that is, in a totality within which only events are conferred with a meaning, then the writing of history does not differ from the activity of creating a myth. In particular, in his view, the idea of "history" always reflects a totalising mode of the organisation of events that is not only particularistic, because, as Foucault proved, each society has its own way of organising knowledge, but is also mythological, because it is based on the exclusion of the perspective of the others (Young 1990).

History, so Young concludes, should be seen as simply a "white mythology", as the "preposterous off-spring of a distorting egocentric illusion to which the children of a western Civilisation have succumbed like the children of all other Civilisations and known primitive societies" (Young 1990: 19). The illusion consists of the identification of the history of provincial Western societies with History writ large. With regard to this view, the emergence of postmodernism is thus the sign of Western culture's awareness that it is no longer the unquestioned and dominant centre of the world (Young 1990: ch. I).

Young is certainly right in his remark that postmodernism has brought about a new self-consciousness about a culture's own historical relativity and thus a loss of the sense of the absoluteness of any Western account of History. This new self-consciousness is perhaps its most permanent result. If, however, one were to ask further in what precisely the mythological aspect of the writing of history consists, two possible answers are available in Young's account. First, Young introduces the concept of mythology by quoting a passage from Derrida's critique of metaphysics as "white mythology". The mythological aspect here consists of the illusion of the universality of metaphysics that calls itself "Reason" but is in fact an "Indo-European Mythology", being the *mythos* of a specific idiom (1990: 7). Myth, however, here is simply used in the polemical sense of illusion and, therefore, can be indifferently applied to both history and metaphysics as expressions of logocentrism. In particular, Young's criticism seems to be directed towards a certain way of writing history, one that surreptitiously presents a specific history as history *sans phrase* (1990: 19); and, indeed, the white mythologies denounced in the title of his book are all those theories that, starting from Marxism, strive towards the idea of a unique "world history", that is, of history as a totality.

A somewhat different argument is put forward, however, in the second chapter of his book, in which he criticises Sartre's attempt to save the Marxist idea of history as a continuous totality. By reading Lévi-Strauss' structuralist critique of Sartre as an example of deconstruction, Young suggests, with Lévi-Strauss, that history in general is the myth of modern man. Now, it is the use of chronology itself, the code most often used by historians, which is said to create the illusory impression of a uniform, continuous progression. Dates, he observes, tell us something only insofar as they are members of a class which, in turn, may or may not correspond to other classes, such as periods, millennia, ages. Thus dates always reflect a specific organisation of an event. This impression of uniform progression is, however, illusory and, in this sense, it is said to be a myth (Young 1990: 45, 46).

This is a crucial point. Even if one rejects Young's polemical usage of the concept of myth as illusion, his remarks on chronology must be further discussed. Young seems to suggest here that the simple organisation of events according to a chronology implies a high degree of choice and interpretation. However, one can object that even the very perception of "one or more events" already implies a process of selection and therefore organisation for what literally comes (*e-venit*). Indeed, as suggested in Chapter 5, there are no events without them being already organised.

On the other hand, while a narrative always implies a certain organisation, "organisation" does not necessarily mean the superimposition of a "dramatised" form, nor even of a "distortion" through the imposition of a "fictitious coherence" that would otherwise lack reality. Indeed, in as far as they mean something to us, events always exhibit some kind of organisation. The point, therefore, is to determine the degree of this organisation. Indeed, if, in order to have a narrative, we merely need a sequence of events, one must then recognise that not all sequences of events constitute a drama. And, as we shall see, in contrast to myth, historical narratives necessarily presuppose the sequence, but not the drama.

Narratives presuppose a plot that organises events: it is the plot that confers events with a meaning as part of a whole. But the point is that this whole does not need to be a dramatic plot, nor even a "coherent" whole, as modernist literature shows. It just needs to be a whole. And, as we shall see, it is only when this whole that constitutes a narrative becomes dramatic that historical narratives can come to work as political myths. In other words, in order to have a historical narrative that works as a myth, something else other than a mere narrative is needed. Let us dwell for a moment on the possible forms of historical narrative. As we will see, different modes of writing history imply different degrees of organisation and, this is my main argument, only some of them can be said to work as political myths.

Hayden White addresses this problem in his work, *The Content of the Form*: narrative – his major argument goes – is not an empty form that can or cannot be added to a given content, but it is already a content in itself (White 1987: x). Thus, if narrative always brings content with it, the problem is to determine what kind of content is entailed in each single form of historical writing. In the first of the essays collected in *The Content of the Form*, White analyses three different examples of historical genres – annals, the chronicle, and narrative history – and looks at the role narrative plays within them.

Annals, he observes, typically consist of a lacunose list of events, in which there are apparently none of the elements that we traditionally associate with narrative: there are no central characters, there is no central subject, no well-marked beginning, middle and end, as well as no narrative voice whatsoever: thus, it appears there is no narrative at all (White 1987: 70). Subsequently, however, he takes a specific example: the *Annals of Saint Gall*. By looking more carefully at this lacunose list of events, it comes to light that there are criteria according to which "events" are ordered as well as a basis from which they are given the status of events (White 1987: 70).

Indeed, in all annals, and this is the meaning of the term, events are registered under the year in which they occurred; the years are then ordered chronologically and for each year only what is held to be most important is actually ranked as an event. In the *Annals of Saint Gall*, we find "Charles fought against the Saxons" next to the year 720, the registration of "great crops" next to "722", and nothing next to "723", "724", and so on, whereas the entry "732" registers that "Charles fought against the Saracens at Poitiers on Saturday", where the fact that the battle took place on Saturday seems to be given the same weight as the "great crops" of 722 or the fact that, in 725, "Saracens came for the first time". Thus, there is a clear organisation of events even in annals: "there is surely a plot," so writes White, "if by plot we mean a structure of relationships by which the events contained in the account are endowed with a meaning by being identified as parts of an integrated whole" (White 1987: 9).

What then differentiates annals from other types of historical genres, such as chronicles or historical narratives? Chronicles, White observes, are held to be superior forms of historical representations because of their greater comprehensiveness, their organisation of the material by topics and reigns and their greater narrative coherence. The chronicle, for instance, has a central subject, such as the life of an individual, a town or an institution, or some great event, such as a war or a crusade (White 1987: 16). Still, White observes, there is something that distinguishes the chronicle from other superior forms of historical narrative: chronicles – like annals, but unlike history – do not less conclude as simply terminate; typically, they lack closure, that summing up of the "meaning" of a chain of events that we normally expect from well-made stories. Chronicles may promise a closure, but usually do not provide it, and this is the reason why the nineteenth century editors of the medieval chronicles denied them the status of genuine history (White 1987: 16).

In contrast to both annals and chronicles, the story told by narrative history does not simply terminate, but actually concludes. All the narrative expectations of a reader are indeed satisfied: there is an identifiable subject, there is a well-constructed plot with a beginning, a middle and a proper end to the story. There is closure, a completeness that was absent in "inferior" forms of historiography. And, according to White, the fullness and completeness of narrative that we experience in "superior" forms of historical narrative signal to us that what was lacking in the incomplete list of events of the annals is indeed the notion of a centre with respect to which to rank events: there is no single perspective that enables the annalist to make a complete story out of scattered events, and these, as a consequence, appear to lack the ethical significance that is provided by a closed story (White 1987).

Going back to the *Annals of Saint Gall*, White argues that there is a correspondence here between the absence of a closed narrative structure and the absence of a social centre that provides a single perspective for ranking events. Without such a social centre, Charles' campaign against the Saxons remains simply a "fight", the invasion of the Saracens simply a "coming", and the fact that the Battle of Poitiers was fought on Saturday is as important as the fact that it was fought at all or the fact that the year 722 witnessed great crops (White 1987: 11). Any well-made story, we can add, has a moral, and the reason why the annals seem to lack the structure of a real story is that they do not have any explicit moral to relate.

This analysis, according to White, suggests that Hegel was right when he stated that a genuinely historical account has to display not only a certain form, namely, the narrative, but also a certain content, and that this content always coincides with a political order. The ranking of events always reflects criteria, and their ranking in the kind of historical narrative that Hegel was referring to clearly reflects a political criterion. Thus, as White points out, for Hegel, the content of the specifically historical discourse was not the story of "what happened", but the peculiar relationship between a public present and a past that a state endowed with a certain political constitution (White 1987: 29). As we read in Hegel's passage from *The Philosophy of History,*

in our language the term *History* unites the objective with the subjective side, and denotes the *historia rerum gestarum,* as much as the *res gestae* themselves; on the other hand, it comprehends not less what has happened, than the narration of what has happened. This union of the two meanings we must regard as of a higher order than mere outwards accident; we must suppose historical narrations to have appeared contemporaneously with historical deeds and events. (Hegel 1956: 60)

According to White, unlike the annals, the historical narrative to which Hegel refers reveals to us a world that is "finished", "done with", "over". They exhibit a narrative closure that, precisely because it is too embarrassing, has to be presented as "found" in the events rather than placed there by narrative techniques. Indeed, it is precisely because narrative history provides us with a degree of coherence to which we ourselves aspire that the events presented by the narrative appear real. As White concludes:

The demand for closure in the historical story is a demand, I suggest, for a moral meaning, a demand that sequences of real events be assessed as to their *significance* as elements of a *moral drama.* Has any historical narrative ever been written that was not informed not only by moral awareness but specifically by the moral authority of the narrator? It is difficult to think of any historical work produced during the nineteenth century, the classical age of historical narrative, that was not given the force of a moral judgment on the events that it related. (White 1987: 22; emphasis mine)

As we have seen, White rightly emphasises that there are different modes of writing history. Among these, only historical narratives and in particular those produced during the nineteenth century, present a mythical organisation. In this case, their "narrative organisation" reflects a need for *significance*, and therefore the need for events to be assessed within the plot of a moral drama. Thus, if political myths are the work on a narrative that responds to a need for significance, and historical narratives also respond to "a demand that sequences of real events be assessed as to their *significance* as elements of a *moral drama*", then there seems to be no difference between the two. However, while White seems to hold persuasively that not all forms of historical writing directly address a need for significance, and seems therefore to limit his claim to narrative history, more recently there have been authors who appear to extend the same remark to all kinds of history.

According to Jonathan Friedman, for instance, history is a mythical construction because it is always a representation of the past subordinated to the establishment of an identity in the present. In his article "Myth, History, and Political Identity", he states that an objectivist history must necessarily be produced in the context of a certain kind of selfhood, namely, one that is based on the radical separation of the subject from any particular identity, and that objectifies and textualises reality (Friedman 1992: 194). In this sense, there would be no difference between myth and history: the common understanding of history as a stream of events or as a temporal continuum whose empirical existence is unquestionable would, in turn, be a mythology – or, rather, the peculiar myth of Western societies (Friedman 1992: 206).

We have seen that Young supports a similar thesis, but he seems to limit it to those accounts that present the history of Western societies as the "History" *sans phrase*. Friedman is an anthropologist and justifies his claim that history is mythical through the analysis of two case studies. In the article, first he analyses the shift in the perception of the eighteenth century Greeks of their previous history from that of "Romans" (*Romoioi*) to that of "Greeks", or the heirs of the Hellenic civilisation. In a second step, he moves on to analyse the Hawaiians'

reconstruction of their history as opposed to Western "history". However, this does not seem to be sufficient to sustain the proposition that
myth and history coincide. This is because both the examples clearly
deal with two particular historical narratives, narratives that are manifestly linked to two situations of struggle for a political identity.

Friedman begins with the observation that the eighteenth century
construction of Greek national identity is largely due to the activity
of a class of expatriate Greek merchants who, in contrast to a discon-
tinuous Roman, Byzantine and Ottoman past, were led to rediscover
Ancient Greece via Western European self-identity: in the building of
the European identity, from the Renaissance onwards, Greece played a
pivotal role as the birthplace of everything specifically Western. Thus,
Greek national identity consisted in the importation and establishment of the European identification of Greece, just as Greek history
became the European history of the ancients (Friedman 1992: 195).
The establishment of a particular history was the work of a process of
construction of political identity, both for Europe and for Greece as
an emergent periphery in the European world system. Thus, as Friedman shows, Greek history internalises the external gaze of its European other, making Greece, in its fashion, the ancestor of Europe
instead of a mere political and economic periphery, while Hawaiian
history extricates itself from Western dominance by projecting a value
system produced in the modern context onto an aboriginal past
(Friedman 1992: 207). From the analysis of these two case studies,
it is clear that – as the very title of the essay also indicates – Friedman's
focus is more on the way in which historical narratives are elaborated
and re-elaborated according to a certain politics of identity rather than
on what characterises historical narratives per se.

If Friedman can conclude that history is largely mythical, it is
because he chooses these two case studies in which historical and mythical narrative do indeed coincide. But can we conclude from these two
examples that history is always mythical? Undoubtedly, history is always
positional.[5] History, as much as myth, always reflects the point of view
of the present and is continuously retold from this point of view.

---

[5] It should be clear from what precedes that when we speak of "history", we do, in fact,
speak of the "writing of history": history exists only inasmuch as it is accessible to us
and therefore only as already interpreted events.

In the first place, historical narratives select what constitutes an "event". In this sense, they are constructed on oblivion as much as on memory (Stråth 2000). The process of the selection of events can go from their deliberated occultation to their effectual perception according to non-intentional criteria. Second, as we have seen, events thus identified also go through a process of further organisation and elaboration – without, in reality, it even being possible to distinguish between the two moments of selection and organisation.

Thus, Friedman is right when he points out that history is always the organisation of the past in terms of a present situation: the selection and organisation of events cannot but reflect our present condition and, as a result, our future hopes and expectations. The past is always constructed according to the conditions and desires of those who produce historical texts in the present. And, as will be discussed further in Chapter 11, identity in the present is also organised in terms of a past (as well as of a future) that is already organised by the present: this is indeed the circularity that is constitutive of the social-historical domain. Political myth – this is the major point – also operates from the point of view of the present, but it does so in a somewhat different way.

Let me illustrate the point by going back to Friedman's two case studies. Both the Greek and the Hawaiian examples point to the fact that the mythical side of the historical narratives analysed consisted precisely in their being part of a politics of identity: in order to construct a common Greek or Hawaiian political identity, the past needed to be anchored to a viable present. In other words, they show that myth is the politics of history: it is precisely in order to spell out this potential political side of the historical narratives analysed that Friedman has recourse to the concept of myth.

Analogously one can argue, for instance, that there is nothing mythical per se in the identification of history with the history of Western societies that Young criticises as "white mythologies". On the other hand, Young is right in saying that this narrative can come to play the role of a political myth. As Sorel would put it, myth always contains a determination to act, and this determination becomes specifically political when it addresses specifically political conditions. Indeed, it is when it comes to political actions and conditions that historical narratives can work as political myths. If myth and history – as we have seen, with some exceptions – share a narrative form,[6] where they differ is that myth, in order to nourish a determination to act, has to put a drama on the stage, or, rather, it has to be received as a drama. Political myths are stories that make their moral explicit in order to prompt political action. Political myths are thus "positional" in a different way to the manner in which history is positional. In other words, political myths must respond directly to a need for significance, although this is not necessarily the case with historical narratives.

Political myths, as we have seen, have a particularistic nature, because they must provide significance here and now, otherwise they cease to be political myths. "To be significant" always means "to be significant for someone and under certain conditions". As a consequence, there are no universal political myths, but only particular ones – and this, at least partially, explains why political philosophy has often neglected the topic. Attempts can be and have been made at a universal history, but not at a universal political myth. What is a political myth for certain subjects, here and now, may well no longer be a political myth even for the same people in another context, or for different people in the same context.

Thus, notwithstanding the fact that political myths and historical narratives are quite often so intermingled as to coincide, analytically speaking we should keep the two categories separate. This will enable us to grasp the differences between certain phenomena that would otherwise be lost. Not all historical narratives are necessarily political myths, and not all political myths are historical narratives. The narrative of the general strike, that of a classless society, and the myth of the millennium, all of which have worked in the past as political myths, are, for instance, all constructed in the future dimension. Thus, even if one could argue that they presuppose certain historical narratives, they are not themselves genuine historical narratives.

This leads us to a crucial point. The work on myth operates with a degree of freedom that is impossible in historical narratives. Undoubtedly, as we have seen, the historian also looks at the past in the light

---

[6] Not all historical writings are indeed narratives. Historical statistics are a good example: one could argue that they are a sequence of events, but they would still lack the plot required before they could be classified as narratives. For a discussion of the concept of narrative, see also Chapter 5.

of the present and future, but, to use Friedrich Schlegel's expression, the historian is a "turned-back prophet."[7] Both historians and ideal-typical myth-makers are prophets since both look at the past and at the present in the light of the future, but the fact that historians are *"turned-back* prophets" places further constraints on them that are not pending on the activity of myth-makers. For instance, myth-makers will be believed because they tell a variant of a story that addresses the need for significance, whereas historians – at least modern historians – will have to rely on method.[8]

Tudor made a similar point when he wrote that the understanding provided by myth is a directly practical understanding, that is, an understanding in which human beings consider the world that confronts them, not as an object of disinterested curiosity, but as the direct material for their activity (Tudor 1972: 123). One can certainly question the idea that the activity of the historian could ever be completely "disinterested", but Tudor points in the right direction when he says that human beings engaged in practical affairs certainly do think, but think in different ways. For instance, he argues, people confronted with the prospect of death, disgrace or serious deprivation will not easily be persuaded to see other people's points of view, nor are they likely to engage in disinterested reflections on human existence. What they require is the confidence to act, and this confidence is often induced by their firm conviction that their cause is just and that they are certain to emerge victorious (Tudor 1972: 134).

This is an extreme case, but it points out that the types of interests at stake, both in the work on myth and in historical research, can coincide, but they may also diverge. However, this does not imply, as Tudor concludes, that in the practical understanding provided by myth, in contrast to history, "no doubt, some distortion of facts does occur" (Tudor 1972: 123). As we have seen, historians, even without

---

[7] The "prophet", in F. Schlegel's use of the term, is a "poet-philosopher" (Schlegel and Schlegel 1992: Frag. 249) and thus something close to an ideal-typical myth-maker. Nevertheless, as we have seen, a myth consists of the work on myth and there is no such thing, therefore, as a single myth-maker.

[8] Ankersmit, too, who sustains that no writing of history is possible without "representation", recognised the centrality of the methodological aspects: it is here that the working of what he calls "transversal reason" can be seen (Ankersmit 2001).

any manipulative intent, also distort facts; or, rather, the very notion of fact always implies a process of selection, choice and organisation, so that it becomes difficult to determine where distortion starts and whether it could have not occurred.

The point, therefore, is not to counterpoise "practical" and thus "distorted" understanding and "disinterested" and thus "faithful" reconstructions of events. Instead, it is to distinguish between a discipline constituted around a method and an activity, the work on myth, that does not follow any given method. Indeed, properly speaking, to talk of a "myth-maker" is an abuse of language: not only, as we have seen, is a myth made by its production-reception, but it is also an entire work on myth that is always at stake. This does not mean that a similar work on historical narrative does not occur. The professional historian does not operate in a social vacuum. However, the very fact that there could be a professional historian is the sign of a difference, namely the fact that the activity of the historian lends itself to a definition through a method. Notwithstanding the discussion that this point may open with regard to the nature of this method, it still remains that the idea of a method implies that of an *organon*, of a series of more or less standardised rules and practices against which the correctness of the account will be assessed.

No "mythical method" exists or has ever existed. And this is probably because most often, as has been observed, political myths operate at the level of unquestioned beliefs held in common by social groups (Flood 1996). Thus, whereas narratives derived from a method are somehow visible, political myths are difficult even to perceive and to determine. As Lance Bennett observed, dealing with the North American case, political myths are difficult to analyse because they are such basic components of everyday perception. They cannot be seen as the things that the people see when they look at the world, because they are the things with which they see. "Myths", he concludes, "are truths about society that often remain unperceived because they are woven throughout everyday social discourse from dinner table conversation, to the morals of television programs, to the lofty policy debates of congress" (Bennett 1980: 167).[9]

---

[9] On Bennett's analysis see in particular Chapter 12.

Undoubtedly, historical narratives are also a part of the social imaginary constituted through different kinds of social practices. And indeed, it is sometimes very difficult in practice to distinguish between historical and mythical discourses, since they are often interwoven in our everyday life. Historical narratives do not live only in the libraries and archives where the modern historian is asked to produce them, but also emerge out of social life. On the other hand, insofar as historical writings have been defined in terms of a method, there has been the possibility of perceiving them and thus criticising them on the basis of their formal correctness: modern historians have to make footnotes, because they are expected to refer to evidence, to other, in principle revisable, narratives. Today, they are normally asked to refer to documents, archives and all the material that constitutes a form of "rationalised memory", that is, the set of information about and accounts of the past as it is contained in the archives, processed in the form of written or visualised narratives that are accessible on demand (White 2000).[10]

To conclude this point, while the work of the historian, at least in modern Western societies, is locatable, the work on myth is difficult even to perceive, and this is the reason why it cannot be formalised through a method. Both, at the same time, are constitutive of the imaginary significations that contribute to the provision of meaning to everyday experience and without which no society could ever survive. After the so-called linguistic turn and the emergence of constructivism, different approaches have been pointing to this crucial dimension of social life. The ever-growing number of publications on "symbolic construction" and the "invention of societies and communities" has pointed out that no social life is possible outside of a symbolic network.[11] But what is social imaginary and how does it relate to the

[10] White distinguishes between "rationalised memory and "traditionalised memory" as information about and accounts of the past latently stored in fables, tales, commonplaces, customs and prejudices. White argues that, while rationalised memory might comprehend traditionalised knowledge, the reverse is not the case. One could criticise this statement but the distinction between the two categories is certainly helpful in order to stress that the two may also come into tension.

[11] On the symbolic dimension of community, see, for instance, Edelman 1976; 1988; and Cohen 1985. Cohen moves from Geertz's definition of the human being as "an animal suspended in a web of significance", but he does not distinguish between significance and meaning, both being conflated under the heading of symbolism.

single individuals that produce it? After discussing this point, we will
be able to restate the difference between mythical and historical narratives from a different perspective.

More than thirty years ago, Cornelius Castoriadis introduced the
concept of social imaginary in order to stress what he perceived
to be a still neglected side of social life. His reasoning was quite
straightforward: all acts, both individual and collective, without which
any society could survive – labour, consumption, love, war, and so on –
are impossible outside of a symbolic network, even though they are
not always directly symbols themselves (Castoriadis 1987: 117ff.). All
functions performed within any society are, in fact, "functions of something", meaning they are functions only in as far as their ends can be
defined. These ends, which vary from society to society as well as from
one epoch to the other, can only be defined at the level of those social
significations without which no social function or need could ever be
defined: this is the level at which the "social imaginary" operates.

Castoriadis moves from the insight that a functionalist view, a view
that reduces the problem of social significations to the ambit of the
functional, is only partially correct; in as far as it aspires to present the
whole truth about the nature of the social-historical, it is a mere pro-
jection. It claims to identify a general rule, but, in fact, it projects over
the whole course of history an idea derived not even from the everyday
life of Western capitalist societies – that, notwithstanding the fact that
the processes of rationalisation are always only partially functional –
but, instead, from what it would like these societies to be (Castoriadis
1987: 131). Capitalist societies are no exception. Given the crucial role
played by the social creation of needs, they exhibit the working of the
social imaginary even more manifestly. Any society continually defines
and redefines its needs, and no society can ever survive outside of the
imaginary significations that constitute it and that are constituted by
it. The institution of a society presupposes the institution of imaginary
significations that must, in principle, be able to provide meaning to
whatever presents itself.

There are, Castoriadis observes, limits to this symbolic order. To put
it in Blumenberg's terms, the world is always a work of art, but it can
never be a total work of art (Blumenberg 1985: 7). The work of the
social imaginary must always start from the material that it finds already
there. Indeed, there are limits posed by nature itself (for example,

societies may define the meaning of nourishment, but they must take the need for it into account), by rationality, that is, the coherence of the symbolic edifice, as well as by the limits imposed by history itself. Every symbol is built on the ruins of the preceding symbolic constructions, and even in order to break with it radically it has to start with these very premises (Castoriadis 1987: 125). Notwithstanding all these limits, the social imaginary has a capacity for virtually universal coverage so that any invasion of the raw world can immediately be treated as a sign of something, that is, it can be interpreted away and thus exorcised. Even that which collides with this order can be subject to a symbolic processing: the transgression of social rule can become an "illness", and completely alien societies that are fundamentally at odds with a given social imaginary can become "strangers", "savages", or even "impious" (Castoriadis 1991).

At the same time, though, Castoriadis observes, the major threat to the instituted society is its own creativity. The merit of Castoriadis' concept of radical social imaginary is to point out that the *instituted* social imaginary is always at the same time *instituting*. No society could ever exist if the individuals created by the society itself had not created it. There seems to be circularity at the basis of the relationship between individuals and the social imaginary. This is the primitive circle of the institution of society that Spinoza also emphasised: society exists only if it can exist in the imagination of individuals who, in turn, cannot exist without the society of which they are a part.[12]

In other words, the individual is not contingent in relation to society. Society can exist concretely only through the fragmentary and complementary incarnation and incorporation of its institution and its imaginary significations in the living, talking and acting individuals of that society. Athenian society is nothing but the Athenians, Castoriadis observes; without them, it is only remnants of a transformed landscape, the debris of marble and vases, indecipherable inscriptions, and worn statues fished out of the Mediterranean. But the Athenians are Athenians only by means of the *nomos* of the *polis*. It is in this relationship between an instituted society, on the one hand – which infinitely transcends the totality of the individuals that "compose" it, but can actually exist only by being "realised" in the individuals that

---

[12] On this point, see Chapter 8.

it produces – and these individuals, on the other, that we experience an unprecedented type of relationship which cannot be thought of under the categories of the whole and its parts, the set and its elements and, even less, the universal and the particular (Castoriadis 1991: 145).

However, Castoriadis seems to open up this circle when he speaks of an "absolute scission" between the two poles of the instituted/instituting social imaginary: the social-historical on the one hand,[13] and what he calls the "psyche" or "psychical monad" on the other (see, in particular, Castoriadis 1987: 204ff.). The psyche is monadic since, in Castoriadis' view, it is "pure representational/affective/intentional flux", indeterminate and, in principle, unmasterable. According to this view, it is only through an always incomplete violent and forceful process of socialisation that a social individual can be produced. This happens through a process of schooling that starts with the very first encounter with language, with the language spoken by the mother. In this way, the psyche is forced to give up its initial objects and to invest in (*cathecting*) socially instituted objects, rules and the world. Thus, it is through the internalisation of the worlds and the imaginary significations created by society that an "individual", properly speaking, is created out of a "screaming monster" (Castoriadis 1991: 148).

As has been observed, Castoriadis' thesis about the monadic isolation and the fundamental "hetereogeneity" between the psyche and society seems to lead to a highly problematic, and thus untenable, metaphysical opposition (Habermas 1987: 327ff.). Once we find ourselves within the monadic isolation of the unconscious, it becomes difficult even to explain how communication is possible in the first place (Whitebook 1989).[14] However, we can recover Castoriadis' insights into the role of the instituting and instituted social imaginary without

---

[13] With regard to the relationship between the terms "society" and the "social-historical", the latter is preferable since, in contrast to the term "society", it does not suggest the idea of an entity endowed with clearcut boundaries, which is contrary to Castoriadis' own idea of magmatic logic.

[14] Whitebook argues that Habermas could not but sharply criticise Castoriadis' theory of the psyche: while Castoriadis starts with the monadic isolation and the problem then becomes to establish how communication is possible, Habermas starts with the fact of communication and the problem then becomes how this can be deformed in the unconscious (Whitebook 1989).

relying on such metaphysical assumptions. What appears at first sight to be a theory deeply dependent on psychoanalysis can, in fact, also be seen from a different perspective.

Arnason, for instance, points out that Castoriadis' major contribution has been to link a radicalised idea of imagination with the problematic of meaning (Arnason 1989). Castoriadis' work has certainly contributed to the recent rediscovery of the importance of images and imagination in social life, as well as to the development of a much more complex view of social imagination.[15] Two aspects of his theory are particularly relevant here: first the idea of a "*radical* imagination", and, second, the emphasis on the idea of the "social *imaginary*".

With regard to the former, the term "radical" has the function of stressing that, as Aristotle held, together with an imitative and reproductive or combinatory *phantasia*,[16] there is also what can be called a primary imagination, namely the faculty of producing images in the largest possible sense (that of "forms", "*Bilder*") without which there would not be any thought at all, and which, therefore, precede any thought (Castoriadis 1997).

The reason why imagination came to be associated with the idea of fictitiousness is that it creates *ex nihilo* – not *in nihilo* or *cum nihilo* – and the Western ensemble logic, which starts with the identity assumption *ex nihilo nihil*, as a consequence, could not but conceive of imagination as essentially non-existence. To this identity and set logic, which could never account for the fact that when "x = x" it is always "x = not X", Castoriadis counterpoises the logic of magmas: this sees significations not as "determinate beings" but as webs of reference (*faisceaux de renvois*) which are certainly always determinable but never determinate (Castoriadis 1987: 221ff.).

To sum up, the expression "radical imagination" has the function of conveying two ideas: the connection with the idea of imagination and creation, and the connection with the "radical" side of it, that is, with the fact that this imagination is before the distinction between "real" and "fictitious". Simply put, it is because radical imagination exists that

---

[15] On the role of imagination in the study of social and political sciences see, recently, Rundell 1994a; 1994b; and Friese 2001.

[16] As Friese notices, it is only in modern times that the term "fantasy" was associated with the ambit of the fictitious and unreal (Friese 2001).

"reality" exists for us – and, therefore, one can add, it exists *tout court* (Castoriadis 1997).

As the concept of the social imaginary points out, there is not a subject and a reality that remains facing it. Instead, the passage from the concept of *imagination* to that of *imaginary* reflects a change from a *subject*-oriented approach to a *context*-oriented one (Arnason 1994). Castoriadis' concept of the social imaginary also has the function of underlining the idea that the definition of "reality" itself depends on the instituting and instituted social imaginary, and not vice versa (Castoriadis 1987: 160; 1991: 147).

The fact that, as we have seen in Chapters 2 and 3, the word "reality" comes into being only relatively late and that it has been conceived in very different ways, is the sign that the emergence of a new word, "reality", was also the emergence of a different conception of the "real". All societies have somehow constituted their "reality" and it is for this reason that any distinction between myth and history as "unreal" and "real" accounts respectively cannot but be of limited efficacy.

On the other hand, by moving from Castoriadis' idea of a radical social imaginary we can now try to restate the difference between political myths and historical narratives. Indeed, if both myths and historical narratives are constitutive of the social imaginary, that is, of the imaginary significations through which any society institutes itself by being simultaneously instituted by them, they are so in a different way. Generally speaking, we can explain the difference between the two by saying that political myths must not only answer the need for meaning for a symbolic mediation of reality, but must also coagulate and produce significance.

As a consequence, political myths can be seen as a site both for the construction of an instituting social imaginary and for the work of a radical political imagination. Myths are not simply symbols, and political myths, in particular, are not just mapping devices. They also contain a determination to act, and this determination can affect the specifically political conditions of a given society.

Therefore, the work on political myths is *radical* in two senses. On the one hand, because it operates at the level of the combination and reproduction of significance as it has been defined in Chapter 6. Thus, in contrast to historical narratives, political myths are often not even perceivable: professional historians can exist, but no professional myth-maker can. Political myths are difficult to analyse because they are not only a part of the world that we experience, they are also, and foremost, the lenses through which we see this world.

If, in this sense, political myths contribute to the self-perpetuation of a given social imaginary, they can also, in another sense, be one of the sites for the questioning of this same imaginary. Moreover, they can be the sites for the questioning of the specifically *political* conditions of an instituting and instituted society. To put it another way, the "not yet determined animal" (of Chapter 6) is an animal that produces myths in order to satisfy his or her need for significance, but precisely because he or she is always not yet determined he or she can also always (potentially) question his or her own conditions of existence.

Put in Castoriadis' terms, the idea of the radical character of imagination is also linked to the project of autonomy. If autonomy must be conceived as the possibility of giving oneself one's law, that is, of instituting a critical relationship with the discourses that are given, then imagination is also radical because, by its own creativity, it can also question not only what is given but also what it produces (Castoriadis 1991; 1997).

If autonomy means interrogation, then political myths can be the site, not only for the instituting of the social imaginary, but also for the opening up of the crucial question: "why *these* significations and not any other?" Clearly, this does not mean that political myths are always a means for interrogation. The work on myth can also tend towards a closure of meaning.[17] As Castoriadis observes, it could even turn out to be the case that no autonomous society has ever existed, since all societies tend to conceal, by different means, the instituting dimension of the social imaginary.[18] However, the concept of the radical imagination points to the fact that the work on political myth can also be the site for interrogation.

---

[17] Some suggestions on the conditions under which political myths produce a closure of meaning can be found in Chapter 2 and, with regard to contemporary societies, Chapter 12.

[18] Since the instituting dimension of the social imaginary is the major threat to the stability of the instituted society itself, it is against this threat that the strongest defences are set up. These consist in the denial and covering up of the instituting dimension of society through the imputation of the origins of the institution and of its social significations to an extra-social source, such as gods, heroes or ancestors (Castoriadis 1991).

Castoriadis sees the creative dimension of imagination essentially as a capacity for interrogation, that is, as a capacity for questioning the given. But there is another dimension of imagination that has been stressed by Ricoeur. In his view, the creativity of imagination is linked to a capacity for fictionalising that we find in the logic of action. There is no action without imagination. As Sorel also has pointed out, people need to represent their upcoming actions in terms of a narrative that makes significance of their conditions. This capacity to fictionalise through the combination of unusual predicates, according to Ricoeur, is a capacity to "radically rethink", which he, employing Mannheim's terminology, calls "utopian" (Ricoeur 1994).

Political myth can be the site for the work of both these creative dimensions of imagination. As we have seen, the myth of the state of nature and that of the general strike, for instance, have been at times both the direct means for questioning what is given as well as for utopian thinking and action. This does not mean that historical narratives are excluded from these dimensions. The concept of political myth simply signals that, in as far as historical narratives come to play this role, they are no longer operating only as historical narratives but also as political myths. In other words, it signals that they are now part of a politics of the past.

11

Myth and Identity

In an early article, "Die politische Theorie des Mythus", Carl Schmitt
supports the existence of a strict relationship between the emergence
of a political theory of myth and the crisis of parliamentarianism. The
theory of myth, he contends, is the most powerful sign of the decline
of the rationalism of parliamentary thought (Schmitt 1988: 17). His
argument can be summarised as follows: if myth is the "symptom of a
form of energy", of an "enormous enthusiasm", then the mechanism
of "the discussing, bargaining and parliamentary procedures" cannot
but appear as a "betrayal of myth" and an act of fundamental infidelity
to the vital enthusiasm from which myth derives (1988: 13).

Schmitt, in the first chapter of his *Political Theology*, identified the
basis for his intellectual enterprise in a "philosophy of concrete life"
(1985b). In his decisionist thesis, which is outlined at the beginning
of the book, he states that he who decides on the state of exception is
sovereign. It is exception that creates the rule, and not vice versa. In his
view, "in the exception, the power of real life breaks through the crust
of a mechanism that has become turbid by repetition"; consequently,
a philosophy of concrete life cannot withdraw from the exception and
the extreme case, but must be interested in it to the highest degree
(1985b: 13–15).

Schmitt, it is well known, is here referring to the debate on the
institutions of the Weimar Republic, and expressions such as "crust of
mechanism" are a form of criticism towards the working of its parliamentary institutions. Parliamentarianism is seen by Schmitt as a form

of "government by discussion"; and the principle of discussion and of reasoning that he saw at work in the institutions of the Weimar Republic is, according to his vitalistic decisionism, the "strongest opposite" to the real life of myth (1988: 11).

Therefore, it is not by chance that his article, "Die politische Theorie des Mythus", also appears as the final chapter of his text, *The Crisis of Parliamentary Democracy* (1985a). Here, significantly, the article appears with another title: "Irrationalist Theories of the Direct Use of Force". Most of the article is devoted to analysing Sorel's view of myth, and it is by presenting his own interpretation of Sorel that Schmitt puts forward his view of political myth as a symptom of national energy. However, as I hope to show in this chapter, this view is based on a problematic conception of the relationship between myth and identity on the one hand, and between the different forms of identity on the other. As we will see, this view, which today still has its supporters, can have very problematic normative outcomes.

Myths, according to Schmitt's reading of Sorel, are the direct expression of concrete life, of a Bergsonian *élan vital* that is alien and also hostile to discussion and rational mediation. For this reason, Schmitt takes the emergence of the theories of myth as the clearest sign of the crisis of parliamentarianism. In Schmitt's reading, Sorel's myth stands to rationality as a decision on the exception stands to parliamentarianism; as a consequence, the rationalism of parliamentary discussion cannot but appear as a "betrayal" of the irrationality of myth.[1] Thus, Sorel's theory of the general strike is necessarily linked not only to Sorel's preference for violence over institutional participation, but also to the intellectual choice of a sort of irrationalism that is substantially at odds with any form of discussion.

The only point where, according to Schmitt, Sorel was wrong was in his diagnosis of the contemporary forces of the production of myth. If myth, as Schmitt argues, is the criterion for deciding whether one nation or social group has a historical mission and has reached its historical momentum (Schmitt 1985a: 68), then we must conclude that the strongest myth of modernity is not that of class conflict, but that of the nation. The myth of class conflict, he observes, was created by the diffusion of an image that was capable of intensifying all the emotions

---

[1] On Schmitt's interpretation of myth as irrationality and particularly on the influence of Nietzsche for the development of this view, see Chapter 2 of McCormick 1997.

of hatred and contempt. This negative image of the bourgeoisie, first fed by literati such as Stendhal, or "the hated socially *déclassé* genius of Baudelaire" was subsequently given a world-historical dimension by Marx and Engels, who declared the bourgeoisie to be "the last representative of a pre-historical humanity divided into classes" (Schmitt 1985a: 74).

However, according to Schmitt, at the beginning of the twentieth century this image of the bourgeoisie as the last *odium generis humani* could no longer thrive from the sheer instinct for class conflict and had to refer to a superior mythology, the national myth.[2] Examples such as Italian fascism, the revolutionary wars of France and Spain, and the German wars of liberation against Napoleon prove the superiority of national myths, because, as Schmitt puts it, they are "symptoms of national energy" (Schmitt 1985a: 74, 75).

If myth is the expression of great enthusiasm, of energy that is already given, then, Schmitt concludes, it is at the "myth of nation", rather than at that of class conflict, that we have to look. What lies at the bottom of this "energy" is clearly stated:

The more naturalistic conceptions of race and descent, the apparently more typical *terrisme* of the Celtic and Romance peoples; the speech, tradition, and consciousness of a shared culture and education, the awareness of belonging to a community of fate [*Schicksalsgemeinschaft*], a sensibility for being different in itself [*Eine Empfindlichkeit für das Verschiedensein an sich*] – all of that tends towards a national rather than a class consciousness today. (Schmitt 1985a: 75; translation modified)

Here myth is the symptom of an irrational force that stems from the consciousness of a common race and descent, traditions, language, the feeling of belonging to the same community of fate, as well as a certain feeling of being different in itself. In other words, national myths are the symptoms of common identities. They are the mere epiphenomenon of a deeper reality, of an identity that is already given and that finds its source in an irrational power that is fundamentally hostile to rational discussion.

In this theory of myth as irrationality, it is not difficult to recognise a familiar discourse. Schmitt's treatment of myth reproduces the

---

[2] One must not forget that, in 1930, seven years after Schmitt's *The Political Theory of Myth*, Rosenberg's *The Myth of the Twentieth Century* appeared. For a discussion of this myth, see Chapter 8.

semantic apparatus and conceptual strategies of the Enlightenment by simply inverting its axiological connotation. In the Enlightenment, myth is the defeat of reason and, thus, the source of all evils. Here, it is the "great enthusiasm" that breaks through the "crust of mechanism" of reason. In both cases, though, myth and rationality are set on two different and opposing grounds so that the two approaches, far from being opposite, converge on a fundamental point: myth and reason are heterogeneous and mutually irreconcilable. However, the suspicion seems to be legitimate that this view is more Schmitt's own, rather than the result of an unbiased reading of Sorel.

As we have seen, Sorel does not appear, in fact, to conceive of myth in this way. Sorel explicitly engages himself in and calls for a rational discussion of the myth of the general strike. His opposition to parliamentarianism stems from a preference for the general strike over institutional participation as a political means for obtaining certain ends, rather than from an intellectual rejection of rationality and discussion per se.

But there is more at stake. Schmitt conceives of myth as the product of a national energy, that is, of a national consciousness that is based on elements – such as language, tradition and consciousness of a common fate – that pre-exist myth. In contrast, Sorel presents the general strike as a means for creating a class consciousness that does not yet exist. The fourth chapter of *Reflections on Violence* is devoted precisely to showing that the general strike, by conveying in a single image all the principles of Marxism, is the best means for creating such a consciousness. Simply put, for Schmitt the myth is a "symptom" because it reflects an identity that is given, whereas for Sorel it is the means for creating an identity yet to come.

The contrast between these two views signals one antinomy of social identity: identity is by definition "that which is identical to itself", but is at the same time "that which is different from itself" since it is necessarily the ever changing product of history. Identity is a choice, if we look at it from Sorel's perspective, but identity is a destiny, if we turn to Schmitt.[3] Political myths also reflect the same antinomy: they can

---

[3] On the idea of the antinomies of identity, see Wagner 2002. He distinguishes between three of them: "identity as choice or as destiny"; "identity as construction or as reality"; and, finally, "identity as autonomy or as domination".

be seen as both a symptom of an already existing identity, but also as a means for creating an identity yet to come.

This antinomy explodes at the end of *The Crisis of Parliamentary Democracy* in which Schmitt, after presenting national myths as the symptom of an already existing national identity, points to the dangers that myth represents. Myth, Schmitt now suggests, is by its very nature *polytheistic*, both because of "the pluralism of an unforeseeable number of myths" and because "every myth is in itself polytheistic" (Schmitt 1985a: 76). Consequently, the feeling of belonging to a single community of fate, which he had before identified as the source and fundament of myth, is now seen as a unity that is crucially endangered by myth. In this way, myth, conceived as the "symptom" of an already existing common identity, comes to be that which, with its intrinsically polytheistic nature, threatens the very deepest reality of which it would be a mere symptom.

If we now go back to the previous chapters of *The Crisis of Parliamentary Democracy*, we see that the same antinomy pervaded Schmitt's treatment of identity and democracy. Schmitt's major point in this text is that parliamentarianism, that is, "government by discussion", is intrinsically linked to liberalism, but not to democracy. Schmitt defines democracy in terms of identity in contrast to liberalism. In particular, by returning to Rousseau's *Social Contract*, he defines democracy as "identity between rulers and the ruled" (Schmitt 1985a: 26, 27).

However, while Rousseau conceived of democracy as identity between rulers and the ruled, in the sense that those who govern and those who are governed must be the same persons (i.e., as identity to themselves), Schmitt uses the expression "identity between rulers and the ruled" in such a way that it comes to signify, not simply identity between individuals, but also identity between these individuals and a *tertium* that is the nation, and even identity of this *tertium* with itself. This is clear later on in the text, when he explains what he means by democracy as identity between rulers and the ruled:

Democracy rests on a string of identities: to this series belong the identity of governed and governing, sovereign and subject, the identity of the subject and object of state authority, the identity of the people with their representatives in parliament, the identity of the state and the current voting population, the identity of the state and the law, and finally the identity of the quantitative (the numerical majority or unanimity) with the qualitative (the justice of the laws). (Schmitt 1985a: 26)

Thus, it is through such a holistic use of the term "identity between rulers and the ruled", which indeed seems to go well beyond Rousseau,[4] that Schmitt can conclude that "democracy requires first homogeneity and – second, if the need arises – elimination or eradication of heterogeneity" (Schmitt 1985a: 9).

If one then further asks how this homogeneity is to be understood, then two opposite answers emerge from the text, and we are faced with another antinomy. On the one hand, Schmitt seems to be quite straightforward in asserting that "the question is not one of abstract, logical-arithmetical games, but is about the *substance of equality*, and, as such, it can be found in certain *physical and moral qualities*" (Schmitt 1985a: 9; emphasis mine). As we have seen, a more detailed list of these qualities includes: race and descent, language, tradition, a consciousness of a shared culture and education, the awareness of a community of fate (*Schicksalsgemeinschaft*), and a sensibility of being different in itself.

On the other hand, though, later on in the text, Schmitt equally strongly asserts that, in fact, such homogeneity never exists *in concreto*. Indeed, he openly states that the various nations or social and economic groups that organised themselves democratically have the same people only "in the abstract", because, *in concreto*, the masses are sociologically and psychologically heterogeneous (Schmitt 1985a: 25).

Indeed, even the passage quoted, in which Schmitt spells out all the series of identities that constitute democracy, is followed by a further fundamental qualification: all these identities, Schmitt writes, are in fact not a "palpable reality" (*handgreifliche Wirklichkeit*) (Schmitt 1985a: 26).

In other words, identity appears here not as a matter of an "objective" legal, political or sociological equality, but as what he calls "identifications" or "recognitions of identity" (*Anerkennungen der Identität*)

---

[4] We cannot enter a discussion of the difference between Rousseau's and Schmitt's treatment of democracy here. Let me just point out that, as is well known, an expression such as "the identity between the people and their representatives in parliament" could not but have appeared suspicious for a critic of representative democracy such as Rousseau.

(Schmitt 1985a: 27).[5] Thus, it is thanks to the idea of "identification" understood holistically that Schmitt can, for instance, conclude that democracy is not antithetical to dictatorship: "the will of the people – so he wrote – is always identical with the will of the people whether a decision comes from the "yes" or "no" of millions of voting papers, or from a *single individual who has the will of the people* even without a ballot, or from the people acclaiming in some way" (Schmitt 1985a: 27; emphasis mine).

This is not the most appropriate place for entering into an accurate discussion of Schmitt's complex view of democracy and identity/identification. But clearly, even from such a brief reconstruction, it is evident that the holistic way in which Schmitt uses the concept of identity can result in very problematic normative outcomes. They become patent in that Schmitt, moving from his definition of democracy in terms of identity between rulers and the ruled, can come to conclude that, in as far as the people "identify" themselves with the *Führer*, he can be said "to *have* the will of the people" and his decision, whatever it will be, is always "democratic" by definition (Schmitt 1985a: emphasis mine).

It might be relevant to remember here that Nazism proposed to outbid democracy through a more authentic identification with the people and popular will, and Schmitt's theory lends itself to such a political project.[6] The assertion that a dictator can "have the will of the people" is, however, very problematic – not exclusively, but primarily due to its political consequences. In dictatorship, identity, and the myth of which this identity should be the symptom, far from being a means for autonomy (as it was for Sorel), is turned into its opposite: identity or identification is the means for domination and, we can add, for the most annihilating form of domination.

Schmitt's treatment of identity and of the relationship between identity and myth brings to light a series of conceptual problems linked

---

[5] To my knowledge, Schmitt's usage of the concept of recognition, in particular, in relation to identity, has not yet been focused on. We cannot enter a full discussion of the issue here, but it is certainly one that deserves further investigation.
[6] Carl Schmitt's adherence to Nazism is one of the most debated issues in the literature. Suffice it to say here that Schmitt's treatment of democracy and its compatibility with dictatorship reminds us that, as many authors have pointed out, Nazi-Fascism attempted to present itself as the savior of democracy. For a discussion of Schmitt's theory from this point of view, see Wolin 1990.

to this use of the concept of identity. First, as we have seen, Schmitt considers myth to be the symptom of an identity that is already given, but, at the same time, one cannot but point to the fact that, as Sorel shows, and Schmitt also seems at certain points to recognise,[7] myth is also the producer of identity. This leads to the problem of the continuity of identity, that is, what we can call the *diachronic antinomy* of identity: identity must exhibit *continuity* in time, it must be identical to itself in order to be "identity", but it is also the ever-changing product of the becoming.

Second, there is what we can call the *synchronic dimension* of this antinomy, which stems from the problem of the *boundaries* of identity. As we have seen in expressions such as "national identity" or "identity between rulers and the ruled", Schmitt combined "identity of singular individual beings with themselves", "their identity with each other", as well as "their identity with a *tertium* (e.g. the general will, the state, the nation)" and even "the identity of this *tertium* with itself in time". This brings forth the problem of the boundaries of identity, and, in particular, the problem of the boundaries between personal and group identities.

Faced with the consequences of Schmitt's holistic use of the concept of identity one would be easily tempted to get rid of the concept altogether. Analogous problems emerge with some of the contemporary uses of the term "identity". Expressions such as "modern identity" (Taylor 1989), "national identity" (Smith 1991), or even the widespread "politics of identity" risk leading us to a holistic understanding of the concept of identity.

In the first place, it should be noted that, even if we are now used to the term "identity" without further qualifications, the concept always denotes a relation rather than a being. "Identity" means that something is identical to something else. Therefore, beyond the widely debated "identity issue", and expressions such as "modern identity",

---

[7] He seems to be aware of this when he analyses the way in which the creation through the work of literati and thinkers of an image of the bourgeoisie as an object of contempt has led to a class consciousness and the way in which this was supplanted by the work of the national myth (Schmitt 1988: 17; 1985a: 74–5). In another crucial passage, after having asserted that a single individual can have the will of the people, he then adds "everything depends on how the will of the people is formed" (Schmitt 1985a: 27).

"gender identity", "class identity" or "the Italian identity", there are possibly interrelated, but fundamentally different, questions: the identity of the singular human being with himself or herself, the identity of different singular human beings with each other, the identity between the same singular human beings with themselves in time, as well as the identity between them and a *tertium* (nation, the gender or another social group) and even the identity of this *tertium* with itself.

Sometimes, as we have seen in the case of Schmitt, this conflation is expressly suggested. A more recent example is Smith's ethno-symbolic view of national identity (Smith 1999). In his *Myths and Memories of the Nation*, Smith constructs his theory on the basis of a parallel between individual and national identity. By using the words of Sophocles' Oedipus in search of his origins, he holds that people need to reconstruct their family origins as much as they need to trace their national roots back to some myth of descent (Smith 1999: 59). However, this analogy between families and ethnic communities is misleading because it obscures the fact that the forms of identity that are at stake in these two instances are fundamentally different: that of an individual, Oedipus, looking for his biological mother and that of collectivities in search of an often invented common origin.[8] At the basis of this view is a further conflation between different forms of the search for meaning. Indeed, Smith postulates a "universal drive for meaning" as a source of myth (Smith 1999: 61), and, as a consequence, he conflates myth with other forms of symbolism that also respond to a need for meaning, but not to a need for significance, and therefore do not generate myths.

It is the possible conflation of all these different problems that renders the expression "identity", without further qualification, so ambiguous. By simply rejecting the notion, though, one would still be left with the problems that the notion addresses. Therefore, a more promising strategy seems to be to take note of the ambiguity generated by these usages of the term, and to start by distinguishing the different problems and issues that are unified here. In other words, we should proceed from the assumption that the term identity, as it emerges in these debates, fundamentally defines a problem rather than an entity.

---

[8] On the extent to which national communities have invented their traditions, see Hobsbawm and Ranger 1983.

According to one view, the emergence of this problem is intrinsically linked to the conditions of modernity.[9] Taylor's influential *Sources of the Self*, whose subtitle is *The Making of Modern Identity*, openly signals this relationship (Taylor 1989). Indeed, as some authors have noticed, it is under specifically modern conditions, that is, in the moment when the individual human being is no longer assigned a specific status by birth, but is instead faced with an expanding myriad possibilities, that the formation of that individual's own identity becomes a problem (Melucci 2000).

This does not mean that personal and social identities did not exist before, or that the issues to which the term identity refers did not exist. It only means that they were not problematic enough to be conceptualised, or that they did not appear as "problematic" as they appear to us now. In other words, we can say that the conditions of modernity rendered personal and social identity fundamentally problematic because they made it clear that our identities are always the instable result of what we are, what we have been and what we want to be.[10] Modernity is, by definition, the "new epoch" (*Neuzeit*), the epoch that aspired to breaking radically with the past and, thus, it can transform identity into a "project". In other words, in an epoch in which the "horizon of expectation" has supplanted the "space of experience", identity has to be a problem because it can no longer be seen as the mere deposit of the past.[11]

This is what we have called the diachronic antinomy of the identity *problematique*. Identity, in whatever way we want to use this term, fundamentally refers to the idea of sameness, to an *idem* that remains the same in time by necessarily being always different at the same time (Friese 2002). Identity is fundamentally a problem: it is the problem of the possible continuity of an *idem* in the becoming, that is, of a possible *idem* in the difference between past, present and future.

Indeed, once one has signalled the dangers implicit in holistic uses of the concept of identity, one must also recognise that, in all different

[9] On this point, see Wagner 2002.
[10] On this point, see Cerutti 1996. Cerutti insists on what he calls the normative and planning side of any group identity: in identifying ourselves with a group we cannot leave aside "what we actually are", or "what we would like to be", or "what we think we ought to be or do" (Cerutti 1996: 7).
[11] I am here referring to Koselleck's thesis as exposed in *Futures Past* (Koselleck 2001).

cases – the identity of the self with itself, the identity of a self with others, or the identity of an abstract notion with itself in space and time – the problem of identity is always the problem of the *idem*. Otherwise stated, whatever qualification we add, the problem of identity is always the problem of the identity in difference, the antinomy of an *idem* that must be identical to itself by being different at the same time.

Clearly, a different "difference" is at stake each time in expressions such as "logical identity", "personal identity", or "group identity". All the same, it should be stressed that if the expression "identity", without further qualifications, has come to be widely employed, it is because it has been suggested that there are no clear boundaries between the various forms of identity. Schmitt's usage of the expression "identity between rulers and the ruled", or common expressions such as "national identity" or "politics of identity" all suggest more or less explicitly that the boundaries between different forms of identity have been challenged.

Therefore, while some authors, when faced with the different forms of identity, simply dispose of the issue by saying that all these forms of identity have nothing to do with one another,[12] one should take note that the problem stems precisely from the relationship between them: an object or a concept is identical to itself or to something else in a different way from that in which one person can be said to be identical to himself or herself or to another person, and the two, in turn, differ from the way in which a group can be said to be identical with itself in space and time. At the same time, to distinguish between the two does not imply a denial of the possible overlaps and convergences.

Let us begin with personal identity. We will then move on to group identity and, finally, look at the way in which myth relates to it. The problem of identity is the problem of an *idem*, but what constitutes the *idem* in the case of personal identity? In what sense and how can the self be said to be identical to itself? Identity, it has been emphasised recently, is "a story of recognitions" (Pizzorno 2000). Ourselves, what "we are", is the result of our living in different circles of recognition, and thus consists of a long series of recognitions by those who are part of these circles.

[12] See, for instance, Bilgrami 2001.

Different traditions, ranging from the philosophical reflections of Rousseau and Hegel to the interactive psychology of Mead, have recently been revisited in order to point to the social dimension of the constitution of our selves, that is, to the fundamental fact that the ways in which we perceive ourselves depend on the ways in which we are and have been perceived by our relevant others (Taylor 1992; Honneth 1995).[13] The concept of recognition points, thus, to the fact that our personal identity is inseparable from our social identity because it is the result of interaction with others.

However, the recourse to the concept of recognition does not imply that personal identity coincides *tout court* with family, gender, national, class or any other form of group identity. The simplest reason for this is that in the case of personal identity the first vehicle of recognition is our body, while in the case of group identity there is not a single visible body that is the object of recognition both by relevant others and by ourselves.[14] The idea of a social body is clearly only a metaphor and, moreover, a much contested one.[15] This is the reason why a politics of recognition based on cultures, such as that proposed by Charles Taylor, can be problematic (Taylor 1992): social groups are not selves that can recognise each other on the basis of a body and of a single narrating voice. As a consequence, for individual human beings, a multicultural politics of recognition, which labels each one as a member of a given culture, may turn into a form of oppressive universalism disguised as cultural particularism.

Our identity is a story of recognition by others, but we interact with many others. Indeed, many theorists have, from different perspectives, underlined the multiplicity of identity: our identity, it has been claimed, is the result of the many different and sometimes contrasting roles and actions that we perform in our lives as well as of the way

---

[13] Notwithstanding the common reference to the concept of recognition, there are many differences between all of these approaches. In the first place, whereas Pizzorno has recourse to this concept from a sociological perspective, in order to explain how society and conflicts emerge (Pizzorno 2000), Honneth and Taylor have a clear normative intent. Second, Honneth explicitly aims to build up an ethic of conflict whose ultimate normative reference point, however, remains the singular human being (Honneth 1995), whereas Taylor, who refers to the Herderian ethic of authenticity, applies the concept of recognition to both individuals and social groups (Taylor 1992).

[14] For a critique of Pizzorno's neglect of the role of the body in the formation of identity, see, for instance, Sparti 2000, as well as Pizzorno's answer in Pizzorno 2000.

[15] For a critique of the analogy of states and individuals, see Bottici 2004.

in which these generate the dynamics of recognition. However, if the word "identity" is to have any meaning whatsoever, if the concept of the "self" is to preserve its semantic core of "sameness", then there must be a unifying moment. The continuity of the body, perceived and recognised by others and by the self, is the first answer.

As Pizzorno points out, the fact that our identity is a story of multiple recognitions also implies that there is only *one* self that knows the whole story and can reconstruct it (Pizzorno 2000: 209). Our identity is not the chaotic juxtaposition of recognitions, because, intertwined with these juxtapositions, there is also self-recognition, a sort of self-attribution of identity. The self appears as a story of recognitions by both us and others, because it is only the self that can reconstruct the whole story by narrating the recognitions that have accumulated in space and time.

"Narrating in order to exist" (Melucci 2000) is the slogan that has been proposed in order to point out that the alternative is not between the Cartesian punctual *ego* and the dissolution of the *idem* in an eccentric identity. What creates an *idem* out of a more or less scattered set of recognitions is the possibility of a narrative. A self implies the possibility of telling a more or less coherent story and the unity of the self is the unity of a possible story. This, however, must be a story that encompasses an endless number of stories: that of a moving, living, interacting body; that of a mother, a daughter, a sister, a worker, a member of a polity, to mention only a few. And the concept of narrative has the advantage of pointing simultaneously to the sameness and to the unavoidable multiplicity of identity.

If identity is the story of recognitions, then the loss of identity is the loss of the possibility of telling a story. According to one view, the pathologies of the self can be considered in terms of an interruption in a narrative or the loss of a coherent story (Ricoeur 1970). The therapeutic impact of psychoanalysis has, consequently, been identified, not in the removal of the cause of the trauma, but in the possibility of narrating a story. Disputes may arise, and in fact have arisen, over the degree to which this rediscovery can be considered as a collective enterprise rather than as an imposition by the therapist of a narrative upon the experience of the patient, but it seems that there can be no definitive answer to this question.

On the other hand, what can be said is that the therapist does play a crucial role in the construction of the plot. The therapist is the one who can help to rebuild a story by providing a narrative plot. In a letter to Einstein, Freud suggests that his theory is nothing but a great mythology (Freud 1941–68). But in what sense can Freud's conception be considered a mythology? The therapeutic impact of the Oedipus complex lies in its power to generate story-plots: the stories of Oedipus and Electra are *mythologems* that can potentially provide a plot to an interrupted life experience. Therefore, a psychoanalytical therapy is successful not when the cause of the trauma is removed, which is impossible since an event has actually occurred, but when it is inserted into a coherent narrative.

Notwithstanding the recent exponential interest in narrative, which has led to talk of a crucial "narrative turn" in the human and social sciences (Aronsson 2001), the narrative core of the self is not a recent discovery. According to Foucault's discussion of the various technologies of the self, this discovery goes back at least as far as Greek-Roman philosophy and Christianity – in the former as philosophical dialogues and letters to friends, in the latter, in the form of confession. In both cases, the self is constructed through narrative practices (Foucault 1988). In modern societies, confessions have been integrated into more or less institutionalised practices such as interviewing, teaching, counselling and therapy, all of which convey what Foucault calls disciplining, that is, normative patterns for what should be told and the ways in which it should be done (Foucault 1988).

Foucault's analysis of the technologies of the self brings us back to a crucial antinomy of identity: if identity is a story of recognition, then we are dominated not only by those who gave us past recognitions, but also by those who can influence our own construction of the plot. In other words, if our public and private selves are intimately linked to conversational practices and cannot be separated from them because it is through these practices that recognition, and thus the constitution of the self, takes place, what margin remains for autonomy? Identity as autonomy and identity as domination: this is perhaps the antinomy of identity that summarises all other possible antinomies: "identity as unity" versus "identity as plurality", "identity as choice" versus "identity as destiny" (Wagner 2002).

Two considerations, concerning the diachronic and the synchronic dimensions of the antinomies of identity respectively, must, however, be added. On the one hand, our identity is not just the story of past and present recognitions (both by others and by ourselves), but is also the story of future and expected recognitions. These expected recognitions may or may not come, and our struggle for recognition may be more or less successful; but it is still true that the project and expectations of future recognitions is also constitutive of our own identity. At the same time, projects and expectations of future recognitions are also dependent on our present and past identities.

This, in turn, brings in the issue of the relationship between personal and group identities. In what sense can a social group, nation or class be said to be an *idem*? Either there can be an answer to this question or expressions such as "group identity", "social identity", and so on are, properly speaking, nonsense. Here the problem is not only that of the narrative synthesis among a more or less scattered set of recognitions. The problem is that there is not a single "self" that can tell the whole story. There is no single body that is the continuous object in the space and time of a set of recognitions and there is, thus, no single self that knows the whole story. While the continuity of the self, and thus of the story that only he or she knows, can be guaranteed by the continuity of the body, in the case of the social group, the idea of the body is, at best, a contestable metaphor. The body, with its precise contours, is, in fact, the first vehicle of recognition by others as well as by the self, but in the case of group identities, we do not have just one, but many living bodies with many different stories of recognitions to tell.

A social group, indeed, is a being of imagination in a different sense to that in which "this table" or "my self" is.[16] Properly speaking, social groups are not beings of *imagination*, because there is no single subject who has this faculty of imagination, but a being of the *imaginary* (Arnason 1994). In the case of social entities such as nations, classes and states, we are not dealing simply with abstract notions, but with socially constructed beings: it is because there are narrating bodies that behave *as if* such beings existed, that they do *actually* exist. They are not,

---

[16] Following the publication of Anderson's influential *Imagined Communities* and the growing interest in social constructivism, there has been a dramatic inrease in the number of publications on the "construction" or "imagination" of social and political communities (Anderson 1983). Spinoza's theory of political myth, as we have seen, contained some fundamental insights in this direction. What we need, though, is a transition, following Castoriadis, from "imagination" to "imaginary".

to use Schmitt's expression, a palpable reality. The recent explosion of literature on various aspects of "the construction of social realities" stems from a new emphasis on this fundamental insight.

If there is an *idem* that can unify the multiplicity of living, acting, moving, narrating bodies, this, again, is a narrative, but it must be a narrative of a different sort: it must be a narrative that recognises that nobody can tell the whole story, and that perhaps there is no story at all to tell. Any form of group identity adds a further dimension to this *problematique* of identity: the possibility of recomposing, not just different stories, but also different narrating voices. The failure to do so results, not simply in a disturbance of identity, but in the absence of a possible story, that is, in the dissolution of a common identity.

This is the reason why an approach to myth in terms of a process can also help clarify the problem of identity. As we have seen, the concept of "work on myth" implies the idea of plurality as well as that of its problematic nature. On the one hand, myth is intrinsically plural, because it is implicit in the concept of myth not only that there can be different variants of myth, but also that there are many different and possible *mythologems*. Plurality is what characterises myth, but it points, at the same time, to a danger: the plurality of stories may turn into the recognition that there is no common story to be told.

On the other hand, myth also implies the possibility of encompass- ing different stories in a common *mythologem*: different stories, stem- ming from different narrative voices, can be recomprised in a single *mythologem*. Myth can, therefore, contribute to a delineation of the always problematic *idem* of any form of group identity. Group identi- ties are often defined in terms of a set of elements. These can be either a set of ethnic features, such as language, history, traditions, as it was for Schmitt, or a set of values and principles, or a combination of the two.[17] However, it is only a common narrative that can make "a sin- gle set" out of a multiplicity of principles, values, memories, symbols. Myth, as a particular kind of narrative, one that provides significance, can also fundamentally contribute to this end.

---

[17] According to Cerutti, for instance, group identity can be defined as a set of values, memories, symbols, etc. that we recognise as common and sufficient for feeling as a "we" (Cerutti 1996: 6).

Myth can, indeed, be one of the means through which a single narrative, which unifies all the various elements that constitute common identity, comes to be recognised and accepted by a plurality of living, acting, narrating bodies. Myth is a narrative that can coagulate and provide *significance*, and significance, as we have seen, is always particularistic in the sense that what is significant for some people in given conditions might not be significant for other people in other conditions, or for the same people in different conditions.

If many forms of group identity rest on a common political myth, we should nonetheless recognise that not all of them do. For example, I can recognise my "Italian identity" without this being a source of significance to me. This, on the other hand, does not mean that political myths are pathological forms of identity building. As we have seen, they are not necessarily deforming and hostile to critical discussion, and can therefore be the non-pathological means for the shaping of common identities.

In particular, group identities that are shaped by the work on a common narrative are not necessarily homogeneous wholes. Indeed, what characterises political myths is precisely their polytheistic nature. The polytheism of myth, which, from the point of view of Schmitt's political theology, was seen as a threat, can be seen as nothing but the reflex of the necessary heterogeneity of group identity. Conversely, to assume that identity necessarily implies homogeneity means to assume the point of view of political theology, which is misleading and problematic from different points of view. All forms of group identity are the result of different stories and different narrative voices whose possible recomposition in a common mythology is never assured.

Typically, however, group identities that rest on a political myth are oriented towards action. Indeed, as narratives that provide significance, political myths not only make sense of experience, they also provide orientation and stimulation for action: they are an invitation to act *here and now*. For instance, the general strike described by Sorel is not a simple narrative that provides meaning to the experience of the proletariat: it is the narrative of its future action because it contains a determination to act.

This example also points out that, from the point of view of a theory of political myth, there can be no sharp separation between cultural and political identity.[18] The myth of the general strike is a specifically political myth because it addresses the need for a common action that affects the specifically political conditions in which this action takes place. The identity that the myth of the general strike contributes to shaping is indeed both cultural and political. What renders a myth specifically political, and, as a consequence, renders political the identity that it can contribute to shaping is the way in which it interacts with the context and, thus, the specifically political conditions that are given each time.

These brief considerations do not pretend to be exhaustive. Clearly, they ask more questions than they answer. They simply suggest that political myths can play an important role in the making of common political identity and that the identities that result thereby are not necessarily homogeneous. Rather, the view of group identity that the concept of work on myth presupposes is in contrast with the idea that group identities are self-like wholes.

There are many variants of this idea today, but the idea of the "clash of civilisations" is perhaps the most striking. Civilisations and cultures can be said "to clash" with each other only if they can be said to "interact" with each other, to "hate" each other, to "perceive" each other in one certain way or another.[19] Expressions such as "nations today raise questions as to *Who we are*", or even "in the world of global politics cultures interact with each other" (Huntington 1996: 21, 43), imply that we attribute to cultural identities all the features of a self: asking questions, providing answers, interacting, and even hating, loving, and perceiving. Undoubtedly, these expressions are *only* metaphors, but the problem is that they are deceptive ones. In particular, they implicitly suggest that group identities can exhibit the same kind of coherence of self-identity. But, in group identities, there is no single narrating body that can tell the whole story, and, therefore, it can always be the case that there is no common story at all.

---

[18] See, for instance, Habermas (1996), who argues that cultural and political identities are separated.

[19] Huntington, going against the German usage, which distinguishes between "civilisation" (*Zivilisation*), as based on material factors, and "culture" (*Kultur*) as based on values, ideals, and other higher intellectual, artistic and moral qualities of a society, defines civilisations as cultural wholes (Huntington 1996: 41).

Thus, the problem with Huntington's paradigm of the "clash of civilisations" is not just that he reduces social action to a unique category of determinations and motivations, that is, culture (Bottici and Challand 2006). Huntington explicitly claims that he merely aims to build a map of reality, which, like all types of maps, is, by necessity, reductive (Huntington 1996: 29). The problem is that the map that he wants to draw is both misleading, because it suggests the existence of clearcut boundaries, and problematic, because it is based on the ascription of the attributes of a self to civilisations.

The antinomies of identity, and, in particular, the attempt to solve them in a definitive way, have certainly helped to create such a hypostatised view of identity. Consequently, a certain degree of scepticism is desirable, and we must never forget that beyond expressions such as "civilisational identities" (Huntington 1996) or "national identity" (Smith 1991; 1999) there might be a conflation between the identity of individuals among each other, their identity with a *tertium* such as culture or nation, but also the identity of this *tertium* with itself. The subjects of social identities are always singular human beings: they are human beings asking questions, providing answers, being the object and subject of the process of recognition. In other words, only singular human narrating bodies can tell the stories of group identities, and there is never the guarantee that all these stories can be reconciled in a single plot.

12

Political Myths Today

The Extraordinary and the Banal

Political myth has often been associated with the extraordinary. Political myths, both when rejected by enlightened thinkers as regression into primitiveness and when acclaimed as symptoms of a great enthusiasm by their sympathisers, were most often seen as manifestations of the extraordinary. According to this view, political myths should have disappeared from modern politics, ruled as it is by an increasing rationalisation and bureaucratisation. However, this does not seem to be the case. Even under conditions of modernity, it seems as if – to paraphrase Geertz – the mythical has not gone out of politics, however much the banal may have entered it (Geertz 1983: 143).

The suspicion emerges that it is precisely through the interplay of the extraordinary and the banal that the work on political myth can, at best, take place today. If this proves to be the case, then by looking for the mythical only in the sites of the extraordinary, in grand parades and blood rituals, one risks overlooking the real sites for political myth. Precisely by rendering banal the extraordinary and vice versa, political myth may come to operate within the ambit of that which is out of question, because it is either apparently irrelevant or too important to be questioned.

It should be remembered here that "banal" literally means "commonplace" in the sense of that which is used by the whole community. According to *The Oxford English Dictionary*, the term "banal", in its first noted usage, denoted something belonging to a compulsory feudal service, where, for instance, the tenants of a certain district were obliged to carry their corn to a certain mill to be ground and to be baked at a certain oven for the benefit of the lord; it is only from the intermediate sense of "open to the use of all the community" that the term comes to mean "commonplace, common, trite, trivial and petty" (Simpson and Weiner 1989: vol. 1, 147).

If banal means this, then the hypothesis seems legitimate that political myth operates by rendering banal, namely commonplace within a community, that which is prima facie extraordinary. On the other hand, it might also be the case that, particularly under contemporary conditions, political myth operates the other way round, that is, by rendering extraordinary what is prima facie banal. The aim of this concluding chapter is to explore this hypothesis, and the way in which it does so is by analysing some of the possible sites for the work on political myth today. As a consequence, this chapter also aims to provide some suggestions for a future sociology of political myth understood as "work on myth".

If the interplay of the extraordinary and the banal proves to be the privileged site for the work on political myth, then political myth assumes a much more sinister light than it ever has in the past. While the grand parades of fascist regimes rendered the role of political myths conspicuous, in the composed discourses of our present-day politicians, there seems to be little place for the great enthusiasm which, according to a romantic view, should characterise political myth. This may, in turn, be the result of the fact that, under contemporary conditions, political myths have become more difficult to perceive and to criticise.

The postmodern attacks on grand narratives, together with the prophecies of a world ruled by specialists without spirit, have, from different sides helped to obscure the possible banality of political myth. By pointing at times towards the dangers of grand political narratives, and at others towards their inevitable decline, both these approaches may have helped to render us myopic in the face of the myths by which we live (Midgley 2003). However, there is the chance that the grand political narratives thrown out the door by post-metaphysical thought have reentered through the window.

We have seen that, when analysing the technique of modern political myths, Cassirer observed that modern politicians fulfil the functions that, in traditional societies, were performed by the *homo magus* and *homo divinans* (Cassirer 1973: 288, 289). Our modern politicians, he observed, not only promise to cure all social evils, but also continually foretell the future: prophecy has become an essential element in the new technique of government, the most improbable and even impossible promises are made, the millennium is predicted over and over again (Cassirer 1973: 289).

If these remarks cannot fully explain why people need such prophecies, they can nevertheless provide some insights as to the forms that political myth can assume under the conditions of modernity. In particular, it seems as if the contemporary conditions of the mediatisation and spectacularisation of politics (Edelman 1988) have indeed increased the potential of prophecy as a technique of government. Indeed, it is precisely under such new conditions that politicians are given unprecedented chances to "make the most improbable, even impossible promises". Our *homines magi* and *divinantes* might have refined their techniques of divination up to a point where they have lost any magical aspect, but while the techniques have changed deeply, the things themselves – to paraphrase Cassirer – have by no means vanished.

It is not only in the discourses of professional politicians that the work of and on political myth can be perceived. Again Cassirer's remarks contain helpful insights in this regard. Let us go back to the passage where he analyses the role played by prophecies:

Curiously enough, this new technique of divination first made its appearance not in German politics, but in German philosophy. In 1918 there appeared Oswald Spengler's *Decline of the West*. Perhaps never before had a philosophical book had such a sensational success. It was translated into almost every language and read by all sorts of readers – philosophers and scientists, historians and politicians, students and scholars, tradesmen and man in the street. What was the reason for this unprecedented success, what was the magic spell that this book exerted over its readers? It seems to be a paradox; but to my mind the cause of Spengler's success is to be sought rather in the title of his book than in its content. The title *Der Untergang des Abendlandes* was an electric spark that set the imagination of Spengler's readers aflame. (Cassirer 1973: 289)

The passage cannot but call our attention to the "sensational successes" of our epoch. Books such as Huntington's *The Clash of Civilisations* also seem to owe their extraordinary success to their titles much more than to their content. Huntington's book is a *mélange* of the methods of political science, history and international relations, but the power of this work rests more on its appeal to the imagination than on the rigour of its scientific arguments. Its title sets the imagination of its readers aflame no less than did Spengler's. The difference between the two is perhaps that, in the space of only a few years, *The Clash of Civilisations* turned into a self-fulfilling prophecy: while the "West" has not declined, "civilisations" appear to have clashed.[1]

Surprisingly enough, Huntington's prophecy of clashing civilisations was strongly criticised in most of the scholarly literature when it first appeared. His reading seemed, to most scholars, to be too simplistic and too reductive an approach to the complexities of world politics. All the same, particularly after 11 September 2001 many people have come to believe that a clash of civilisations is taking place. Two independent surveys of the US media's reaction to the September 11 attacks, for instance, showed that the events were framed entirely within the paradigm of the clash of civilisations (Abrahamian 2003; Seib 2004).

Immediately after the attacks, the *New York Times* launched a new section entitled "A Nation Challenged" hosting articles that framed the events within the idea of a clash between Islam and the West. Titles such as "Yes, This Is about Islam", "Jihad 101", "Barbarians at the Gates", "The Age of Muslim Wars", "This Is a Religious War" all referred to cultural and religious factors, leaving politics completely aside (Abrahamian 2003). Similar articles appearing in other newspapers also depicted such a clash, and were accompanied by pictures of religiously motivated atrocities, hate and fanaticism. For instance, the article "This is a Religious War" was illustrated with pictures of atrocities from Medieval Europe such as Goya's *Spanish Inquisition* (Sullivan 2001), while an article entitled "A Fervour America Should Easily Recognise", which appeared in the *Washington Post*, was accompanied by a photo of hooded men carrying the Koran and a hatchet (Morgan 2001).

This approach differed from the early reaction of the European media, which seemed at first to reject the idea of a clash of civilisations as an interpretative framework. In their reading of September 11

---

[1] In the analysis of the clash of civilisations as a political myth I will follow Bottici and Challand 2006.

events, they tended to privilege political factors over cultural factors. All the same, within a few years, many Europeans have also come to believe that a clash between Islam and the West is taking place (Bottici and Challand 2006). In September 2004, an article in the *Times* emphatically stated that "Islamic fundamentalism is causing a clash between liberal democracies and Muslims" and quoted a poll that revealed that 48 per cent of Italians believed that a clash of civilisations is under way and that Islam is a religion intrinsically more fanatical that any other (Bremner 2004).

Within a few years a theory that was so strongly criticised when it first appeared became a very successful narrative through which many people came to interpret the contemporary world. The clash of civilisations has become the lens through which many people perceive the world, and feel and act within it. This is, to a great extent, the result of a work on this myth that started long before and that was actually only intensified after September 11. The events of that day certainly charged this narrative with strong emotional reinforcement, but the reasons why people were ready to see "civilisations clashing with each other" instead of singular individuals acting out of a complex set of motivations have a much longer history. In other words, they are part of a work on a myth that started long before Huntington launched his prophecy, a work on a myth that took place in the media, in intellectual discourses and in other kinds of social practices.

Intellectual discourses have, for instance, played a crucial role. As we have seen, political myth and theory regularly coexist and reinforce each other (Chapter 9). Political myths are simply the work on a common narrative that provides significance to present, past and future experience. As such, they are not opposed to rational theorising, as an enlightened view would maintain, but, instead, are quite often intermingled with it. "Political myth", Tudor observed thirty years ago, "supplies the theoretical argument with a concrete reference and a temporal perspective it would otherwise lack; on the other hand, the theoretical argument endows myth with academic respectability and a certain timeless significance" (Tudor 1972: 126).

Indeed, in the scholarly literature on Islam there is a whole series of *topoi* that are more or less directly recalled by icons, such as the image of the fanatical bearded man with an open mouth and eyes wide open, or the hooded men holding copies of the Koran and hatchets.[2] The idea that Islam is a religion more fanatical than any other, or that it is fundamentally hostile to modernity, is part of a long tradition of "orientalist" discourses (Said 1978). Orientalism is a mechanism at work in social sciences, literature, music and visual arts whereby the "Orient" becomes the mirror of what the Occident is not. Through such a mechanism, the variety of a multifaceted experience is reduced to a fixed and immutable block, the "Orient", which, as its very geographical definition shows, can only exist as a negative reflex of an "Occident" perceived as the starting point. Discourses about a presumed "Arab mind", depicted as violent, backward and resistant to civic order (Patai 1973), or about Islam as being intrinsically violent (Pipes 1983) are examples of an orientalist approach. The result is a Eurocentric and negatively biased representation of the "Other", through which Islam is portrayed as a fixed blueprint that determines an entire way of life for hundreds of millions of Muslims all over the world.

The clash of civilisations, on the other hand, is not a "Western" product that has been exported to non-Western countries. Rather, together with "Western" orientalist literature there is also a whole series of "oriental" orientalist discourses that depict Islam and the Arab world in the same way (Sadiki 2004). Many Islamist militants striving for power (be they Middle Eastern or "Western" based) also create simplified blocks by portraying the "West" and "modernity" as a threat *to* Islam and to their worldviews.[3] The result of the work of the myth of the clash is that in many Arab countries Islam is becoming one of the first factors of self-identification. While there has always been a variety of possibilities for self-identification in Arab countries, more and more Arabs are now identifying themselves as Muslim first according to a survey conducted in six countries in June 2004 (Telhami 2004).

Intellectual discourses have therefore contributed to rendering banal, that is commonplace, that which is prima facie extraordinary within a community. On the other hand, the sites for the work on the

---

[2] For a more detailed analysis of this point, see Bottici and Challand 2006.
[3] Halliday (2003) deals with this point in his chapter, "Islam and the West: 'Threat of Islam' or 'Threat to Islam'?"

political myth of the clash of civilisations are not just explicit statements about Islam. As we have seen, this work is much more powerful, precisely because it also operates through icons that are more or less consciously associated with explicit statements. Particularly today, political myths are most often apprehended through a cumulative exposure to them.

For instance, as Geisser observed when analysing the sources of what he calls "media Islamophobia", French journalists are very cautious in their statements and even explicitly deny the paradigm of the clash. The sources of Islamophobia are rather the continual insistence in the media on the need for more security and the parallel, only occasionally related, media demonisation of Muslims (Geisser 2003: 25). As a consequence, icons such as the *Marianne voilée*, which appeared in *Figaro* on 26 October 1985, are much more powerful conveyers of the myth of the clash between civilisations than any overt statement: by representing the female symbol of the French Republic wearing the Muslim veil, orientalist discourses about the incompatibility of Islam and modernity are recalled by means of a synecdoche.

Furthermore, the development of new technologies of communication and the increased role that they play in our lives have provided an ever-growing number of other sites for the work on the myth of the clash. For instance, Geisser observed that the French media have operated a sort of media systematisation of a general discourse about Islam that depicts it as an immutable and conflictual block. The "mediatic Muslim" is indeed always represented in the same postures – believers praying seen from the back; crying and threatening groups; veiled women; fanatical bearded men (Geisser 2003: 24). In this way, not only what is extraordinary, that is, the violence of the "Other", is reduced to being commonplace because it is continually put on our screens, but the reverse is also the case. By charging these icons with all the fears and emotions associated with the idea of a clash between civilisations, what is apparently banal, such as a believer praying, is infused with an aura of the extraordinary.

Thus, the myth of the clash of civilisation not only highlights the interplay between myth and theory but also what can be called the condensational capacity of political myths, that is, their capacity to be conveyed through icons that more or less consciously recall them. Indeed, this power seems to be increased under conditions of modernity and it is from this very observation that a sociology of contemporary political myths should commence.

If political myths have always been the work on a common narrative that responds to a need for significance, it is perhaps the privilege of our time to have pushed the pervasiveness of this work to the extreme. Suspicious as we have become of any grand narratives, we have developed political myths that, in comparison with those of the past, tend to exasperate their form of archipelago. While the grand political myths of the past were as conspicuous as continents, and therefore were evident, today, it is usually only by travelling from one island to another that we apprehend them. The risk, however, is that we may see only single islands, and no longer perceive the entire archipelago.

A rejection of grand narratives, on the one hand, and the emergence of new powerful technologies, on the other: both seem to have rendered the work on political myth less and less perceivable, and therefore more subtle. The work of political myth has always been the work on significance, and, as a consequence, political myths have always been difficult to analyse, precisely because the work on significance can take place at a more or less conscious level. Political myths are part of the basic components of our everyday perception of politics and for this reason they tend to remain unquestioned. They are not only what we perceive about the world of politics, but also the lens through which we perceive it. They are the basic assumptions of a society and they are woven throughout all sorts of social discourses and practices (Chapter 9).

However, if, to paraphrase Spinoza, all societies are and have been, in a sense, "mythical", what they differ in is the degree to which this mythical dimension can generate critical discussion. In other words, political myths can be the vectors of the project for autonomy, but, in order to be so, they must work as means for interrogation. The problem emerges, however, that under the contemporary conditions of a globalised spectacle (Edelman 1988) this becomes more and more difficult.

According to Bennett, it is because of the absence of formalised political ideologies in American politics that political myths surreptitiously tend to guide the whole process in which policies are made and public opinion is formed (Bennett 1980: 167). Their systematic effect on public thinking, communication and action explains, in Bennett's

view, a number of characteristics of American politics, including the
narrow range of public debates, the restricted scope of political conflict, the tendency of political institutions to produce and implement
policies that embody stabilising images of political order, independent of whether they have any impact on underlying social problems
(Bennett 1980: 167).

In the process of growing up in contemporary mediatic societies,
Bennett observes, most people encounter an overwhelming number
of myths that gradually slip into their subconscious thinking (Bennett
1980). Young children are exposed to a battery of these myths through
schools, parents, cartoons, films, advertisements, icons, and so on.
These myths may recount the extraordinary vicissitudes of groups such
as the Puritans, the Founding Fathers, the slaves, the Western pioneers
or the European immigrants. Whether these groups and their heroes
are black or white, rich or poor, great leaders or humble citizens, their
dramatised experiences, according to Bennett, illustrate a remarkably
similar set of virtues. In other words, their extraordinary adventures
serve to transmit those models of conduct that are destined to uphold
their future everyday banality. It is through these models of virtues –
which Spinoza called the "exemplars of human nature" – that people first encounter models of life centred on free enterprise, industry,
tolerance, perseverance and individualism (Bennett 1980). Again, we
face interplay between the extraordinary and the banal: it is through
exposure to the extraordinary adventures of their mediatic heroes that
people learn those models of life that they will apply in their banal
everyday life.

Some of these myths, Bennett observes, point, for instance, to the
causes of poverty and other social adversities and show how people
overcome them; others teach the principles of politics, the standards
of civility and the nature of society. The range of different myths available to make essentially similar points makes it possible for cultural
perspectives to be transmitted in forms that are suited to the experiences of different social groups, so that it is legitimate to assert that
there is a clear body of myth at the basis of American society (Bennett
1980).

One could not object that these are cultural but not truly political
myths: the concept of political myth shows precisely how problematic any sharp distinction between political versus cultural myths and

identities can be. There is, for instance, a whole range of literature that shows how the work on apparently cultural myths alone can come to influence the specific political settings and conditions of a society, and thus also the common sense of belonging to a community as much as do the distribution of power and other limited resources (Bennett 1980; Yanarella and Siegelman 1988; Edelman 1988).

This literature has started to explore how, for instance, in mass-oriented American Westerns, the myth of the frontier addressed political issues such as the nature of society and the persisting problem of balancing the social need for law and the human desire for justice (Moeller 1988). Similarly, the problematic and undecided relationship between politics and sports fiction should also be explored: both when dealing with overtly political material and when not, works in the genre of sports fiction can be the site for the work on political myths. Among the narratives that have been able to coagulate significance, Shevory mentions the heroism of individual aspiration, the participation in the community or rather the heroism of individuals equipped with extraordinary qualities, and the team as a utopian ideal (Shevory 1988).

Bennett also provides another example of the way in which political myths succeed in structuring political processes: their presence is not only evident in the production of equally acceptable policy alternatives, but also in the generation of intolerance for political options that fall outside the range of the myth-sanctioned choices. The work on political myth is locatable in "what is not said" as much as in "what is overtly said". For instance, in the 1972 US presidential election, George McGovern elicited strong public rejection and confusion by proposing a guaranteed minimum income for every American. The total failure of the proposal is even more striking if compared with the success of Nixon's 1968 proposal for a guaranteed annual income.

The difference between the two was not the amount of the stipend, which was the same, but the different terms in which the proposals were presented. Nixon put it in the mythically acceptable terms of a "Family Assistance Plan" and never mentioned the concept of a "minimum guaranteed income". McGovern's proposal, explicitly cast in the terms of a "guaranteed income", was, in contrast, unacceptable to a diffused mythical understanding of poverty, which attributed poverty to individual failings on the part of the poor.

As Bennett further points out, the diffused belief in the individual causes of poverty is the result of a political myth. Even if there is nothing "political" per se in the claim that the poor are poor because of their individual failures, and thus in the films, icons, and other fragmentary islands of this archipelago, it is clear that the context in which the work on myth operates and the way in which this myth is received and re-elaborated can come to render it crucially political. Furthermore, precisely because its work is dispersed and pervasive, and therefore not so easily locatable, it tends to remain unquestioned and, thus, to reinforce itself. According to Bennett, there is no success or failure in policy that could contradict this myth today: if policies against poverty – most of them generally aimed at correcting "individual attitudes" – are seen to fail, they are easily interpreted as proof of the incorrigibility of individuals (Bennett 1980: 172).

Thus, it seems as if the logic of mass communication tends to enhance the circularity of reasoning on social problems and political solutions. Among the factors that promote this circularity, two deserve further comment. The first of these is what has been called "the primacy effect" (Flood 1996: 87). This term has been coined in order to stress the power of a person's earliest perceptions of a phenomenon to function as the basis for generalisations, categorisations and expectations that are not easily or adequately revised in the light of subsequent observation. Through a process of continual exposure that starts from childhood itself, the work of and on political myth assumes particularly insidious forms since it drastically reduces the possibility of perceiving and therefore dismissing certain cognitive and practical *schemata.*

The primacy effect is exacerbated under the contemporary conditions of a globalised spectacle. In a society of spectacle, the possibilities of rendering the banal extraordinary, and vice versa, are enormously increased. As we have seen, for instance, one does not need to read Huntington to begin to perceive the clash of civilisations. The latter is continually put on our screens, and is thereby banalised, that is, rendered commonplace through continual usage. One just needs to watch the news, children's cartoons or Hollywood films, or merely walk in the street: everywhere, there are innumerable examples of the mediatic constructions of such a clash and of icons recalling it. As a consequence of this work on myth, people no longer see single individuals acting in one way or another; they actually see civilisations clashing with each other (Bottici and Challand 2006).

However, we do not need to look among bloody clashes in order to see the work of and on a political myth. One can see the work on political myth even in political routines such as elections. In many countries, political elections and the spectacle that usually accompanies them, instead of being a moment for questioning a certain model of society, are the means through which this model is reproduced: elections are its visible continuity.

And this brings us to our second consideration – the role of rituals. If political myths are the models that a society or social group constructs *of* itself and *for* itself (Lincoln 1989: 24), rituals such as elections are social routines through which these models are reproduced within society. Indeed, by virtue merely of their repetition, rituals powerfully contribute to reinforcing the circularity of political processes.

However, as we have seen, political myth and rituals are not coextensive concepts (Chapters 6 and 9). Whereas myths have to change with the changing of the political conditions for which they must provide significance in order to be effective, rituals must remain unchanged for the same purpose. Rituals indeed represent the stability acted out and re-enacted: by virtue of their repetition they tend to deny the passage of time, the nature of change and the implicit extent of indeterminacy in social relations (Moore 1975).

Rituals, together with other icons, and various fragments of the archipelago, are the means through which the work on political myths can take place. As Spinoza pointed out when analysing the political myths of the nation of Israel, it is through social rituals, which recall the pact with God in everyday life, that this political myth works. As we have seen (Chapter 8), for instance, the obsessive character of Jewish rituals, according to Spinoza, by virtue of the obsessive repetition of gestures – when eating, ploughing, sowing – had the precise function of implicitly annihilating the sense of individual autonomy; in their everyday gestures, the Jews had to confess that they were not their own masters, but entirely under the control of others (Spinoza 1951b: 76).

However, this does not mean that political myths, since they are often transmitted through rituals, are destined to inhibit social change. If political myths are models both of a society and for a society, and

if these models are transmitted through social routines and apprehended through cumulative exposure to them, how is it possible to
account for social change? How can this circularity be opened? Under
contemporary conditions, the problem seems destined to be even
more insidious. A sociology of contemporary political myths therefore
cannot avoid facing this normative question.

The enormous potentialities of the new mediatic technologies, their
possible global range, the increasing role that they play in our everyday
life, not to mention the alarming possibilities opened by biopolitics,
could all render the work of myth incomparably more sinister than it
has ever been in the past. The work on myth is no longer restricted to
a few disparate, fragmentary appearances that recall each other, nor is
it limited to a few political rituals. We live in a world made of icons, of
potential conveyers of the work of myth. Moreover, the work on myth
is rendered less and less accessible in the form of the great narratives
of the past: the attacks against them, far from being liberating, have
rendered it more insidious although seemingly banal.

We have also seen that the logic of mass communication tends to
render the work of political myth much more insidious because, in a
way, it hides its own political character. There may be nothing overtly
"political" per se in a Western, a sports fiction or any other sort of
Hollywood film that does not openly deal with political material; but
when it comes to the justification of certain policies over others, or even
to the a priori denial of certain political options, then these works do
reveal their political character.

Yet, as has been suggested, even in sports fiction germs of political
criticism may be present (Shevory 1988). Even in the contemporary
condition of mass communication, there may be a chance for the
work of what Castoriadis called the "radical imagination" (Castoriadis
1987). However insidious the new conditions might render the work
on political myth, there may still be space for the critique. The slogan "another world is possible", which is the icon of a new possible
political myth, is a symptom of the radical imagination. The work of
imagination is radical not only because it radically shapes our social
imaginary, but also because it can create *ex nihilo* (not *in nihilo* or *cum
nihilo*), and thus always has the potential to question its own products. Imagination becomes radical when it becomes the means for
interrogation.

There is no general and definitive answer to the question of how this is possible. Political myths, as well as political imagination in general, are destined to remain prey to the antinomies that we have seen at work in the concept of identity: the work on political myth can mean unity and plurality, choice and destiny, the spaces for autonomy as well as for the most totalitarian of dominations. But we do not need grand parades or blood rituals to witness the work on political myths: they are simply part of our banal political life.

The question of how questioning is possible is rendered even more complicated by the fact that the work on political myth is never pure, but is always interwoven with other kinds of discourses. It is not only difficult to locate the work on political myth: it must also be distinguished from the other kinds of discourses in which it is most often wrapped. Therefore, it is from a classification of the possible types of work on a political myth that a sociology of political myth should start in order to face the question of how and when questioning is possible.

For example, religious political myths are typically myths that aspire to provide an ultimate meaning and unique truth: this is true, for example, of the Jewish theocracy analysed by Spinoza (Chapter 8), as well as for the contemporary myth of martyrdom, against which Palestinian suicide attacks can be read (Larzillière 2003). Typically, these are political myths that tend to escape the possibility of critical discussion.

Scientific political myths, on the other hand, are those that present a narrative of events intermingled with chains of relationship of cause and effect. For example, the myth of the Aryan race that Cassirer analyses is based on a mixture of narrative and scientific "findings", such as the biological superiority of the Aryan race (Rosenberg 1941; Chapter 8). Similarly, many contemporary nationalist myths of descent are intermingled with biological claims (Smith 1999). Clearly, the two discourses bring different issues to the fore and call for different tools of evaluation.

Finally, there are historical political myths. In these cases, political myths are fused with historical narratives. Historical political myths are narratives that produce significance and that can come to affect political conditions. For instance, most national myths, such as the Italian Resistance or the French Revolution, are derived from historical narratives (Chapters 9 and 10). In the case of historical narratives, the great advantage, with regard to other forms of political myth, is that there is a moment in which these narratives are given visibility since they can be put in the form of a rationalised memory (White 2000). In these cases, the work on myth can be more easily located, formalised and discussed.

Each of the types of political myth described brings further considerations to the fore, and therefore also calls for different tools of evaluation: the very possibility of an ultimate meaning in the face of a plurality of sacred stories, the correctness of scientific theory with regard to the current paradigms, or the accuracy of the historical reconstruction with regard to the current methods. Their possible fusion with political myths, however, points to their intrinsic plurality – the plurality of the sacred stories, the probability of scientific findings, as well as the never ending character of historical interpretation.

When the plurality of political myth is denied, this is the sign that the instituted dimension of the social imaginary is denied. Political myths live out of history: they have to remain open to change because they must provide significance to changing circumstances. In contrast, when political myths attempt a closure of meaning, then no more work is possible and the myths in question cannot be revised, but only dismissed together with the political regimes that have produced them. Well-known examples include the myth of Jewish theocracy, the myth of the Aryan race and the Italian fascist myth of the glorious Roman past. These are myths which, by attributing the origins of the social significations of a society to an *extra-social* source (Gods, heroes, ancestors), have covered up the instituted dimension of society, and thus subtracted it from the possibility of interrogation.

Bibliography

Abbagnano, N., 1971, *Dizionario di filosofia*, Turin, Utet.

Abrahamian, E., 2003, "The US Media, Huntington and September 11", in *Third World Quarterly*, 24, 2, pp. 529–44.

Adorno, F., 1961a, *La filosofia antica. I. La formazione del pensiero filosofico dalle origini a Platone VI–VI secolo a.C.*, Milan, Feltrinelli.

———, 1961b, *La filosofia antica. II. Filosofia, cultura, scuole tra Aristotele e Augusto IV–II secolo a.C.*, Milan, Feltrinelli.

Adorno, T. W., and Horkheimer, M., 1997, *Dialectic of Enlightenment*, Eng. trans. by J. Cumming, London, Verso (1969, *Dialektik der Aufklärung. Philosophische Fragmente*, Frankfurt a. M., Fisher Verlag).

Aldrich, C. R., 1931, *The Primitive Mind and Modern Civilisation*, London, Kegan Paul.

Anderson, B., 1983, *Imagined Communities: Reflections on the Spread of Nationalism*, London, Verso.

Angehrn, E., 1996, *Die Überwindung des Chaos. Zur Philosophie des Mythos*, Frankfurt a. M., Suhrkamp.

Ankersmit, F. R., 2001, *Historical Representation*, Stanford, Stanford University Press.

Aquinas, T., 1975, *Summa theologiae. English and Latin*, ed. and trans. by J. Cunningham, London, Blackfriars.

Aristotle, 1970a, *The Physics*, Eng. trans. by P. H. Wicksteed and F. M. Cornford, Cambridge, Mass., Harvard University Press, Loeb Classical Library, vols IV and V.

———, 1970b, *Poetics*, Eng. trans. by W. H. Fyfe, Cambridge, Mass., Harvard University Press, Loeb Classical Library, vol. XXIII.

———, 1974, *Aristotle's Categories. De Interpretatione*, Eng. trans. by J. L. Ackrill, Oxford, Clarendon.

———, 1975, *The "Art" of Rhetoric*, Eng. trans. by J. H. Freese, Cambridge, Mass., Harvard University Press, Loeb Classical Library, vol. XXII.

———, 1977, *The Metaphysics*, Eng. trans. by M. A. Tredennick, Cambridge, Mass., Harvard University Press, Loeb Classical Library, vols XVII–XVIII.

Arnason, J. P., 1989, "The Imaginary Constitution of Modernity", in G. Busino et al. (eds), *Autonomie et autotransformation de la société. La philosophie militante de Cornelius Castoriadis*, Geneva, Libraire Droz, pp. 323–39.

———, 1994, "Reason, Imagination, Interpretation", in G. Robinson and J. Rundell (eds), *Rethinking Imagination: Culture and Creativity*, London, Routledge, pp. 155–70.

Aron, R., 2001, *The Opium of the Intellectuals*, Eng. trans. by D. J. Mahoney and B. C. Anderson, New Brunswick, Transaction Publishers (1955, *L'opium des intellectuels*, Paris, Hachette).

Aronsson, K., 2001, "Narrative, Sociology of", in N. J. Smelser and P. B. Baltes (eds), *International Encyclopedia of the Social and Behavioural Sciences*, Amsterdam, Elsevier. vol. 15, pp. 10286–291.

Assmann, J., 1997, *Das kulturelle Gedächtnis. Schrift, Erinnerung und politische Identität in frühen Hochkulturen*, Munich, Beck.

———, 2000, *Herrschaft und Heil: politische Theologie in Altägypten, Israel und Europa*, Munich, Carl Hanser.

Astius, F., 1836, *Lexicon Platonicum sive Vocum Platonicorum Index*, Leipzig, Weidmann.

Audi, R., (ed.), 1999, *The Cambridge Dictionary of Philosophy*, Cambridge, Cambridge University Press.

Auerbach, E., 1944, "Figura", in *Neue Dantestudien*, Istanbul.

———, 1953, *Mimesis: The Representation of Reality in Western Literature*, Eng. trans. by W. R. Trask, Princeton, Princeton University Press (1946, *Mimesis*, Berne, Franke).

Augustine, Saint, 1970, *Confessiones*, Eng. trans. by W. Watts, Cambridge, Mass., Harvard University Press, Loeb Classical Library.

Bacon, F., 1963, *Novum Organon*, vol. IV in *The Works of Francis Bacon*, London, Longman.

Balibar, E., 1985, *Spinoza et la politique*, Paris, PUF.

Bartlett, R. C., 2000, "Introduction", in P. Bayle, *Various Thoughts on the Occasion of a Comet*, Eng. trans. by R. C. Bartlett, New York, State University of New York, pp. xxiii–xlvii.

Barthes, R., 1972, *Mythologies*, Eng. trans. by A. Lavers, New York, Hill and Wang (1957, *Mythologies*, Paris, Seuil).

———, 1977, *Image, Music, Text*, Fontana, Collins.

———, 1986, "The Discourse of History", Eng. trans. by R. Howard, in *The Rustle of Language*, Oxford, Blackwell (1984, "Le discours de l'histoire", in R. Barthes, *Le Bruissement de la langue*, Paris, Edition du Seuil).

Bayle, P., 2000, *Various Thoughts on the Occasion of a Comet*, Eng. trans. by R. C. Bartlett, New York, State University of New York (1994, *Pensées diverses écrites à un Docteur de Sorbonne, à l'occasion de la comète qui parut au mois de décembre 1680*, Paris, Société de Textes Français Modernes).

Bell, D., 1960, *The End of Ideology: On Exhaustion of Political Ideas in the Fifties*, London, Free Press of Glencoe.

Bennett, W. L., 1980, "Myth, Ritual, and Political Control", in *Journal of Communication*, 30, pp. 166–79.

Bilgrami, A., 2001, "Identity and Identification: Philosophical Aspects", in N. J. Smelser and P. B. Baltes (eds), *International Encyclopedia of the Social and Behavioural Sciences*, Amsterdam, Elsevier, vol. 11, pp. 7148–54.

Bloch, M., 1973, *The Royal Touch: Sacred Monarchy and Scrofula in England and France*, Eng. trans. by J. E. Anderson, London, Routledge (1924, *Le rois thaumaturges: Etude sur le caractère surnaturel attribué à la puissance royale, particulièrement en France et en Angleterre*, Strasbourg, Librairie Istra).

Bloch, M., 1977, "The Past and the Present in the Present", in *Man*, 12, 2, pp. 278–82.

Blumenberg, H., 1971, "Wirklichkeitsbegriff und Wirkungspotential des Mythos", in M. Fuhrmann (ed), *Terror und Spiel. Probleme der Mythenrezeption*, Munich, Fink, pp. 11–66.

―――, 1983, *The Legitimacy of the Modern Age*, Eng. trans. by R. Wallace, Cambridge, Mass., MIT Press (1966, *Die Legitimität der Neuzeit*, Frankfurt a. M., Suhrkamp).

―――, 1985, *Work on Myth*, Eng. trans. by R. Wallace, Cambridge, Mass., MIT Press (1979, *Arbeit am Mythos*, Frankfurt a. M., Suhrkamp).

Bohrer, K. H. (ed.), 1983, *Mythos und Moderne. Begriff und Bild einer Rekonstruktion*, Frankfurt a. M., Suhrkamp.

Bonitz, H., 1955, *Index Aristotelicus, Secunda Editio*, Graz, Akademische Druck-U. Verlagsanstalt.

Bottici, C., 2003, "The Domestic Analogy and the Kantian Project of Perpetual Peace", in *Journal of Political Philosophy*, 11, 4, pp. 392–410.

―――, 2004, *Uomini e Stati. Percorsi di un'analogia*, Pisa, ETS.

Bottici, C., and B. Challand, 2006, "Rethinking Political Myth: The Clash of Civilisations as a Self-Fulfilling Prophecy", in *European Journal of Social Theory*, 9, 3, pp. 315–36.

Boudon, R., 1999, "Local vs General Ideologies: A Normal Ingredient of Modern Political Life", in *Journal of Political Ideologies*, 4, 2, pp. 141–61.

Bouveresse, J., 1982, "L'animal cérémoniel: Wittgenstein et l'anthropologie", in *Ludwig Wittgenstein. Remarques sur le Rameau d'Or de Frazer*, Editions l'Age d'Homme, pp. 41–124.

Brandwood, L., 1976, *A Word Index to Plato*, Leeds, W. S. Maney and Son.

Braudel, F., 1980, *On History*, London, Weidenfeld and Nicolson.

Bremner, C., 2004, "Stoned to Death . . . Why Europe is Starting to Lose Its Faith in Islam", in www.timesonline.co.uk, 4 December.

Burnet, J., 1920, *Early Greek Philosophy*, London, A. & C. Black.

Bultmann, R., 1962, "Zum Problem der Entmythologisierung", in *Il problema della demitizzazione. Atti del convegno indetto dal Centro Internazionale di Studi Umanistici e dall'Istituto di Studi Filosofici*, Rome, Archivio di Filosofia, pp. 19–35.

―――, 1984, *New Testament and Mythology and Other Basic Writings*, Eng. trans. by S. M. Ogden, Philadelphia, Fortress Press.

Bultmann, R., and K. Jaspers, 1954, *Die Frage der Entmythologisierung*, Munich, Piper Verlag.

Callimachus, 1958, *Aetia, Iambi, Lyric Poems, Hecale, Minor Epic and Elegiac Poems, Fragments of Epigrams, Fragments of Uncertain Location*, Eng. trans. by C. A. Trypanis, Cambridge, Mass., Harvard University Press, Loeb Classical Library.

Cantelli, G., 1986, *Mente. Corpo. Linguaggio. Saggio sull'interpretazione vichiana del mito*, Florence, Sansoni.

Cassirer, E., 1951, *The Philosophy of the Enlightenment*, Eng. trans by C. A. Koelln and J. P. Pettergrove, Princeton, Princeton University Press (1932, *Die Philosophie der Aufklärung*, Tübingen, Mohr).

———, 1968, *An Essay on Man: An Introduction to a Philosophy of Human Culture*, New Haven, Yale University Press.

———, 1973, *The Myth of the State*, New Haven, Yale University Press.

———, 1977, *Philosophie der symbolischen Formen*, Darmstadt, Wissenschaftliche Buchgesellschaft.

———, 1981, *Kant's Life and Thought*, Eng. trans. by J. Haden, New Haven, Yale University Press.

Castoriadis, C., 1986, "Institution de la société et religion", in C. Castoriadis, *Domaines de l'homme. Le carrefour du labyrinthe*, Paris, Seuil, pp. 455–81.

———, 1987, *The Imaginary Institution of Society*, Eng. trans. by K. Blamey, Cambridge, Polity Press (1975, *L'institution imaginaire de la société*, Paris, Seuil).

———, 1991, "Power, Politics, Autonomy", in C. Castoriadis, *Philosophy, Politics, Autonomy – Essays in Political Philosophy*, Oxford, Oxford University Press, pp. 143–75.

———, 1997, "Radical Imagination and the Social Instituting Imaginary", in C. Castoriadis, *The Castoriadis Reader*, Oxford, Blackwell, pp. 319–38.

Cavell, S., 1979, *The Claim of Reason: Wittgenstein, Scepticism, Morality and Tragedy*, Oxford, Clarendon Press.

Cazes, B., 2001, "Utopias: Social", in N. J. Smelser and P. B. Baltes (eds), *International Encyclopedia of the Social and Behavioural Sciences*, Amsterdam, Elsevier, vol. 24, pp. 16123–7.

Cerutti, F., 1996, "Identità e politica", in F. Cerutti (ed.), *Identità e politica*, Bari, Laterza, pp. 5–43.

———, 2003, "A Political Identity of the Europeans?", in *Thesis Eleven*, 72, London, Sage, pp. 26–45.

Chantraine, P., 1984, *Dictionnaire étymologique de la langue grecque. Histoire des mots*, Paris, Edition Klincksieck.

Churchill, J., 1989, "If a Lion Could Talk . . .", in *Philosophical Investigations*, 12, 4, pp. 308–24.

Clack, B. R., 1999, *Wittgenstein, Frazer and Religion*, London, Macmillan.

Cohan, S., and L. Shires, 1988, *Telling Stories: A Theoretical Analysis of Narrative Fiction*, New York, Routledge.

Cohen, A. P., 1985, *The Symbolic Construction of Community*, London, Routledge.

Cohn, N., 1970, *The Pursuit of the Millennium*, London, Paladin.

Cole, T., 1983, "Archaic Truth", in *Quaderni Urbinati di Cultura Classica*, 13, pp. 7–28.

Colli, G., 1975, *La nascita della filosofia*, Milan, Adelphi.

———, 1977, *La sapienza greca I: Dioniso, Apollo Eleusi, Orfeo, Museo, Iperborei, Enigma*, Milan, Adelphi.

———, 1978a, *La sapienza greca II: Epimenide, Ferecide, Talete, Anassimandro, Anassimene, Onomacrito*, Milan, Adelphi.

———, 1978b, *La sapienza greca III: Eraclito*, Milan, Adelphi.

Cornford, F. M., 1952, *Principium Sapientiae: The Origins of Greek Philosophical Thought*, Cambridge, Cambridge University Press.

Cosmas Indicopleustes, 1897, *The Christian Topography of Cosmas, an Egyptian Monk*, Eng. trans. by J. W. McCrindle, London, Hakluyt Society.

Coulter, J., 1999, "Discourse and Mind", in *Human Studies*, 22, pp. 163–81.

Courtine, J.-F., 1992a, "*Realitas*", in G. Gabriel, K. Gründer, and J. Ritter (eds), 1971–, *Historisches Wörterbuch der Philosophie*, Darmstadt, Wissenschaftliche Buchgesellschaft, vol. VII, pp. 178–85.

———, 1992b, "Realität/Idealität", in G. Gabriel, K. Gründer, and J. Ritter (eds), 1971–, *Historisches Wörterbuch der Philosophie*, Darmstadt, Wissenschaftliche Buchgesellschaft, vol. VII, pp. 185–93.

Dante, A., 1984, *The Divine Comedy*, Eng. trans. by M. Musa, Harmondsworth, Penguin (1988–9, *La Divina Commedia*, ed. by U. Bosco and G. Reggio, Florence, Le Monnier).

———, 1995, *Epistola a Cangrande*, ed. by E. Cecchini, Florence, Giunti.

Das, V., 1998, "Wittgenstein and Anthropology", in *Annual Review of Anthropology*, 27, pp. 171–95.

Delatte, L., C. Rutter, S. Govaerts, and J. Denooz, 1984, *Aristoteles Metaphisica. Index Verborum. Listes de Fréquence*, Hildesheim, Olms-Weidmann.

Deleuze, G., 2006, *Nietzsche and Philosophy*, Eng. trans. by H. Tomlinson, New York, Columbia University Press (1962, *Nietzsche et la philosophie*, Paris, Presses Universitaires de France).

Denooz, J., 1988, *Aristote ⟨⟨Poetica⟩⟩. Index Verborum. Liste de fréquence*, Liege, Centre Informatique de Philosophie et Lettres.

Descartes, R., 1984, *Meditations on First Philosophy*, Eng. trans. by J. Cottingham, in *The Philosophical Writings of Descartes*, vol. 2, Cambridge, Cambridge University Press, pp. 1–62 (1973, *Meditationes de prima philosophia*, Paris, Librairie Philosophique Vrin).

———, 1985, *Discourse on the Method*, Eng. trans. by R. Stoothoff, in *The Philosophical Writings of Descartes*, vol. 1, Cambridge, Cambridge University Press, pp. 111–51 (1973, *Discours de la Méthode*, Paris, Librairie Philosophique Vrin).

Detienne, M., 1967, *Les Maîtres de la vérité dans la Grèce archaïque*, Paris, Maspéro.

———, 1986, *The Creation of Mythology*, Eng. trans. by M. Cook, Chicago, University of Chicago Press.

Diels, H., and W. Kranz, 1951, *Fragmente der Vorsokratiker*, Zurich, Weidmannsche Verlagsbuchhandlung.

Dierse, U., 1976, "Ideologie" in G. Gabriel, K. Gründer, and J. Ritter (eds), 1971–, *Historisches Wörterbuch der Philosophie*, Darmstadt, Wissenschaftliche Buchgesellschaft, vol. IV, pp. 157–86.

Döner, A., 1996, *Politischer Mythos und symbolische Politik*, Reinbeck, Rowolt.

Dörrie, H., 1972, *Der Mythos und sein Funktion in der antiken Philosophie*, Innsbruck, Innsbrucker Beiträge zur Kulturwissenschaft.

Dubois, M., 2001, "Ideology, Sociology of", in N. J. Smelser and P. B. Baltes (eds), *International Encyclopedia of the Social and Behavioural Sciences*, Amsterdam, Elsevier, vol. 11, pp. 7177–82.

Duhem, P., 1965, *Le système du monde: histoire des doctrines cosmologiques de Platon à Copernic*, Paris, Herman.

Eagleton, T., 1991, *Ideology: An Introduction*, London, Verso.

Edelman, M., 1967, "Myth, Metaphors and Political Conformity", in *Psychiatry*, 30, 3, pp. 217–28.

———, 1976, *The Symbolic Uses of Politics*, Urbana, University of Illinois Press.

———, 1988, *Constructing the Political Spectacle*, Chicago, University of Chicago Press.

Eliade, M., 1954, *The Myth of the Eternal Return, or Cosmos and History*, Princeton, Princeton University Press.

———, 1957, *Mythes, rêves et mystères*, Paris, Gallimard.

Evans-Pritchard, E. E., 1948, *The Divine Kingship of the Shilluk of Nilotic Sudan*, Cambridge, Cambridge University Press.

Finnegan, R., 1988, *Literacy and Orality, Studies in the Technology of Communication*, Oxford, Blackwell.

Fisch, J., 1992, "Zivilisation, Kultur", in O. Brunner, W. Conze, and R. Koselleck (eds), 1974–1997, *Geschichtliche Grundbegriffe: Historisches Lexikon zur politischensozialen Sprache in Deutschland*, Stuttgart, Klett, vol. 7, pp. 679–774.

Flood, C. G., 1996, *Political Myth: A Theoretical Introduction*, New York, Garland.

Foucault, M., 1988, "Technologies of the Self", in L. H. Martin, H. Gutman, and P. Hutton (eds), *Technologies of the Self: A Seminar with Michel Foucault*, Amherst, University of Massachusetts Press, pp. 9–15.

Frandsen, S. B., 2000, "Italian Fascism and Roman Heritage: The Third Rome of Mussolini", in B. Stråth, B. (ed.) *Myth and Memory in the Construction of the Community*, Brussels, Peter Lang, pp. 157–69.

Frank, M., 1982, *Der kommende Gott. Vorlesungen über die Neue Mythologie*, Frankfurt a. M., Suhrkamp.

Frazer, J. G., 1922, *The Golden Bough, a Study in Magic and Religion*, London, Macmillan.

Freeden, M., 2001, "Ideology: Political Aspects", in N. J. Smelser and P. B. Baltes (eds), *International Encyclopedia of the Social and Behavioural Sciences*, Amsterdam, Elsevier, vol. 11, pp. 7175–7.

Freeman, K., 1966, *The Pre-Socratic Philosophers: A Companion to Diels' Fragmente der Vorsokratiker*, Oxford, Blackwell.

Freud, S., 1937, *The Interpretations of Dreams*, Eng. trans. by A. A. Brill, London, Allen & Unwin (1941–1968, "Die Traumdeutung", in *Gesammelte Werke*, Frankfurt a. M., Fischer, vols II–III).

———, 1941–1968, "Warum Krieg?", in *Gesammelte Werke*, Frankfurt a. M., Fischer, vol. XVI, pp. 13–27.

———, 1950, *Totem and Taboo*, Eng. trans. by J. Strachey, New York, Norton (1941–1968, "Totem und Tabu", in *Gesammelte Werke*, Frankfurt a. M., Fischer, vol. IX).

———, 1959, *Group Psychology and the Analysis of the Ego*, Eng. trans. by J. Strachey, New York, Norton (1941–1968, "Massenpsychologie und Ich-Analyse", in *Gesammelte Werke*, Frankfurt a. M., Fischer, vol. XV).

———, 1966, *Introductory Lectures on Psychoanalysis*, Eng. trans. by J. Strachey, New York, Norton (1941–1968, *Vorlesungen zur Einführung in die Psychoanalyse – Neue Folge*, vol. XI in *Gesammelte Werke*, Frankfurt a. M., Fischer).

———, 1989, *Civilisation and Its Discontents*, Eng. trans. by J. Strachey, New York, Norton (1941–1968, *Das Unbehagen in der Kultur*, vol. XIV in *Gesammelte Werke*, Frankfurt a. M., Fischer).

Friedman, J., 1992, "Myth, History, and Political Identity", in *Cultural Anthropology*, 7, 2, pp. 194–210.

Friese, H., 2001, "Imagination: History of the Concept", in N. J. Smelser, and P. B. Baltes (eds), *International Encyclopedia of the Social and Behavioural Sciences*, Amsterdam, Elsevier, vol. 11, pp. 7197–201.

——— (ed.), 2002, *Identities: Time, Difference, and Boundaries*, Oxford, Berghahn Books.

Friese, H., and P. Wagner, 2002, "Survey Article: The Nascent Political Philosophy of the European Polity", in *Journal of Political Philosophy*, 10, 3, pp. 342–64.

Fuhrmann, M. (ed.), 1971, *Terror und Spiel. Probleme der Mythenrezeption*, Munich, Fink.

Gadamer, H. G., 1988, *Truth and Method*, London, Sheed and Ward (1975, *Wahrheit und Methode*, vol. I in *Gesammelte Werke*, Tübingen, Mohr).

———, 1993a, "Der Mythos im Zeitalter der Wissenschaft", in *Gesammelte Werke*, Tübingen, Mohr, vol. VIII, pp. 180–8.

———, 1993b, "Mythologie und Offenbarungsreligion", in *Gesammelte Werke*, Tübingen, Mohr, vol. VIII, pp. 174–80.

———, 1993c, "Mythos und Logos", in *Gesammelte Werke*, Tübingen, Mohr, vol. VIII, pp. 170–4.

Galilei, G., 2005, *Opere*, vol. I, Torino, Utet.

Geertz, C., 1964, "Ideology as a Cultural System" in D. E. Apter (ed.) *Ideology and Discontent*, London, Free Press of Glencoe, pp. 47–76.

———, 1973, *Interpretation of Cultures*, New York, Basic Books.

———, 1983, *Local Knowledge*, New York, Basic Books.

———, 1995, *After the Fact: Two Countries, Four Decades, One Anthropologist*, Cambridge, Mass., Harvard University Press.

———, 2000, *Available Light: Anthropological Reflections on Philosophical Topics*, Princeton, Princeton University Press.

Gehlen, A., 1980, *Man in the Age of Technology*, Eng. trans. by P. Lipscomb, New York, Columbia University Press (1994, *Urmensch und Spätkultur: philosophische Ergebnisse und Aussagen*, Wiesbaden, Aula Verlag).

———, 1988, *Man, His Nature and Place in the World*, Eng. trans. by C. Mcmillan and K. Pillemer, New York, Columbia University Press (1997, *Der Mensch: seine Natur und eine Stellung in der Welt*, Wiesbaden, Quelle und Meyer).

Geiser, K., 1963, *Platons ungeschriebene Lehre*, Stuttgart, Klett Verlag.

Geisser, V., 2003, *La nouvelle islamophobie*, Paris, Editions La Découverte.

Gliozzi, G., 1977, *Adamo e il nuovo mondo. La nascita dell'antropologia come ideologia coloniale dalle genealogie bibliche alle teorie razziali (1500–1700)*, Florence, La Nuova Italia.

Gockel, H., 1981, *Mythos und Poesie. Zum Mythosbegriff in Aufklärung und Frühromantik*, Frankfurt a. M., Klostermann.

Goody, J., 1977, *The Domestication of the Savage Mind*, Cambridge, Cambridge University Press.

———, 1986, *The Logic of Writing and the Organisation of Society*, Cambridge, Cambridge University Press.

Goody, J., and I. Watt, 1968, "The Consequences of Literacy", in J. Goody (ed.), *Literacy in Traditional Societies*, Cambridge, Cambridge University Press, pp. 27–68.

Gramsci, A., 1975, *Quaderni del carcere. Edizione critica dell'Istituto Gramsci*, Turin, Einaudi.

Grünepütt, K., 1992, "Realität der Außenwelt", in G. Gabriel, K. Gründer, and J. Ritter (eds) 1971–, *Historisches Wörterbuch der Philosophie*, Darmstadt, Wissenschaftliche Buchgesellschaft, vol. VII, pp. 206–11.

Habermas, J. 1987, *The Philosophical Discourse of Modernity: Twelve Lectures*, Eng. trans. by F. Lawrence, Cambridge, Polity Press (1985, *Der philosophische Diskurs der Moderne. Zwölf Vorlesungen*, Frankfurt a. M., Suhrkamp).

———, 1996, "Citizenship and National Identity", in J. Habermas *Between Facts and Norms*, Eng. trans. by W. Rehg, Cambridge, Mass., MIT Press (1992, *Faktizität und Geltung*, Frankfurt a. M., Suhrkamp), pp. 491–515.

Halliday, F., 2003, *Islam and the Myth of Confrontation*, London, Tauris.

Havelock, E. A., 1963, *Preface to Plato*, Oxford, Oxford University Press.

———, 1983, "The Linguistic Task of Presocratics", in K. Robb (ed.), *Language and Thought in Early Greek Philosophy*, La Salle, Hegeler Institute.

———, 1986, *The Muse Learns to Write: Reflections on Orality and Literacy from Antiquity to the Present*, New Haven, Yale University Press.

Hegel, G. W. F., 1931, *The Phenomenology of Mind*, Eng. trans. by J. B. Baillie, London, Allen & Unwin (1971, *Phänomenologie des Geistes*, vol. III in *G. W. F. Hegel: Werke in Zwanzig Bänden*, Frankfurt a. M., Suhrkamp).

———, 1956, *The Philosophy of History*, Eng. trans. by J. Sibree, New York, Dover Publications (1971, *Vorlesungen über die Philosophie der Geschichte*, vol. XII in *G. W. F. Hegel: Werke in Zwanzig Bänden*, Frankfurt a. M., Suhrkamp).

———, 1991, *Elements of the Philosophy of Right*, Eng. trans. by H. B. Nisbet, Cambridge, Cambridge University Press (1970, *Grundlinien der Philosophie des Rechts*, vol. VII in *G. W. F. Hegel: Werke in Zwanzig Bänden*, Frankfurt a. M., Suhrkamp).

———, 1995, *Lectures on the History of Philosophy*, Eng. trans. by E. S. Haldane, Lincoln, University of Nebraska Press (1971, *Vorlesungen über die Geschichte der Philosophie*, vols XVIII–XX in *G. W. F. Hegel: Werke in Zwanzig Bänden*, Frankfurt a. M., Suhrkamp).

Hegel, G. W. F, F. Hölderlin, and F. W. J. Schelling, 1971, *Das älteste System-programm des deutschen Idealismus*, in *G. W. F. Hegel: Werke in Zwanzig Bänden*, vol. I, Frankfurt a. M., Suhrkamp, pp. 234–7.

Heidegger, M., 2002a *Being and Time*, Eng. trans. by J. Stambaugh, Chicago, University of Chicago Press (1993, *Sein und Zeit*, Tübingen, Max Niemeyer Verlag).

——, 2002b, *The Essence of Truth: On Plato's Cave Allegory and Theaetetus*, Eng. trans. by T. Sadler, London, Continuum (1988, *Vom Wesen der Wahrheit: zu Platons Höhlengleichnis und Theätet*, in *Gesamtausgabe*, Frankfurt a. M., Kloster-mann, vol. 34).

Henry, B., 1986, *Libertà e mito in Cassirer*, Naples, ESI.

——, 2000, *Mito e identità. Contesti di tolleranza*, Pisa, ETS.

——, 2001, "The Role of Symbols for European Political Identity – Political Identity as a Myth?", in F. Cerutti and E. Rudolph (eds), *A Soul for Europe*, Leuven, Peeters, vol. 2, pp. 49–70.

Herodotus, 1920–4, *Historiae*, Eng. trans. by A. D. Godley, London, Heine-mann, Loeb Classical Library.

Hesiod, 1977, *The Homeric Hymns and Homerica*, Eng. trans. by H. G. White, London, Heinemann, Loeb Classical Library.

Hick, J. (ed.), 1977, *The Myth of God Incarnate*, London, SCM Press.

——, 1982, *God Has Many Names*, Philadelphia, Westminster Press.

Hippler, T., 2000, "Spinoza on Historical Myth", in B. Stråth (ed.), *Myth and Memory in the Construction of the Community*, Brussels, Peter Lang, pp. 95–112.

Hirsch, W., 1971, *Platons Weg zum Mythos*, Berlin, De Gruyter.

Hobbes, T., 1985, *Leviathan*, London, Penguin.

——, 1994, *The Elements of Law, Natural and Political*, Oxford, Oxford University Press.

Hobsbawm, E. J., 1963, *Primitive Rebels: Studies in Archaic Forms of Social Movement in the Nineteenth and Twentieth Centuries*, Manchester, Manchester University Press.

——, 1990, *Nations and Nationalism since 1780*, Cambridge, Cambridge University Press.

Hobsbawm, E. J., and T. Ranger, 1983, *The Invention of Tradition*, Cambridge, Cambridge University Press.

Hölderlin, F. 1966, *Poems and Fragments*, Eng. trans. by M. Hamburger, London, Routledge & Kegan Paul (1981, *Sämtliche Werke und Briefe*, Munich, Hanser).

Hoffmann, F. et al., 1992, "Realismus", in G. Gabriel, K. Gründer, and J. Ritter (eds), 1971–, *Historisches Wörterbuch der Philosophie*, Darmstadt, Wissenschaftliche Buchgesellschaft, vol. VII, pp. 148–70.

Homer, 1978, *The Iliad*, Eng. trans. by A. T. Murray, Cambridge, Mass., Harvard University Press, Loeb Classical Library.

——, 1995, *The Odyssey*, Eng. trans. by A. T. Murray and G. E. Dimock, Cambridge, Mass., Harvard University Press, Loeb Classical Library.

Honneth, A. 1995, *The Struggle for Recognition: The Moral Grammar of Social Conflicts*, Eng. trans. by J. Anderson, Cambridge, Polity Press (1992, *Kampf um Anerkennung*, Frankfurt a. M., Suhrkamp).

Hübner, K. 1985, *Die Wahrheit des Mythos*, Munich, Beck.

———, 1994, *Die zweite Schöpfung. Das Wirkliche in Kunst und Musik*, Munich, Beck.

Hume, D., 1985, *A Treatise of Human Nature: Being an Attempt to Introduce the Experimental Method of Reasoning into Moral Subjects*, London, Penguin.

Huntington, S. P., 1996, *The Clash of Civilizations and the Remaking of World Order*, New York, Simon & Schuster.

Husserl, E., 1954, *The Crisis of the European Sciences and Transcendental Phenomenology*, Eng. trans. by D. Carr, Evanston, Northwestern University Press (1992, "Die Krisis der europäischer Wissenschaften und die transzendentale Phänomenologie", in *Gesammelte Schriften*, Hamburg, Meier, vol. VIII).

———, 1973, *Cartesian Meditations: An Introduction to Phenomenology*, Eng. trans. by D. Cairns, The Hague, Nijhoff (1992, *Cartesianische Meditationen*, vol. VIII in *Gesammelte Schriften*, Hamburg, Meier).

———, 1992, "Idee zu einer reinen Phänomenologie", in *Gesammelte Schriften*, Hamburg, Meier, vol. V.

———, 2001, *Logical Investigations*, Eng. trans. by J. N. Findlay, London, Routledge (1992, *Logische Untersuchungen*, vols II–III–IV in *Gesammelte Schriften*, Hamburg, Meier,).

Iser, W., 1976, *Akt des Lesens*, Munich, Fink.

Jamme, C., 1991, *Einführung in die Philosophie des Mythos*, Darmstadt, Wissenschaftliche Buchgesellschaft.

———, 1999, *"Gott an hat ein Gewand". Grenzen und Perspektiven philosophischer Mythos-Theorien der Gegenwart*, Frankfurt a. M., Suhrkamp.

Jenkins, K. (ed.), 1997, *The Postmodern History Reader*, London, Routledge.

Jenkins, R., 1996, *Social Identity*, London, Routledge.

Jost, J. T. 1995, "Towards a Wittgensteinian Social Psychology of Human Development", in *Theory and Psychology*, 5, 1, pp. 5–25.

Joyce, J., 1957, *Letters of James Joyce*, ed. by R. Ellmann, London, Faber & Faber.

Jung, C. G., 1981, *Archetypes of the Collective Unconscious*, Eng. trans. by G. Adler and R. F. C. Hull, in *The collected Works of C. G. Jung*, Princeton, Princeton University Press, vol. 9.

Kahn, C. H., 1973, *The Verb "Be" in Ancient Greek*, Dordrecht, Reidel.

Kaiser El-Safti, M., 1992, "Realität, formale/objektive" in G. Gabriel, K. Gründer and J. Ritter (eds), 1971–, *Historisches Wörterbuch der Philosophie*, Darmstadt, Wissenschaftliche Buchgesellschaft, vol. VII, pp. 194–206.

Kant, I., 1991a, "An Answer to the Question: 'What is Enlightenment?'" Eng. trans. by H. B. Nisbet, in *Political Writings*, Cambridge, Cambridge University Press, pp. 54–60 (1912–13, "Beant wortung der Frage: Was ist Aufklärung?" in *Gesammelte Schriften*, hrsg. Königlich Preußischen Akademie der Wissenschaft (=Akademie-Ausgabe), Berlin, Walter de Gruyter, vol. VIII, pp. 15–32).

———, 1991b, *Metaphysics of Morals*, Eng. trans. by M. Gregor, Cambridge, Cambridge University Press, pp. 131–175 (1912–13, *Metaphysik der Sitten, erster teil: Metaphysische Anfangsgründe der Rechtslehre*, vol. VI in *Gesammelte Schriften*, hrsg. Königlich Preußischen Akademie der Wissenschaft (= Akademie-Ausgabe), Berlin, Walter de Gruyter, pp. 203–372).

———, 1991c, *On the Common Saying: 'This May Be True in Theory, But It Does Not Apply in Practice'*, Eng. trans. by H. B. Nisbet, in *Political Writings*, Cambridge, Cambridge University Press, pp. 61–93 (1912–13, *Über den Gemeinspruch: Das mag in der Theorie richtig sein, taugt aber nicht für die Praxis*, in *Gesammelte Schriften*, hrsg. Königlich Preußischen Akademie der Wissenschaft (= Akademie-Ausgabe), Berlin, Walter de Gruyter, vol. VIII, pp. 273–313).

———, 1991d, *Perpetual Peace: A Philosophical Sketch*, Eng. trans. by H. B. Nisbet, in *Political Writings*, Cambridge, Cambridge University Press, pp. 93–131 (1912–13, *Zum ewigen Frieden. Ein philosophischer Entwurf*, in *Gesammelte Schriften*, hrsg. Königlich Preußischen Akademie der Wissenschaft (= Akademie-Ausgabe), Berlin, Walter de Gruyter, vol. VIII, pp. 341–86).

———, 1993, *Critique of Practical Reason*, Eng. trans. by L. White Beck, New York, Macmillan (1912–13, *Kritik der Praktischen Vernunft*, in *Gesammelte Schriften*, hrsg. Königlich Preußischen Akademie der Wissenschaft (= Akademie-Ausgabe), Berlin, Walter de Gruyter, vol. V, pp. 1–164).

———, 1998, *Critique of Pure Reason*, Eng. trans. by P. Guyer and A. W. Wood, in *The Cambridge Edition of the Works of Immanuel Kant*, Cambridge, Cambridge University Press (1912–13, *Kritik der reinen Vernunft*, in *Kants Werke*, vols III–IV in *Gesammelte Schriften*, hrsg. Königlich Preußischen Akademie der Wissenschaft (= Akademie-Ausgabe), Berlin, Walter de Gruyter, vols III–IV).

———, 2000, *Critique of the Power of Judgment*, Eng. trans. by P. Guyer and E. Matthews, in *The Cambridge Edition of the Works of Immanuel Kant* Cambridge, Cambridge University Press (1912–13, *Kritik der Urteilskraft*, in *Gesammelte Schriften*, hrsg. Königlich Preußischen Akademie der Wissenschaft (= Akademie-Ausgabe), Berlin, Walter de Gruyter, vol. V, pp. 175–485).

Kantorowicz, E., 1957, *The King's Two Bodies: A Study in Medieval Political Theology*, Princeton, Princeton University Press.

Kavka, G., 1986, *Hobbesian Moral and Political Theory*, Princeton, Princeton University Press.

Kemper, P. (ed.), 1989, *Macht des Mythos – Ohnmacht der Vernunft?*, Frankfurt a. M., Fischer Taschenbuch Verlag.

Kenny, A. J. P., 1973, *Wittgenstein*, London, Penguin.

Kerényi, K., 1963, Prolegomena, in K. Kerényi, and C. G. Jung, *Essays on a Science of Mythology*, Eng. trans. by R. F. C. Hull, Princeton, Princeton University Press.

Kersting, W., 1992, "Politics, Freedom and Order: Kant's Political Philosophy", in P. Guyer (ed.), *The Cambridge Companion to Kant*, Cambridge, Cambridge University Press.

Kirk, G. S., 1970, *Myth: Its Meaning and Functions in Ancient and Other Cultures*, Berkeley, University of California Press.

———, 1974, *The Nature of Greek Myth*, Hardmondsworth, Penguin.

Kirk, G. S., J. E. Raven, and M. Schonfield, 1983, *The Presocratic Philosophers*, Cambridge, Cambridge University Press.

Koselleck, R., 2004, *Futures Past*, Eng. trans. by K. Tribe, New York, Columbia University Press (1979, *Vergangene Zukunft*, Frankfurt a. M., Suhrkamp).

Koyré, A., 1957, *From the Closed World to the Infinite Universe*, Baltimore, Johns Hopkins University Press.

Krämer, H. J., 1982, *Platone ed i fondamenti della metafisica*, Milan, Vita e Pensiero.

———, 1995, *Platons ungeschriebene Lehre*, in T. Kobusch and B. Mojsisch (eds.), *Platon. Seine Dialoge in der Sicht neuer Forschungen*, Darmstadt, Wissenschaftliche Buchgesellschaft.

Krois, J. M., 1979, "Der Begriff des Mythos bei Ernst Cassirer", in H. Poser (ed.), *Philosophie und Mythos: Ein Kolloquium*, Berlin, De Gruyter, pp. 199–218.

Labov, W., 1972, *Language in the Inner City*, Philadelphia, University of Pennsylvania Press.

La Caze, M., 2002, *The Analytic Imaginary*, Ithaca, Cornell University Press.

Landucci, S., 1972, *I Filosofi e i selvaggi*, Bari, Laterza.

Lang, B., 1989, "The Politics of Interpretation: Spinoza's Modernist Turn", in *Review of Metaphysics*, reprinted in G. Lloyd (ed.) 2001, *Spinoza: Critical Assessments*, London, Routledge, vol. III, pp. 293–318.

Larzilliére, P., 2003, "Le ⟨⟨martyr⟩⟩ palestinien, nouvelle figure d'un nationalisme en échec", in A. Dieckhoff and R. Leveau (eds), *Israéliens et Palestiniens: la guerre en partage*, Paris, Editions Balland, pp. 89–119.

Leghissa, G., 2002, "Mito, dogma e genesi del moderno in Hans Blumenberg", in H. Blumenberg, *Il futuro del mito*, Milan, Medusa, pp. 5–35.

Le Goff, J., 2000, "The Medieval West and the Indian Ocean: An Oneiric Horizon", in A. Pagden (ed.), *Facing Each other: The World's Perception of Europe and Europe's Perception of the World*, Aldershot, Ashgate, pp. 1–21.

Lentin, A., 2004, *Racism and Anti-Racism in Europe*, London, Pluto Press.

Lévi-Strauss, C., 1962, *La pensée sauvage*, Paris, Plon.

———, 1964, *Mythologiques: Le cru et le cuit*, Paris, Plon.

———, 1968, *Structural Anthropology*, Eng. trans. by C. Jacobson and B. Grundfest Schoepf, London, Allen Lane (1958, *Anthropologie structurale*, Paris, Plon).

———, 1978, *Myth and Meaning*, London, Routledge.

———, 1987, *Anthropology and Myth: Lectures, 1951–1982*, Eng. trans. by R. Willis, Oxford, Blackwell.

———, 1990, *The Naked Man*, Eng. trans. by J. Weightman and D. Weightman, Chicago, University of Chicago Press (1965, *Mythologiques: L'Homme nu*, Paris, Plon).

Liddell, H. G., R. Scott, and J. H. Stuart, 1968, *A Greek-English Lexicon*, Oxford, Clarendon Press.

Lincoln, B., 1989, *Discourse and the Construction of Society: Comparative Studies of Myth, Ritual, and Classification*, Oxford, Oxford University Press.

Locke, J., 1997, *An Essay Concerning Human Understanding*, London, Penguin.

Lotito, L., 2002, "Introduzione", in *Schelling. Introduzione filosofica alla filosofia della mitologia*, Milan, Bompiani, pp. v–xli.

Löwith, K., 1965, *From Hegel to Nietzsche*, London, Constable (1941, *Von Hegel zu Nietzsche*, Zürich, Europa Verlag).

———, 1949, *Meaning in History: The Theological Implication of the Philosophy of History*, Chicago, University of Chicago Press.

Macpherson, C. B., 1964, *The Political Theory of Possessive Individualism*, London, Oxford University Press.

Maffey, A., 1989, "Utopia", in N. Bobbio, N. Matteucci, and G. Pasquino (eds), *Dizionario di Politica*, Turin, Utet, pp. 1214–20.

Maltese, C., 1992, *Storia dell'arte in Italia 1785–1943*, Turin, Einaudi.

Malinowski, B., 1992 *Magic, Science and Religion and Other Essays by Bronislaw Malinowski*, Illinois, Waveland Press.

Mannheim, K., 1960, *Ideology and Utopia*, London, Routledge & Kegan Paul.

Marconi, D., 1999, *La filosofia del linguaggio. Da Frege ai giorni nostri*, Turin, Utet.

Marcuse, H., 1980, *Das Ende der Utopie*, Berlin, Verlag Neue Kritik.

———, 1991, *One Dimensional Man: Studies in the Ideology of Advanced Society*, Boston, Beacon Press.

Marquard, O., 1979, "Lob des Polytheismus: Über Monomythie und Polymythie", in H. Poser (ed.), *Philosophie und Mythos: Ein Kolloquium*, Berlin, De Gruyter, pp. 40–59.

Martin, R. P., 1989, *The Language of Heroes: Speech and Performance in the Iliad*, Ithaca, Cornell University Press.

Marx, K., 1969, *The Eighteenth Brumaire of Louis Bonaparte*, in *Karl Marx and Frederick Engels: Selected Works in Three Volumes*, vol. I, Moscow, Progress, pp. 394–488 (1978, *Der achtzehnte Brumaire des Louis Bonaparte*, in *Marx Engels Werke*, Berlin, Dietz Verlag, vol. VIII, pp. 11–194).

———, 1975, *Contribution to the Critique of Hegel's Philosophy of Law*, in *Karl Marx Frederick Engels Collected Works*, vol. III, Moscow, Progress, pp. 3–129 (1982, *Zur Kritik der Hegelschen Rechtphilosophie*, in *Karl Marx Friderich Engels Gesamtausgabe* (MEGA), vol. I–2, Berlin, Dietz Verlag).

Marx, K., and F. Engels, 1976, *The German Ideology*, in *Karl Marx Frederick Engels Collected Works*, vol. V, Moscow, Progress, pp. 19–452 (1978, *Die deutsche Ideologie*, in *Marx Engels Werke*, Berlin, Dietz Verlag, vol. III).

McCormick, J. P., 1997, *Carl Schmitt's Critique of Liberalism: Against Politics as Technology*, Cambridge, Cambridge University Press.

Mead, G. H., 1934, *Mind, Self and Society*, Chicago, University of Chicago Press.

Meier, C., 1990, *The Greek Discovery of Politics*, Eng. trans. by D. McLintock, Cambridge, Mass., Harvard University Press (1980, *Die Entstehung des Politischen bei den Griechen*, Frankfurt a. M., Suhrkamp).

Melucci, A., 2000, "Costruzione di sé, narrazione, riconoscimento" in D. Della Porta, M. Greco, and A. Szakolczai (eds), *Identità, riconoscimento, scambio. Saggi in onore di Alessandro Pizzorno. Con una risposta e un saggio autobiografico di Alessandro Pizzorno*, Bari, Laterza, pp. 30–45.

Messeri, M., 1997, *Verità*, Florence, La Nuova Italia.

Midgley, M., 2003, *The Myths We Live By*, London, Routledge.

Moeller, J., 1988, "Nature, Human Nature, and Society in the American Western", in E. J. Yanarella and L. Siegelman (eds), *Political Mythology and Popular Fiction*, New York, Greenwood Press, pp. 19–38.

Moneti, M., 1992, *Il pease che non c'è e i suoi abitanti*, Florence, La Nuova Italia.

Moore, S. F., 1975, "Epilogue", in S. F. Moore and B. Meyerhoff (eds), *Symbol and Politics in Communal Ideology*, Ithaca, Cornell University Press.

Moravcsik, J., 1992, *Plato and Platonism: Plato's Conception of Appearance and Reality in Ontology, Epistemology, and Ethics, and its Modern Echoes*, London, Blackwell.

Moreau, P.-F., 1994, *Spinoza: L'expérience et l'éternité*, Paris, PUF.

Morgan, D., 2001, "A Fervour that America Should Easily Recognize", *Washington Post*, 2 November.

Morgan, K., 2000, *Myth and Philosophy from Presocratics to Plato*, Cambridge, Cambridge University Press.

Mosse, G. L., 1974, *The Nationalization of Masses: Political Symbolism and the Mass Movements in Germany from Napoleonic Wars through the Third Reich*, New York, Howard Ferting.

Nestlé, W., 1942, *Vom Mythos zum Logos: die Selbstentfaltung des griechischen Denkens von Homer bis auf die Sophistik und Sokrates*, Stuttgart, Kröner.

Neumann, K., 1972, "Idee", in G. Gabriel, K. Gründer and J. Ritter (eds.), 1971–, *Historisches Wörterbuch der Philosophie*, Darmstadt, Wissenschaftliche Buchgesellschaft, vol. VII, pp. 55–134.

Nietzsche, F., 1984, *Nietzsche Briefwechsel. Kritische Gesamtausgabe*, ed. by G. Colli and M. Montinari, Berlin, De Gruyter.

———, 1994, *On the Genealogy of Morality*, Eng. trans. by C. Diethe, Cambridge, Cambridge University Press (1973, *Zur Genealogie der Moral. Eine Streitschrift*, in *Nietzsche Werke, Kritische Gesamtausgabe*, ed. by G. Colli and M. Montinari, Berlin, De Gruyter).

———, 1999, *The Birth of Tragedy and Other Writings*, Eng. trans. by R. Geuss and R. Speirs, Cambridge, Cambridge University Press (1973, *Die Geburt der Tragödie, oder: Griechentum und Pessimismus*, in *Nietzsche Werke, Kritische Gesamtausgabe*, ed. by G. Colli and M. Montinari, Berlin, De Gruyter).

———, 2002, *Beyond Good and Evil*, Eng. trans. by J. Norman, Cambridge, Cambridge University Press (1973, *Jenseits von Gut und Böse*, in *Nietzsche Werke, Kritische Gesamtausgabe*, ed. by G. Colli and M. Montinari, Berlin, De Gruyter).

Norris, C., 1991, *Spinoza and the Origins of Modern Critical Theory*, Oxford, Blackwell.

Nussbaum, M., 1986, *The Fragility of Goodness: Luck and Ethics in Greek Tragedy and Philosophy*, Cambridge, Cambridge University Press.

———, 2001, *Upheavals of Thought: The Intelligence of Emotions*, Cambridge, Cambridge University Press.

Olson, D. R., and N. Torrance (eds), 1991, *Literacy and Orality*, Cambridge, Cambridge University Press.

Onions, C. T., 1966, *The Oxford Dictionary of English Etymology*, Oxford, Clarendon Press.

Pagden, A., 1982, *The Fall of Natural Man*, Cambridge, Cambridge University Press.

—— (ed.), 2000, *Facing Each Other: The World's Perception of Europe and Europe's Perception of the World*, Aldershot, Ashgate.

Paggi, L. (ed.), 1999, *Le memorie della Repubblica*, Florence, La Nuova Italia.

Panikkar, R., 1962, "La demitologizzazione nell'incontro tra Cristianesimo e Induismo", in *Il Problema della demitizzazione. Atti del convegno indetto dal Centro Internazionale di Studi Umanistici e dall'Istituto di Studi Filosofici*, Rome, Archivio di Filosofia, pp. 243–66.

——, 1964, *The Unknown Christ of Hinduism*, London, Darton, Longman and Todd.

Passerini, L. (ed.), 2003, *Figures d'Europe: Images and Myths of Europe*, Brussels, P.I.E.- Peter Lang.

Pavone, C., 1991, *Una Guerra civile. Saggio storico sulla moralità nella resistenza*, Turin, Bollati Boringhieri.

——, 1995, *Alle origini della repubblica: Scritti su fascismo, antifascismo e continuità dello stato*, Turin, Bollati Boringhieri.

Pellegrin, P., 2001, *Le Vocabulaire d'Aristote*, Paris, Ellipses.

Pieper, J., 1965, *Über die platonischen Mythen*, Munich, Kösel Verlag.

Patai, R., 1973, *The Arab Mind*, New York, Scribner.

Pipes, D., 1983, *In the Path of God: Islam and Political Power*, New York, Basic Books.

Pizzorno, A., 1993, *Le radici della politica assoluta e altri saggi*, Milan, Feltrinelli.

——, 2000, "Risposte e proposte", in D. Della Porta, M. Greco, and A. Szakolczai (eds), *Identità, riconoscimento, scambio. Saggi in onore di Alessandro Pizzorno. Con una riposta e un saggio autobiografico di Alessandro Pizzorno*, Bari, Laterza, pp. 197–246.

Plato, 1989, *The Collected Dialogues of Plato Including the Letters*, ed. by E. Hamilton and H. Cairns, New Haven, Princeton University Press.

Poser, H. (ed.), 1979, *Philosophie und Mythos: Ein Kolloquium*, Berlin, De Gruyter.

Preus, S., 1989, "Spinoza, Vico, and the Imagination of Religion", in *Journal of the Histories of Ideas*, 50, pp. 71–93.

Pulcini, E., 2001, *L'individuo senza passioni*, Turin, Bollati Boringhieri.

Rath, I. W., 1992, *Die verkannte mythische Vernunft. Perspektiven einer vernünftigen Alternative*, Wien, Passagen Verlag.

Rawls, J., 1973, *A Theory of Justice*, London, Oxford University Press.

——, 1993, *Political Liberalism*, New York, Columbia University Press.

Reale, G., 1986, *Per una nuova interpretazione di Platone. Rilettura dei grandi dialoghi alla luce delle dottrine non scritte*, Milan, Vita e Pensiero.

——, 1991, *Platone. Tutti gli scritti*, Milan, Rusconi.

Ricoeur, P., 1970, *Freud and Philosophy: An Essay on Interpretation*, Eng. trans. by D. Savage, New Haven, Yale University Press (1965, *De l'interprétation: Essai sur Freud*, Paris, Seuil).

——, 1986, *Du texte à l'action*, Paris, Editions du Seuil.

————, 1994, "Imagination in Discourse and in Action", in G. Robinson and J. Rundell (eds), *Rethinking Imagination: Culture and Creativity*, London, Routledge, pp. 118–35.

Rorty, R., 1989, *Contingency, Irony, and Solidarity*, Cambridge, Cambridge University Press.

Rosenberg, A., 1941, *Der Mythus des 20. Jahrhunderts – Eine Wertung der seelisch-geistigen Gestaltenkämpfe unserer Zeit*, München, Hoheneichen-Verlag.

Rosenthal, M., 1997, "Why Spinoza Chose the Hebrews: The Exemplary Function of Prophecy in the *Theological-Political Treatise*", in *History of Political Thought*, 18, reprinted in G. Lloyd (ed.), 2001, *Spinoza: Critical Assessments*, London, Routledge, vol. III, pp. 245–81.

Ross, W. D., 1951, *Plato's Theory of Ideas*, Oxford, Clarendon Press.

Rousseau, J. J., 1997a, "Discourse on the Origin and Foundations of Inequality Among Men", Eng. trans. by V. Gourevitch, in *The Discourses and Other Early Political Writings*, Cambridge, Cambridge University Press, pp. 111–230 (1996, *Discours sur l'origine et les Fondements de l'inégalité parmi les hommes*, Paris, Librairie Générale Française).

————, 1997b, "Of The Social Contract", Eng. trans. by V. Gourevitch, in *The Social Contract and Other Later Political Writings*, Cambridge, Cambridge University Press (2001, *Du Contract Social*, Paris, Flammarion).

Rundell, J., 1994a, "Creativity and Judgment: Kant on Reason and Imagination", in G. Robinson and J. Rundell (eds), *Rethinking Imagination: Culture and Creativity*, London, Routledge, pp. 87–117.

————, 1994b, "Introduction" in G. Robinson and J. Rundell (eds), *Rethinking Imagination: Culture and Creativity*, London, Routledge, pp. 1–11.

Russell, B., 1922, "Introduction", in L. Wittgenstein, 1961, *Tractatus logico-philosophicus*, Eng. trans. by D. F. Pears and B. F. McGuinness, London, Routledge, pp. ix–xxii.

Said, E., 1978, *Orientalism*, Routledge, London.

Sabbatucci, D., 1978, *Il mito, il rito e la storia*, Rome, Bulzoni Editore.

Sadiki, L., 2004, *The Search for Arab Democracy: Discourses and Counter-Discourses*, London, Hurst and Company.

Schelling, F. W. J., 1856–1861, *Philosophische Einleitung in die Philosophie der Mythologie oder Darstellung der reinrationalen Philosophie*, vol. XI in *F. W. J. Schellings Sämtliche Werke*, Stuttgart, Cotta.

Scheman, N., 1996, "Forms of Life: Mapping the Rough Ground", in H. Sluga and D. Stern (eds), *The Cambridge Companion to Wittgenstein*, Cambridge, Cambridge University Press, pp. 383–410.

Schlegel, F. S., and A. W. Schlegel, 1992, *Athenäum. Eine Zeitschrift von A. W. Schlegel und F. S. Schlegel*, Darmstadt, Wissenschaftliche Buchgesellschaft.

Schneider, H. J., 1999, "Creation and Recreation: The Interplay of Activity and Structure in Language", in *Journal of Pragmatics*, 31, pp. 669–84.

Schmitt, C., 1985a, *The Crisis of Parliamentary Democracy*, Eng. trans. by E. Kennedy, Cambridge, Mass., MIT Press (1926, *Die geistesgeschichtliche Lage des heutigen Parlamentarismus*, Berlin, Dunker und Humblot).

———, 1985b, *Political Theology*, Eng. trans. by G. Schwab, Cambridge, Mass., MIT Press (1922, *Politische Theologie*, Berlin, Dunker und Humblot).

———, 1988, "Die politische Theorie des Mythus", in *Positionen und Begriffe im Kampf mit Weimar-Genf-Versailles*, Berlin, Dunker und Humblot, pp. 9–18.

Seib, P., 2004, "The News Media and the Clash of Civilisations", in *Parameters*, Winter 2004–5, pp. 71–85.

Shevory, T. C., 1988, "Winning Isn't Everything: Sport Fiction as a Genre of Political Criticism", in E. J. Yanarella and L. Siegelman (eds), *Political Mythology and Popular Fiction*, New York, Greenwood Press, pp. 61–80.

Shils, E., 1958, "Ideology and Civility: On the Politics of the Intellectual", in *Sewanee Review*, 66, pp. 450–80.

Simpson, J. A., and E. S. C. Weiner (eds), 1989, *The Oxford English Dictionary*, Oxford, Clarendon Press.

Smith, A. D., 1986, *The Ethnic Origins of Nations*, Oxford, Blackwell.

———, 1991, *National Identity*, London, Penguin.

———, 1999, *Myths and Memories of the Nation*, London, Routledge.

Sorel, G., 1975, *Reflections on Violence*, Eng. trans. by T. E. Hulme, New York, AMS Press (1990, *Réflexions sur la violence*, Paris, Seuil).

Sparti, D., 2000, "Il riconoscimento dal volto umano", in D. Della Porta, M. Greco, and A. Szakolczai (eds), *Identità, riconoscimento, scambio. Saggi in onore di Alessandro Pizzorno. Con una risposta e un saggio autobiografico di Alessandro Pizzorno*, Bari, Laterza, pp. 45–65.

Spinoza, B., 1951a, *Political Treatise*, Eng. trans. by R. H. M. Elwes, in *A Theologico-Political Treatise and a Political Treatise*, New York, Dover Publications, pp. 267–387 (1924, *Tractatus Politicus*, vol. III in *Spinoza Opera*, ed. by C. Gebhardt, Heidelberg, Carl Winters Universitätsbuchhandlung).

———, 1951b, *A Theologico-Political Treatise and a Political Treatise*, Eng. trans. by R. H. M. Elwes, New York, Dover Publications, pp. 1–266 (1972, *Tractatus Theologico-Politicus*, in *Spinoza Opera*, ed. by C. Gebhardt, vol. III, Heidelberg, Carl Winters Universitätsbuchhandlung).

———, 1985, *Ethics*, Eng. trans. by E. Curley, in *The Collected Works of Spinoza*, Princeton, Princeton University Press, vol. I, pp. 401–617 (1924, *Ethica*, in *Spinoza Opera*, ed. by C. Gebhardt, vol. II, Heidelberg, Carl Winters Universitätsbuchhandlung).

Stoppino, M., 1989, "Ideologia", in N. Bobbio, N. Matteucci, and G. Pasquino (eds), *Dizionario di Politica*, Turin, Utet, pp. 483–95.

Stråth, B. (ed.), 2000, *Myth and Memory in the Construction of the Community*, Brussels, Peter Lang.

Sullivan, A., 2001, "This Is a Religious War", *New York Times*, 7 October.

Taylor, C., 1989, *Sources of the Self: The Making of the Modern Identity*, Cambridge, Cambridge University Press.

———, 1992, *Multiculturalism and the "Politics of Recognition"*, Princeton, Princeton University Press.

———, 1995, *Philosophical Arguments*, Cambridge, Mass., Harvard University Press.

Taylor, J. T., 1986, "Do You understand? Criteria of Understanding in Verbal Interaction", in *Language and Communication*, 6, 3, pp. 171–80.

Tebben, J. R., 1994, *Concordantia Homerica. Pars I Odissea*, Hildesheim, Olms-Weidmann.

———, 1998, *Concordantia Homerica. Pars II Ilias*, Hildesheim, Olms-Weidmann.

Telhami, S., 2004, "Arabs Increasingly Define Themselves as Muslim First", in *Daily Star*, 16 July 2004.

Thesaurus Linguae Graecae, 1992, CDROM, Irvine, University of California.

Thomas, R., 1992, *Literacy and Orality in Ancient Greece*, Cambridge, Cambridge University Press.

Thompson, J. B., 2001, "Ideology: History of the Concept", in N. J. Smelser and P. B. Baltes (eds), *International Encyclopedia of the Social and Behavioural Sciences*, Amsterdam, Elsevier, vol. 11, pp. 7170–4.

Thorsen, A., 2000, "Foundation Myth at Work: National Day Celebrations in France, Germany and Norway in a Comparative Perspective" in B. Stråth (ed.), *Myth and Memory in the Construction of the Community*, Brussels, Peter Lang, pp. 331–51.

Thucydides, 1919, *History of the Peloponnesian War*, Eng. trans. by C. F. Smith, London, Heinemann, Loeb Classical Library.

Tomashevski, B., 1965, "Thematics", in L. Lemon and M. Reis (eds), *Russian Formalist Criticism: Four Essays*, Lincoln, University of Nebraska Press, pp. 61–95.

Toolan, M. J., 1988, *Narrative: A Critical Linguistic Introduction*, London, Routledge.

Tudor, H., 1972, *Political Myth*, London, Macmillan.

Vattimo, G., 1999a, "Estetica", in *Enciclopedia di filosofia*, Milan, Garzanti, pp. 340–5.

———, 1999b, "Immaginazione", in *Enciclopedia di filosofia*, Milan, Garzanti, pp. 528–30.

Vernant, J. P., 2006, *Myth and Thought Among the Greeks*, Eng. trans. by J. Lloyd and J. Fort, New York, Zone Books (1990, *Mythe et pensée chez les Grecs. Études de psychologie historique*, Paris, La Découverte.

Veyne, P., 1988, *Did Greeks Believe in Their Myths?*, Eng. trans. by P. Wissing, Chicago, University of Chicago Press.

Vico, G., 1999, *New Science*, Eng. trans. by D. Marsh, London, Penguin Books (1992, *Principi di scienza nuova*, Milan, Mondadori).

Vlastos, G., 1965, "Degrees of Reality in Plato", in R. Bambrough (ed.), *New Essays on Plato and Aristotle*, London, Routledge.

Volkmann-Schluck, K.-H., 1969, *Mythos und Logos. Interpretationen zu Schellings Philosophie der Mythologie*, Berlin, De Gruyter.

Von Savigny, E., 1991, "Common Behavior of Many a Kind", in R. L. Arrington and H. J. Glock (eds), *Wittgenstein's Philosophical Investigations: Text and Context*, London, Routledge, pp. 105–119.

Wagner, P., 1994, *A Sociology of Modernity*, London, Routledge.

———, 2002, "Identity and Selfhood as a Problematique", in H. Friese (ed.), *Identities: Time, Difference, and Boundaries*, Oxford, Berghahn Books, pp. 32–56.

———, 2004, "Palomar's Question: The Axial Age Hypothesis: European Modernity and Historical Contingency", in J. Arnason, S. Eisenstadt, and B. Wittrock (eds), *Axial Civilisations and World History*, Leiden, Brill, pp. 87–121.

Wallace, R., 1984, "Introduction to Blumenberg", in *New German Critique*, 32, pp. 93–108.

Walzer, M., 1964, "On the Role of Symbolism in Political Thought", in *Political Science Quarterly*, 82, June, pp. 120–203.

Warrender, H., 1957, *The Political Philosophy of Thomas Hobbes*, Oxford, Clarendon.

Wartelle, A., 1982, *Lexique de la ⟨⟨Rhétorique⟩⟩ d'Aristote*, Paris, Les Belles Lettres.

Weber, M., 1969, *On Charisma and Institution Building*, ed. by S. Eisenstadt, Chicago, University of Chicago Press.

———, 1976, *The Protestant Ethic and the Spirit of Capitalism*, Eng. trans. by T. Parsons, London, Allen & Unwin (1984, *Die protestantische Ethik und der Geist des Kapitalismus*, vol. 17 in *Max Weber Gesamtausgabe*, ed. by H. Baier et al. Tübingen Mohr).

———, 1978, *Economy and Society*, Eng. trans. by E. Fischoff et al. Berkeley, University of California Press (1984, *Wirtschaft und Gesellschaft*, vol. XXII 1–XXII 5 in *Max Weber Gesamtausgabe*, Abteilung I).

———, 2004, *The Vocation Lectures: Science as Vocation, Politics as Vocation*, Eng. trans. by R. Livingstone, Indianapolis Cambridge, Hackett.

White, H., 1973, *Metahistory: The Historical Imagination in Nineteenth-Century Europe*, Baltimore, Johns Hopkins University Press.

———, 1987, *The Content of the Form: Narrative Discourse and Historical Representation*, Baltimore, Johns Hopkins University Press.

———, 2000, "Catastrophe, Communal Memory and Mythic Discourse: The Uses of Myth in the Reconstruction of Society", in B. Stråth (ed.), *Myth and Memory in the Construction of the Community*, Brussels, Peter Lang, pp. 49–75.

Whitebook, J., 1989, "Intersubjectivity and the Monadic Core of the Psyche: Habermas and Castoriadis on the Unconscious", in G. Busino et al. (eds), *Autonomie et autotransformation de la société. La philosophie militante de Cornelius Castoriadis*, Geneva, Librarie Droz, pp. 225–45.

Wingo, A. H., 2003, *Veil Politics in Liberal Democratic States*, Cambridge, Cambridge University Press.

Wittgenstein, L., 1961, *Tractatus logico-philosophicus*, Eng. trans. by D. F. Pears and B. F. McGuinness, London, Routledge (1995, *Tractatus logico-philosophicus*, in *Werkausgabe*, Frankfurt a. M., Suhrkamp, vol. I, pp. 7–87).

———, 1967, *Zettel*, Oxford, Blackwell.

———, 1969, *On Certainty*, Oxford, Blackwell.

———, 1974, *Philosophical Grammar*, Eng. trans. by A. Kenny, Oxford, Blackwell (1969, *Philosophische Grammatik*, ed. by R. Rhees, Oxford, Blackwell).

————, 1976, *Philosophical Investigations*, Eng. trans, by G. E. M. Ascombe, Oxford, Blackwell (1995, *Philosophische Untersuchungen*, in *Werkausgabe*, Frankfurt a. M., Suhrkamp, vol. I, pp. 225–581).

————, 1979, *Remarks on Frazer's Golden Bough*, Eng. trans. A. C. Miles, Retford, Brynmill.

Wolin, R., 1990, "Carl Schmitt, Political Existentialism and the Total State", in *Theory and Society*, 19, pp. 389–416.

Yanarella, E. J., and L. Siegelman (eds), 1988, *Political Mythology and Popular Fiction*, New York, Greenwood Press.

Young, R., 1990, *White Mythologies: Writing History and the West*, London, Routledge.

Index

Mannheim, K., 188, 192–3, 197, 226
Marconi, D., 86
Marcuse, H., 87, 198
Marquard, O., 50, 77
Martin, R. P., 20
Marx, K., 160, 162, 186–93, 229
McCormick, J. P., 228
Mead, G. H., 238
Melucci, A., 236, 239
Messeri, M., 43
Midgley, M., 112, 139, 247
Moeller, J., 255
Moneti, M., 198
Moore, S. F., 129, 257
More, T., 197–8
Moravcsik, J., 41
Moreau, P. F., 164
Morgan, D., 249
Morgan, K., 28–9
myth
  definition of, 4, 10, 99, 115, 207
  historical, 183, 259 (*see also* history, myth and)
  political (*see* political myth)
  reality of, 12, 44–62, 104–5
  religious, 44–61, 259 (*see also* religion, and political myth)
  and ritual (*see* ritual)
  scientific, 259
  truth of, 77, 44–61, 83 ff, 110
  work on, 7, 8, 12, 15, 82, 99, 130, 133, 143, 145, 149, 158, 179, 181, 200, 216–19, 225, 242, 244, 247, 256, 257–8
mythos, 10, 18, 20–44, 81, 208
mythosdebatte, 8
  see also Blumenberg

Nestlé, W., 22
Neumann, K., 41, 64

Nietzsche, F., 10, 17, 81, 121, 128, 195, 228
Norris, C., 166
Nussbaum, M., 126–7

ousia, 25

Pagden, A., 141–2, 148
Paggi, L., 183
Panikkar, R., 60–1
Passerini, L., 111
Pavone, C., 183
Pellegrin, P., 36
Pieper, J., 31, 33
Patai, R., 251
Pipes, D., 251
Pirandello, L., 205
Pizzorno, A., 237–9
Plato, 10, 21, 26, 28–35, 39–42, 67
Plutarch, 62
political myth, 3–4, 8–9, 130, 134–50, 151–76, 177–85, 210, 213–16, 224–6, 228, 231, 243–4, 246–60
  classical theories of, 151–77
  contemporary, 183, 202, 246–60
  definition of, 3–9, 179–85
  see also Cassirer; Flood; Lincoln; myth; politics; Sorel; Spinoza; Tudor
politics, 1, 131–3, 151, 154, 159, 170, 177, 180, 246
  definition of, 180
  of identity, 204, 214, 234, 237 (*see also* identity)
  and media, 246–60
  modern, 3, 131–4, 154, 170, 246–60
  of the past, 203, 226
  and Romanticism, 75–80
Poser, H., 100
Preus, S., 165–6, 170

Lightning Source UK Ltd.
Milton Keynes UK

174946UK00001B/80/P

9 780521 182751